Financial Mail on Sunday

Guide to Running Your Own Business

Ruth Sunderland

RANDOM HOUSE
BUSINESS BOOKS

Ruth Sunderland has asserted her rights under the Copyright, Designs and Patents Act, 1988, to be identified as the author of this work.

First published in 2001 by Random House Business Books,
Random House, 20 Vauxhall Bridge Road, London SW1V 2SA

Random House Australia (Pty) Limited
20 Alfred Street, Milsons Point,
Sydney, New South Wales 2061, Australia

Random House New Zealand Limited
18 Poland Road, Glenfield,
Auckland 10, New Zealand

Random House (Pty) Limited
Endulini, 5a Jubilee Road, Parktown 2193, South Africa

The Random House Group Limited Reg. No. 954009

Papers used by Random House are natural, recyclable
products made from wood grown in sustainable forests.
The manufacturing processes conform to the environmental
regulations of the country of origin.

ISBN 0 7126 8003 9

Companies, institutions and other organizations wishing to make
bulk purchases of books published by Random House should
contact their local bookstore or Random House direct:

Special Sales Director
Random House, 20 Vauxhall Bridge Road, London SW1V 2SA
Tel 020 7840 8470   Fax 020 7828 6681

www.randomhouse.co.uk
businessbooks@randomhouse.co.uk

Typeset in Sabon by MATS, Southend-on-Sea, Essex
Printed and bound in Great Britain by
Mackays of Chatham PLC, Chatham, Kent

Contents

Acknowledgements

I would like to thank my family, friends and colleagues for their support – and tolerance – during the writing of this book. In particular, I would like to thank Stephen Pegge of Lloyds TSB for reading the manuscript and giving me his valuable criticisms, suggestions and encouragement, and Valerie Thompson of Business Link London Central, for her help on my chapter on marketing. The remaining errors and deficiencies are all mine.

Introduction

Growth Is Good

> It is Enterprise which builds and improves the world's possessions ... if Enterprise is afoot, wealth accumulates ... and if Enterprise is asleep, wealth decays ...
> John Maynard Keynes, *Treatise on Money*.

> Entrepreneurs are the new frontline troops for Britain's new economy.
> Tony Blair

This book is for anyone who is serious about owning or working for a true growth business.

Many people dream of making millions by making a success of their own business venture, and then retiring after a few years to the Bahamas.

The reality is that on the road to growth, entrepreneurs will work very hard, take nerve-racking risks and surmount many difficulties. Many will fall by the wayside and only the most talented, determined and best-prepared will make the grade. Even if you do succeed, getting rich is far more likely to happen gradually, after years of hard graft and ploughing profits back into the company, than it is to occur overnight.

The business world is changing rapidly. Entrepreneurs today must contend with new technology, e-commerce, fresh competition, new regulations and a host of other challenges. It is also becoming more competitive. In today's world of global commerce, firms face rivalry not just within the UK, but from the rest of Europe and beyond.

Here at *Financial Mail on Sunday*, we meet and talk to hundreds of businessmen and women, from the bosses of FT-SE 100 companies to entrepreneurs running the tiniest firms, along with leading experts at the UK's biggest banks, accountancy firms, venture capitalists and business advice agencies. *Financial Mail* also runs a unique Enterprise Awards programme, specially designed to encourage, recognise and reward growing businesses. This has given us an unrivalled insight into the secrets of success behind Britain's fast-growth firms, the pitfalls they face and the hurdles they must overcome.

Encouraging enterprise and growth matters to all of us, because fast-growing, flexible companies are the engine of the UK economy. We depend on them increasingly for jobs, for the innovations that improve our lives and for our ability as a nation to compete on the global stage.

Thirty years ago, most of the working population expected 'jobs for life', climbing tortuously up the career ladder at a big corporation. The shift away from old, male-dominated heavy industries in the Eighties has been painful for many, but has also transformed the economic landscape. We are all now likely to be involved in enterprise at some stage in our working lives, as an entrepreneur ourselves, or as an employee, customer or supplier of a growing business. Official statistics bear this out.

By the late Nineties there were an estimated 3.7 million businesses in the UK, according to the Department of Trade and Industry. That is 1.6 million more than in 1980 – and 99% of those businesses were classified as small firms with fewer than fifty employees, accounting for 45% of private-sector jobs and 40% of private-sector sales.[1]

In 1998, small firms created 1.64 million new jobs and those in their first year of trading generated sales of more than £58 billion.[2]

Enterprise has been a liberating force for many. Talented individuals no longer have to spend years engaging in office politics in the hope of clawing their way to the top of a large company, but are opting to build their own businesses instead. The UK's embrace of the enterprise culture has also given opportunities to many people who may have been held back by prejudice or rigid structures in the traditional workplace. Almost a third of new firms are set up by women, while mature business people aged over fifty and ethnic-minority entrepreneurs account for almost 20% of small and medium enterprises between them.

Anyone can run a growth business, whether he or she is old or young, black or white, male or female – provided that person has the drive, the skills and the right advice. This book aims to be a straightforward practical guide, with case studies drawing on the experiences of real companies, for those who are truly committed to growth. It will guide entrepreneurs from the exciting start-up stage, through early growth, consolidation, maturity and exit routes, examining key areas such as marketing, the Internet, finance for growth and dealing with risk. It will also focus on the often neglected human issues involved in running a successful growth business, such as stress, balancing work and family life, and giving staff a stake in the business.

While it cannot hope to address every point that will arise on the road to growth, it will try to point the reader to sources of further expert help and advice. We hope that using it will help you grow your business into a powerhouse for the future.

Notes

1   Small and Medium Enterprise Statistics for the United Kingdom, 1997, SME Statistics Unit, Department of Trade and Industry, July 1998.
2   Barclays Bank Research Review, *Starting up in Business*, July 1999.

1

From Dream to Reality

No one is genetically programmed to be an entrepreneur. It is not something you are born with. We have found little to suggest that most people cannot emulate the behaviour of successful entrepreneurs. It is more a matter of will, persistence and environment.

Daniel F. Muzyka, *Insead Management School, Fontainebleau, France*

Building up small businesses is the toughest job in the world.

Tim Waterstone, *Founder of the Waterstone bookshop chain*

1   Are you an entrepreneur?

The most important factor in building a successful growth business is not finance, products or marketing.

It is you.

Your personality, ambition and skills are what will drive the business forward – or not. It makes sense, therefore, to embark on some self-analysis before plunging into a business venture. The idea is not to match yourself against some ideal blueprint of an 'entrepreneurial personality' – there is no such thing – but to clarify your motivations, your aims, your strengths and weaknesses, and how you might address them. This exercise is particularly helpful for people considering setting up a business for the first time and may help them to assess whether or not to go ahead. But it is also useful for existing business owners wanting to expand their operations. As part of this process, we will look at the characteristics of successful entrepreneurs and the sort of enterprise they typically run.

This chapter will also help you to identify your motives – why you believe you want to run a growth business – and your aims, or what you want to get out of it for yourself. It will help you to look objectively at the positive qualities that will help you to succeed and the negative characteristics that could lead to you failing.

No one, of course, can create a growth business all on his or her own. Relationships with other people and the ability to build high-performance teams are key to entrepreneurial success. This is not a 'soft' issue – your ability to forge productive relationships with business partners, staff, customers, suppliers and the wider community is a major determinant of how your business will grow.

The chapter will also examine common problems faced by most entrepreneurs. This is not merely a theoretical exercise. Throughout the chapter we will look at the real-life experiences of entrepreneurs – some household names, others lesser known – who look to be on course to be the entrepreneurial stars of tomorrow.

The *Financial Mail on Sunday* Enterprise Programme

Financial Mail began the Enterprise programme in 1997 with the aim of encouraging and honouring the elite of fast-growth firms that have the potential to become the powerhouses of the next millennium. We believed that these entrepreneurial companies were not receiving the public recognition they deserved.

Our initiative struck a chord. Since the programme began, hundreds of firms have participated and it has won the support of some of the UK's most successful entrepreneurs, including James Dyson, who built a multimillion-pound business with his revolutionary vacuum cleaner, Sir Tom Farmer, Founder of the Kwik-Fit auto-repair group, Pam Bader, Chief Executive of domestic cleaning franchise empire Molly Maid and Tim Waterstone, founder of Waterstone's bookshops.

The *Financial Mail* and Lloyds TSB, the lead sponsor of the awards, conduct continuous research tracking the winners' progress, attitudes and confidence.

The *Financial Mail*/Lloyds TSB Enterprise Index, which charts the progress of the winners, shows that Enterprise companies are outstanding exporters who invest a much higher proportion of turnover in training than their peers. They display a higher than average level of business confidence and are better placed to seize opportunities than their peers, even in tough economic conditions.

The Enterprise Awards have provided us with unique insights into what makes Britain's best-performing growth businesses tick.

We believe that many other business people who aspire to fast-track growth can learn a great deal from their experiences, which we will be sharing with readers of this book. One of the aims of the programme is that entering the awards should help entrepreneurs focus on their business, thereby highlighting its strengths and weaknesses. Many of the entrants have reported that going through the entry process has helped them to become orientated towards growth.

2   So what exactly is an entrepreneur?

Perhaps the most popular stereotype of the entrepreneur is of a brash, pushy, ruthless young man who drives a fast car and has a mobile phone grafted on to his ear, down which he constantly barks orders. It is not an attractive image and it is often a completely false one. An entrepreneur nowadays is just as likely to be a hard-working wife and mother, a retired manager or a young Bangladeshi hoping to revitalise the family curry house. Entrepreneurs come from all age groups, social classes, educational backgrounds and have a wide range of previous experience.

That does not mean, however, that being an entrepreneur is easy – quite the reverse. One of the issues facing entrepreneurs in the UK is that running a business is not a respected occupation. Research by the London Business School,[1] shows that there is a collective desire in this country to maintain the status quo. People want to preserve their existing social status and in general prefer to work in established organisations. There is also a strong fear of the social consequences of failing in business, with people fearing that they may be shunned or stigmatised if they do not make a success of a venture.

In the past, this has deterred many talented people from becoming entrepreneurs, though thankfully there is evidence that these attitudes are changing. Many people are realising for the first time that there is an entrepreneur inside them struggling to get out. To explore what qualities are needed to be a successful entrepreneur, it is helpful to define the term.

First, not all small businessmen are entrepreneurs. According to the Centre for Growing Businesses at Nottingham Trent Business School, around 90% of firms start small and stay small. Many are content to run a 'lifestyle business', which provides them with a comfortable standard of living, and are not particularly interested in growing it. That is a perfectly reasonable stance to take, but it is not entrepreneurship.

There is a great deal of academic debate as to what exactly does constitute an entrepreneur. In the Enterprise programme, we use a straightforward definition: an entrepreneur is an individual who attempts to create a business with a view to achieving significant growth. The entrepreneur may act alone or as part of an entrepreneurial team. He or she might want to start a new venture totally from scratch, or may focus instead on expanding an existing business.

But the key question is, what makes them successful? There are no hard and fast rules, but most, in our experience of running

the Enterprise programme, share the following six key characteristics:

- *Ambition, drive and achievement.* Successful entrepreneurs
  are people with energy and drive. They display high levels of
  initiative and self-belief. Money, though important to them, is
  not normally their primary motivation. Instead, they are
  driven by a need for self-fulfilment.

- *Vision, business planning and clear objectives.* Entrepreneurs
  who succeed typically have a well-defined vision for their
  businesses, supported by clear plans on how to realise it. They
  are good at addressing the practicalities in achieving their
  aims. They realise the importance of strategic thinking and
  view time spent on planning as an integral part of running
  their companies.

- *Mature attitude to risk.* Risk is an integral part of being an
  entrepreneur. The best business people will take a measured
  attitude and will attempt to manage risk. They will try to
  assess the inevitable risks they face and to neutralise them as
  much as possible. Unnecessary gambles will be avoided.

- *Valuing others.* Entrepreneurs are often egocentric individuals
  who want to be in control. That can be a virtue in driving a
  business forward, but there is a need for balance. One of the
  striking themes to emerge from the Enterprise programme is the
  number of successful growth businesses run by teams, and the
  high degree of recognition and encouragement of the contribution to growth that can be made by managers and staff.

- *Innovation and willingness to embrace change.* Successful
  entrepreneurs are open to innovation and try to foster an
  innovative culture within their companies. They see the
  positive, rather than the negative aspects of change and are
  often at the forefront of new developments such as e-
  commerce. They see change as giving them opportunities to
  gain an edge on the competition, rather than focusing on the
  inconvenience or expense.

- *Bouncing back.* Failure, like risk, is an inevitable part of
  business life. Effective entrepreneurs realise, however, that

most failures need not be catastrophic. When presented with what looks like a failure, they will persevere and are prepared to employ non-traditional thinking to find solutions.

Case Study 1: From beach bum to the BAFTAs

Terry Murtha, Nigel Smith and Christopher Horrell are unlikely candidates to become business heroes. But a brilliant business idea, backed by hard work and unflagging customer service, propelled the three men from Ilfracombe in Devon out of dead-end jobs and into the limelight.

In the early Nineties Murtha was a seaside deckchair attend-ant and confesses to being a 'beach bum' for ten years. The other two looked as if they had similarly inauspicious prospects. Smith made a living mending fruit machines and Horrell was a factory maintenance man. But the three set up a lighting effects company, SH Technical Support, whose expertise has been used at the BAFTA awards, the Royal Variety Show and the National Lottery television show. 'Every week we are doing another show,' says Terry. Their business, based in Ilfracombe, has now achieved sales of more than £1 million a year.

Smith and Horrell, who did lighting work for music events in their spare time, met Murtha at a soul concert he was helping to organise. They told him they had a revolutionary idea for 'star-cloth', the backdrop with lights used in theatres and on television. The method already in existence involved attaching the bulbs to the cloth with a time-consuming soldering process. Smith and Horrell invented a purpose-built bulb holder which meant that lights could simply be pushed in and then out again when they needed changing. Their technique was to push the lights into small sockets in the material, rather than soldering them on. Murtha was impressed by the idea and his granny came to their aid with a loan of £15,000, allowing the trio to set up SH in 1993.

SH scooped two awards in the 1998 Enterprise 2000 programme, for competitive advantage and customer orientation. Smith and Murtha (Horrell has since retired) work seventy-hour weeks and are prepared to devote as much time as it takes to service their clients. They continue to innovate and have recently invented a remote control operating system for pin spotlights, tiny lights that can enable them to be adjusted without engineers having to clamber up ladders.

'We are an unorthodox bunch but we always deliver the best to our clients,' says Murtha. 'Service is where we have delivered the most. We always give 110%. Nine out of ten companies like ours we deal with don't give good service, so it can be a great selling point for growing firms.'

3   Routes to growth

A popular myth is that to be entrepreneurial, you must be involved in a start-up business. This is not the case. Entrepreneurs may operate in any of the following situations:

- *A start-up*. Some entrepreneurs may be first-timers embarking on a completely fresh venture. Others may be experienced or serial entrepreneurs, setting up a new company, possibly in a new field. Or an entrepreneur may start up a new business which is part of an existing group, such as Richard Branson's forays into cola or cosmetics under his Virgin brand.

- *A family business*. Some entrepreneurs operate in businesses which have been owned and run by their families for one or more generations. Younger family members may want to revitalise a business when they take over, but the family culture and web of relationships can make this difficult. Equally, the family may have to wrestle with the knotty issue of bringing in outsiders to achieve the growth they want.

- *Franchising*. This is where an original business owner, or franchisor, replicates a single business concept through a network of individual entrepreneurs or franchisees, who each run their own outlet or outlets. Examples include fast food chain McDonald's. Franchising has benefits for both franchisor and franchisee. For franchisors, it is an increasingly popular route to growing a business. Franchisees have the incentive and motivation associated with owning their own businesses, but with the added benefit of an established name and continuing support from the franchisor.

- *A management buyout or buyin.* A buyout is the term for a group of managers who purchase the business they are running from its existing owners. That business is often a subsidiary or a division of a larger company. Having purchased the business, the new owner-managers will try to run it as an independent, growth-orientated enterprise. A management buyin is a similar proposition, except that the management team that buys the business is from outside the organisation.

- *Triggers to growth.* Events that frequently act as triggers to growth include a change in ownership, either because a family firm is inherited by the younger generation, or because a business is sold to a new entrepreneur, who is hoping to achieve growth through the acquisition.

  Growth may also be triggered by an entrepreneur spotting a new market opportunity or threat, or by a major life event, such as reaching a milestone birthday, or children leaving home.

4   What are my motives?

Not everyone who sets up or runs a business has the necessary personal qualities to achieve growth. Motivation is a key factor here. If you feel you want to run a growth business, it is worth examining your motives closely before taking on the inevitable challenges and personal sacrifices involved. Research by consultants Business Planning and Research International for the *Mail on Sunday* and leading accountant BDO Stoy Hayward among growth firms[2] shows that there are five main reasons people set up in business: to be their own boss, spotting a good market opportunity, to become rich, it runs in the family and redundancy or some other financial necessity.

Perhaps your motivations are a combination of those listed above, or there may be other factors driving your decision. But before setting off on the challenging path to growth, think about which of these apply to you and whether there are perhaps other more suitable ways of meeting your needs. This will help you to be sure that you are truly committed to going for growth, with all the personal demands that entails. It is also important that you define what success means to you and, therefore, what are your goals.

- *I want to be the boss.* The desire for independence is the biggest motivating factor for people setting up their own businesses. The *Mail on Sunday*/BDO research showed that 37% of growth business owners set up their companies because they wanted to be their own bosses. A further one in five did so because they disliked working for others. People often have feelings like this for years while working for others, but do not act on them. Often the impulse to go it alone comes when they are passed over for promotions they believe they deserve, when they suddenly have to work for a new and uncongenial boss, or when they are assailed with feelings that life is passing them by without them having achieved their full potential. This can often happen at particular 'land-mark' ages, such as forty or fifty.

    In addition, talented people from ethnic minority groups, the gay community, older age groups and the disabled may be motivated to set up their own businesses because they feel they experience discrimination or prejudice in the workplace. Just under a third of new firms are founded by women, often because they feel they have hit the 'glass ceiling' at work or that work is not flexible enough to accommodate their role within the family.

    If you believe you want to start a growth business because of your need for independence, the questions you need to ask yourself are:

    (i)　Would I be able to work with partners?
    (ii)　Am I happy delegating authority and responsibility to others?
    If the answer to these two questions is 'no', you might

consider solving your problems by getting another job with more autonomy, or solo self-employment rather than setting up a business. Remember that although you are your own boss when you set up a business, you never have total autonomy – you still have to deal with customers, employees, financiers and others. It is more a question of being able to determine your long-term direction, rather than day-to-day 'freedom'.

- *I have spotted a market opportunity.* More than one in five growth entrepreneurs started up because they spotted a market opportunity. But what exactly does this mean? Some people are inspired to go into business because they have come up with a completely new idea for a product or service. That can be the route to making a fortune. But trying to sell something no one has ever heard of before is often difficult, and an entrepreneur in this position is likely to face scepticism from investors, customers and suppliers. Possibly, there will also be high costs involved in marketing, to make customers realise they can't survive without your offering.

  An idea does not need to be totally innovative to succeed. 'Copycat' products abound in many areas of commercial life from washing powder to financial services and many are very successful. Ideally, however, you should differentiate your product or service from the competition by means other than simply offering the cheapest price. Many people with a particular skill from consultancy to carpentry decide to set up in business by themselves. Unless they have very clear ideas on how they are going to create a growth business out of this, however, these people often end up as self-employed operators rather than entrepreneurs, albeit sometimes highly paid. If you are tempted to set up in business based on a market opportunity, you need to research the real viability of your idea:

  (i)   How big is the potential market, who are your competitors and why would customers come to you instead of to them?

(ii)   If you can fill a particular market niche, how would you stop rivals copying you and nabbing your customers?

(iii)   What is the shelf-life of your idea? Can it sustain a business in the long run, or is it a 'one-hit wonder'?

● *I want to get rich.* 'I find the whole concept of starting a business just to make money very odd.' That comment comes from James Dyson, one of the UK's most successful entrepreneurs. In spite of achieving sales of his bagless vacuum cleaner amounting to more than £300 million a year, Dyson claims to have been motivated by the desire to design a product people would enjoy.

Of course, there is nothing wrong with wanting to be a millionaire. But founding and running a business is not a way to achieve effortless, Lottery-style riches overnight. Dyson himself invented his vacuum cleaner in 1979 and it took him years of struggle to make it a best-seller.

One in five entrepreneurs list getting rich as a motivation. We have all read stories about 'dot.com' entrepreneurs who have become paper millionaires in a matter of months by dreaming up a new Internet venture. In most cases the operative word here is paper – the real money often proves more elusive. In the early years and perhaps for longer, most entrepreneurs find money is frequently tight. You may have to live on less than if you were working for someone else and you do not have the security or regularity of a pay packet. Your earnings are likely to fluctuate and you will probably find you are keener to plough money back into the business, at least at first, than you are to go out and buy a Porsche. In addition, you are likely to have to take on more financial risks and responsibilities than ever before.

As a business owner, you may have to take on larger debts than you are used to and maybe put up your home as security for your borrowings. You will also be responsible for personal financial affairs that might have been taken care of by an employer, such as your tax bills, pension, sickness insurance and life assurance. If you employ other people, you will also have to pay their wages. This can be a source of stress and worry, particularly if things go wrong, or if you hit a bad patch.

Ask yourself whether you are prepared to go through all this. If the answer is no, keep on buying those Lottery tickets.

- *Business runs in my family.* Some 12% of the growth entre-preneurs in the *Mail on Sunday*/BDO Stoy Hayward research claimed that business was in their blood. Being brought up in an entrepreneurial family can bring great advantages. It may give you more confidence in starting a growth enterprise for yourself, and can, too, provide a ready-made network of people you trust who can give you support and the benefit of their experience. But family firms can also be doubly difficult, as problems at work inevitably spill over into the home and can, in the worst cases, irretrievably sour relationships. Decisions about promo-tions and succession lines can also be clouded by personal emotions and jealousies that are driven by a familial, rather than a professional, dynamic. Sometimes the younger generation is pushed into taking over the family business against its will or, on the other hand, ambitious children may be prevented from taking a larger role by dominant parents unwilling to relinquish control. The arrival of in-laws and the issue of what role, if any, they will have in the family business, adds to the complexity of the issues involved.

  In reality, there is no such thing as having business in your blood. Being surrounded by entrepreneurial relatives does not mean you have what it takes too – you may be far more suited to another career. Many successful entrepreneurs are the first in their families to go into business and, by the same token, there are plenty of people born into business families who have no inclination to be entrepreneurs themselves. The questions here are whether you want to go into the family business and, if so, what role you will play, and how it will fit in with your parents, brothers, sisters and other relatives. Or do you want to set up your own, separate enterprise? These questions need careful consideration, not only with regard to your ambitions, but also to your family relationships.

There may also be a need for outside skills to be imported into a family business. Can they be attracted?

- *I need to set up a business because I have been made redundant.* Around 12% of growth entrepreneurs said they went into business out of necessity, usually because they had lost their jobs. Going into business because you've been made redundant sounds negative – and if you are treating it as a last-resort option, it probably is. A business set up with that attitude is unlikely to achieve growth. But for many people the cash payment they receive when they are made redundant can provide start-up capital not available before. The nasty shock and blow to the self-esteem involved can provoke in some a strong urge to 'fight back' and prove their worth. This can all be very positive.

At the extreme, it is noticeable that immigrants and refugees often start successful businesses. Conventional routes of employment may be closed to them, and they have a powerful incentive to work hard in order to establish themselves in their new home.

A significant trend in recent years is the number of over fifties who have set up in business. These are often highly qualified and motivated individuals who have been made redundant and find it hard to get another job, but are by no means ready to retire.

Ao suffering a trauma such as redundancy is not necessarily a bad motive for setting up in business, provided you channel the experience in a positive way. But going into business ill prepared, with the view that it is a last resort, is more likely to end in failure than to solve your problems.

Case Study 2: If at first . . .

Richard Branson, owner of the Virgin airlines to cola group, is probably Britain's best-known entrepreneur. He started his first business venture at the age of twelve, planting seedlings that he was convinced would make him a killing selling Christmas trees. They were eaten by rabbits. The next year he tried again, with a scheme involving budgies, and failed again. His achievements at exclusive private school Stowe were undistinguished and he left saying, 'Having left without going to university I decided to make money. I never considered failure.'

Starting in the Sixties as a hippie entrepreneur, Branson is said to be relatively indifferent to his material wealth and to be concerned that everyone in his empire is having 'fun'. Practical jokes and parties are a frequent feature of life at Virgin. The growth of his empire has been marked by setting up a range of businesses in areas as diverse as financial services and cosmetics, and giving a stake to top management who are then expected to make the company a success.

Although few will achieve Branson's fame and riches, he displays the characteristics we have identified as key to entre-preneurial success: ambition, vision, bouncing back and involving others.

5   What are my aims?

Making a list of your aims will help you assess how realistic they are and how likely you are to achieve them through setting up a business. They might include:

- *Money.* How much money do you need/want to make from your business? If you are married or in a partnership, how much does your partner want/need? If he or she is earning, will financial support be forthcoming if cash runs short? It is worth having a serious talk about finances with your husband, wife or partner before taking the plunge, as difficulties or different expectations about money can cause serious difficulties in a relationship.

    You also need to think about when you want the money and what you want it for. If, for instance, you are in your thirties and your priority is to build a business which will provide you with a prosperous retirement, you will have a longer business time horizon than if you want the money in time to pay your children's school fees. Think also about how much risk you are prepared to take to get the money and discuss the issue frankly with your husband, wife or partner.

- *More flexibility.* Do you want more flexibility over how long you work, when you work, where you work, how much you travel on business, what holidays you take? Will you be able to achieve this, given that most business owners work a 51.5-hour week and take a mere five days' holiday in the first year of trading, according to Barclays Bank?[3]

- *Autonomy and achievement.* Do you feel that you can only fulfil your personal and financial potential by working for yourself? Are you tired of pointless office politics and other people messing things up? Going into business may be the answer, but you will probably need to deal with customers who are every bit as demanding and irrational as your former boss and colleagues. You may also need to become a good boss yourself for the first time – and that is not as easy as it seems.

- *Recognition and respect.* Do you want to become an entrepreneur to win the respect of your peers, friends and neighbours? Do you want to be a person of note in your local community? On the other hand, are you prepared to handle the situation if your reputation, however unfairly, is attacked?

    You may well have other aims as well as these. If so, think about them carefully and consider whether they are compatible with running your own business.

- *How will I deal with problems.* Each business, like each individual, has its own distinctive set of problems. But some are common to virtually all, and it is a good idea to think about how you will deal with them at an early stage and to work out what support networks you will have. Be prepared for cash-flow problems, customers or suppliers going bust, failing to control costs, conflicts with staff or business partners, dealing with government or European Union red tape and inspectors. Other common difficulties include stress, not having time for your family, friends or a social life. Think about whom you could turn to for help and advice, or even just a shoulder to cry on. Being in business on your own can be very lonely. Perhaps you need a confidant or mentor with whom you can discuss business issues. Is there someone with experience or just good listening skills whom you could consult?

6 Personal strengths – and weaknesses

Your personal strengths and weaknesses will determine those of your business, so it is worth assessing them as honestly as you can. It is a good idea to ask a frank but sympathetic friend to give his or her views, which might differ somewhat from your own! The areas to consider are both personal and professional, and include:

- *Your skills.* These might consist of professional qualifications, expertise, knowledge and contacts acquired through previous businesses or employment, skills learned as a hobby or leisure pursuit. They will also include your business skills, such as expertise at marketing, financial planning or sales, for instance.
- *Your personal characteristics.* These include traits such as tenacity, single-mindedness, willingness to work hard, attention to detail, flair and creativity, ability to motivate people, caution and dislike of risk.

  Remember that these characteristics can be virtues in some circumstances, but vices in others. For example, single-mindedness can be an asset when a business first starts, giving you the energy to drive it forward. But it can also become a damaging trait as the business grows, hampering your relationship with others and acting as a barrier to growth as you insist on keeping sole control to yourself.
- *Your ability to relate to others.* If you are part of an entrepreneurial team, the members may be able to compensate for each other's deficiencies and blind spots. It is a

good idea to carry out this exercise together, as it can help you assign the roles within the business – for instance, finance director, sales director, operations director – most effectively.

If you conclude, after going through the self-analysis exercises above, that you had better not go ahead, don't give up on your dream. It may be that you are just not ready to be an entrepreneur *yet*. In a few months or years, your circumstances, skills and attitudes may have changed, making you far better prepared for success. Plan how you might address your shortcomings. You might embark on a course, a secondment, or some private study.

7   The big idea

Some famous entrepreneurs have built their fortunes on a revolutionary product idea. James Dyson, the inventor of the bagless vacuum cleaner, is one. Others, such as Charles Dunstone, the founder of Carphone Warehouse, spotted that customers were not able to buy an existing product, in this case mobile phones, in a way that suited them. He said, in an interview with the *Financial Mail on Sunday*, 'During the Eighties the big businesses who bought mobile phones were well looked after, but small businesses had to go to some tacky car stereo shop under the railway arches. And that is where we came in. It was a real business opportunity.' His big idea was to set up shops offering customers independent advice on which phone package is best for them.

Perhaps the largest group of entrepreneurs are those who have an idea to run a familiar business in a fresh and appealing way. An example in this category is Julian Metcalfe and Sinclair Beecham, who set up the Pret A Manger sandwich bar chain in 1986. There were plenty of sandwich bars already in existence when they started, but the key to Pret's success was that it promised freshly prepared, high-quality and healthy ingredients. With no previous catering experience they made their own sandwiches and salads. Now their company has scores of outlets and a multimillion-pound annual turnover. Recently they sold a 33% stake for £26 million to McDonalds. 'As consumers we believed what was on offer to workers at lunchtime was not very good. The fact that we had no catering experience was in part an advantage because there were no borders to what we did,' Beecham has said.

When you are assessing whether your big idea will make the transition from nice thought to viable money earner, sit down and write out an outline of how it will work. Address the following issues:

- What exactly is your product and service?
- Why will people buy it?
- Who will buy it?
- How much will they pay?
- How often will they buy?
- How will you sell it? For instance, in shops, over the Internet, mail order?
- How much do you think you can sell?
- What raw materials will you need?
- How much will it cost to make?
- How will you have it made?
- Are there obvious add-ons you could introduce at a later stage?
- What capital will you need and can you raise it?

Carrying out this rough exercise will give you a sense of whether you have a realistic idea on your hands. If so, you can move on to more detailed business planning, which will be dealt with later in this chapter.

Case Study 3: I made my mother-in-law a millionaire

A business idea hatched up over a game of squash with a friend made Mark Jackson's mother-in-law a millionaire. Jackson, a former GP from Bath, Somerset, was on the squash court mulling over business ideas with his solicitor friend Michael Symons in 1992 when the two hit on the concept of providing services designed to help people out in the aftermath of a car crash. He persuaded his mother-in-law to invest £10,000 in the venture. Her stake in the company, now a stock market-quoted business named Helphire, grew to more than £2 million.

Helphire now sells insurance policies which are an add-on to conventional motor insurance and cover all aspects of a claim where the motorist has not been at fault, from arranging repairs to replacing the vehicle with a car of equivalent status. The business, based in Bath, began life in a converted barn and achieved sales of £100,000 in its first year, rising to £1 million in three years. In the first two years following its stock market debut in 1997 its shares grew in value by 800%. That phenomenal growth helped the company to scoop the overall winner's award and the category award for vision, business planning and clear objectives in the 1999 *Financial Mail* Enterprise Awards. 'I must be the only man in Britain whose mother-in-law thinks he walks on water,' says Jackson. In the year to March 2000, profits at the once tiny business grew by nearly a third to £6 million.

But it has not been all plain sailing. In spite of the profit growth, the company's shares dropped in 2000 amidst rows over the pricing of its services. Jackson says, 'It is all part of the growing pains of being a new business. The very fact that you create a new market means that you will be attacked by existing players. In business one of the things you learn is that you need to be very resilient. The secrets of our success are always being clear in our own minds about where we are going and how we are going to get there, which is harder than it sounds. I would also urge growing companies always to use their advisers. When things are going well you think you rule the world. But when you have problems, especially as a public company, your advisers are very useful people indeed. You might think your problems are unique, but they have seen it all many times before.'

8   What type of business entity?

The legal form your business takes is an important issue to consider at this stage. It will have major implications for the extent of your personal liability if things go wrong, taxation, how private you can keep your business affairs and how much legislation you will have to comply with. There are three main types of business entity: sole trader, partnership and limited company. Each has pros and cons, and which is best will depend on your own circumstances.

- *Sole trader.* This is the simplest and least formal type of business entity and may be the best option when you first set up. You may be a sole trader and employ other people, or simply work on your own. The set-up costs are low and there is little bureaucracy, though you do need to inform the Inland Revenue, the National Insurance Contributions Agency and possibly Customs and Excise, if you are likely to fall into the VAT net. There is no obligation on you publicly to disclose information about your business affairs, giving you complete privacy.

  The downside is that the business and the owner are effectively one and the same, so any claims against the business are claims against its owner. In practice, this means that your personal liability for business debts is unlimited. Sole traders may also have an 'image problem' in that they are seen by some outsiders as lacking the credibility of a limited company.

- *Partnership.* This structure is similar to that of a sole trader except that the business has two or more owners. Partnerships can be quite small, such as a local firm of solicitors, or very large, such as the global accountancy firms including PriceWaterhouseCoopers or Deloitte & Touche. Partners do not need to have an equal stake in the business in terms of their financial input or the time they devote to the business. The business relationship should be recorded in a partnership agreement. As with sole traders, start-up costs and bureaucracy are low, and you can also keep your business affairs private.

  Partners are jointly and severally liable for business debts out of their personal assets. Other disadvantages can emerge if there are disputes or power struggles between partners. Partners who are not active in the business and have no say over decision-making can still be personally liable for debts incurred by the business.

- *Limited company.* A limited company is a separate legal entity from its owner or owners, who have shares in the company. The directors who run it need not be owners. The 'veil of incorporation', as accountants call it, means that the shareholders' private assets and debts are separate from those of the company. Shareholders are not personally liable for any debts the company incurs. Most large companies such as ICI or Marks & Spencer are public limited companies, listed on the stock market and owned by a large number of shareholders. But many smaller businesses not listed on the stock market have private limited company status.

  The main advantages are that the owners' liability is limited to the amount they have invested in the business. If it goes under, their personal assets are not on the line, unless they have given personal guarantees or the business has been run improperly. For example, directors may be personally liable for debts if the company has been trading fraudulently or while insolvent. The business will also still exist even if the owners sell out, leave it or die. Limited company status is also often viewed as giving credibility.

  On the downside, the legislation a limited company must deal with is greater than a sole trader or partnership, creating higher costs. Limited companies must file information including their accounts at Companies House, where any member of the public, press or competitors has access to it. Companies also are liable for corporation tax, rather than income tax.

9   Sources of support

It never hurts to seek advice and support. Indeed, getting the right support can be an important factor in achieving growth. The main source of advice for growing firms is Business Link in England, a nationwide network of advice centres. Business Link offers a range of core services on behalf of the Department of Trade and Industry, and specialised services geared to meeting local demand. These include: advice and information for start-ups, training and consultancy services, and specialist services such as exporting for small and medium businesses. The charges vary according to which services you need. Link is meant to be a 'one-stop shop' which can signpost businesses to the help they need and is usually the best place to start.

The equivalent in Scotland is Business Shops, Business Connect in Wales and the Local Economic Development Unit (LEDU) in Northern Ireland. Learning and Skills Councils, formerly known as Training and Enterprise Councils, oversee the availability of training, counselling and advice. Services vary locally. Enterprise agencies are independent agencies to help and advise small and medium businesses, focusing on pre-start, start-up and early-stage enterprises. Banks are also a useful source of help, information and advice. They produce a range of leaflets and guides for customers, and a good relationship with your bank manager can be an invaluable mine of good counsel.

Young people aiming to set up in business can turn to the Prince's Trust, which provides loans and grants to eighteen-thirty-year-olds who cannot get funding from the banks, and mentoring from a business adviser. The Prince's Trust is also involved in pilot schemes offering similar help to mature entrepreneurs, which should be available nationwide in the next year or so. The Shell LiveWIRE project runs several schemes for young entrepreneurs.

Business Links and other agencies offer special help for ethnic minority entrepreneurs in areas where there is a strong concentration of ethnic groups.

See Appendix 2, Useful Contacts, at the end of this book for contact details.

10   Your business plan

Why plan? You will be sure to come across people who tell you about tycoons who made their millions without ever giving a moment's thought to planning. These are like the people who tell you their granny smoked three packets of cigarettes a day and lived to be a hundred – listen politely and don't even think of emulating them. The reason you should plan is so that you are clear about where you want your business to be and how you are going to get there.

Many business people find that they are so absorbed in the day-to-day dramas of running the company that they lose sight of their true objectives. They are so busy fire-fighting that the company can easily end up drifting in no particular direction. A business plan helps avoid this as, by formally writing down your plan, you have clear targets that everyone in the business can aim for. At any time you can check your progress against the plan and see how well or badly you are doing.

A plan is also a living document, not a list of prescriptions set in stone for all time. You should revisit it, review and adapt it as your business evolves. Business plans have great value for those within the business but are also essential when dealing with outsiders. When you are raising money, from a bank or from investors, they will want to see a business plan, which should help make the case for why they should risk their money on you. A good one will:

- set out your strategy and your action plan, usually for the next three to five years;
- explain your aims and how you hope to achieve them;
- help you identify priorities and avoid wasting time on non-priority areas;
- help you involve employees in your strategy and enable you to build a committed team;
- provide a benchmark against which you can judge business performance.

The golden rules

Banks, business advisers and professionals such as accountants can help you to prepare a plan. But it helps if you have an understanding of the basic principles.

- *Keep it short.* Concentrate on what the reader needs to know and do not indulge in verbiage. Detailed supporting information can be supplied in appendices.
- *Presentation matters.* Check carefully for good grammar, spelling and clear expression. Present the plan in a binder or cover. Supply a contents page and a summary. Remember that numerical information can often be more easily grasped in chart or graph form. Avoid jargon and ask an outsider to read it and tell you anything they do not understand.
- *Be realistic.* Readers are not fools and will normally be able to detect over-optimistic forecasts.

The contents of a good plan

A business plan should draw the reader logically through your vision for your business, its environment, its structure, how it focuses on customers' needs, the competition, its strategic position, a SWOT – Strengths, Weaknesses, Opportunities, Threats – analysis, its objectives, its marketing mix, its operational plan, its finances, and risks and contingencies.

The following is a bit of a shopping list of what should be included in a plan, but you can use it as a prompt when drawing up your own, which should not be schematic but a genuine reflection of your business vision.

Your business

- A history of the business, including when it began trading and progress until now.

    Explain the current business and ownership structure.
- A description of your product or service, saying what differentiates it from the competition. Explain its weak and strong points, and your plans to develop it.

Your market

- An account of the market in which you sell or want to sell. Explain how large the market is, and quantify your share or expected share. This section should also contain information on key market trends, for example, the public's growing awareness of organic food in the light of recent food scares and the drive for healthier eating and fitness.
- A description of your customers and of the customer groups you hope to attract in future.
- An outline of your main competitors. Explain who supplies competing products or services, and their strengths and weaknesses compared with yours. Explain why customers buy from you.

Your sales

- An outline of where your product or service is positioned in the market, for instance whether it is high or low quality/price. What is your unique selling point?
- An explanation of how price-sensitive your product is, in other words, how much the price affects customers' willingness to purchase. Identify where you can increase profit margins or sales.
- A description of how you promote your products or services, through public relations, advertising or other methods.
- Explain the channels through which you sell to your customers, for instance, from your own shop, the Internet, mail order, via a wholesaler to retailers. How does this compare with your competitors and with possible alternative methods?
- Explain how cost-effective your selling is.

Your management

- Outline your management structure, and the key skills of the management team and staff. Identify weak spots and say how you propose to remedy them.

- Analyse the efficiency of your workforce compared with competitors'.
- Outline your salary structure and how it compares with competitors', explaining any significant differences.
- Describe schemes to encourage worker commitment such as share ownership schemes or Investors In People standard.

Your operations

- Describe your premises and your long-term property commitments.
- Explain how production is organised. Are your equipment and capacity geared to meeting current and future demand?
- Describe your management information systems and show that they are capable of delivering high-quality information in a timely fashion.
- Identify any quality or regulatory standards the business has achieved.

Your financial performance

- Provide historic financial information, if available, for the last three to five years (Profit and loss account, cash-flow statement, balance sheet).
- Break down sales figures into components, for instance, sales by product group, geographic area or customer segment.
- Provide your gross profit margins.
- Provide information on stock turnover, debtor days and creditor days.
- Give details of any major capital expenditure.
- Explain any divergences in profitablity, cash flow or working capital from industry norms.
- Give forecasts for the next three to five years, using the same format as your historic information so the two can be easily

compared. State the assumptions you have made.

- If you are using your business plan to raise money, say why you need it.

SWOT

- Provide a brief analysis of your business's strengths and weaknesses, the opportunities open to it and the threats it faces. SWOT analysis – standing for strengths, weaknesses, opportunities, threats – will be dealt with in more detail later in the book.

11   Getting personal

Many people think of business as an impersonal, objective and professional sphere where emotions do not, or at least should not, intrude. Of course, this is a convenient fiction. The reality is that business life is full of emotional drama. Many business people describe running their own companies as 'an addiction' that they cannot live without.

When you become an entrepreneur, you are likely to experience an emotional roller coaster, with feelings of intense excitement and elation when you succeed, and the depths of despair when you do not. Along the way you will almost certainly feel at times lonely, frustrated, overwrought and angry, as well as powerful, proud and in control. Running a business can be an isolating experience as family and friends who still work for an employer are not sharing your experiences and may not be able to identify or sympathise.

It will also make enormous demands on your time and energy. Many entrepreneurs work a sixty-hour week or more and often take hardly any holiday. More than 60% find running a business stressful and family life can easily suffer. Even conventional financial success, amazingly enough, can be a problem in emotional terms. If you do make your millions, it can create jealousy among family and friends, and divide you from people with whom you once had a great deal in common. Female entrepreneurs in particular report that their partners are often unable to cope when they succeed, with the men perhaps feeling that they have been left behind in terms of earnings and status, and that their traditional role has been undermined. It is not possible to guard against all these possibilities and for most the buzz of running a business will more than compensate.

But it is possible to make your own life easier. The more you talk and communicate with those close to you, the more support and understanding they are likely to give you. Running a business demands a great deal, not just of the owner, but of those close to him or her, who often also find themselves reshaping their lives around the needs of the business. You must acknowledge that your business can affect them too – the most common way being long hours and preoccupation on the part of the person involved in the business. Take care not to damage your health and relationships through overwork, and always try to set aside uninterrupted time with your family and friends. It is worthwhile taking steps to manage stress. Physical exercise such as playing sport is often helpful, as are therapies such as massage or reflexology.

Finally, a key exercise is to talk about what business success means to you with your spouse, partner or someone else you can trust. Remember that your success is not defined by outsiders who might measure it by their own yardsticks of profits, power or status. It is defined by you.

Notes

1 Global Entrepreneurship Monitor, 1999 UK Executive Report, London Business School and Babson College, sponsored by Apax Partners & Co.
2 *Mail on Sunday*/BDO Stoy Hayward Business Monitor, April 1999.
3 Barclays Research Review, *Starting up in Business*, July 1999.

2

Making Your Business Special

Give them quality. That's the best kind of advertising.
Milton Hershey, *American industrialist*

Only the paranoid survive.
Andy Grove, *Chief Executive, Intel*

Your business is up and running, you have your strategic plans in place and you're determined to grow.

But wait. What is special about you? What we are really asking here is: why should customers buy your products and services instead of going to your competitors? What is your competitive advantage? Building a competitive advantage is a vital element of the early growth phase and will determine a great deal of your future performance. Your business does not exist in splendid isolation. Rivals will be circling from the day you start in business, striving to overtake you.

And what about the future? With the pace of change in today's markets, the biggest competitors to your business may not be here yet, but they could be just around the corner. It may not always seem like it, but commercial competition is healthy as it results in better choice, prices and services for customers and motivates enterprises constantly to improve. As Andy Grove's maxim suggests, a dose of paranoia – continually asking whether your business is doing well enough, whether someone else is doing better – is no bad thing in an entrepreneur. You can gain competitive advantage through innovation, operational excellence, differentiation, cost leadership and customer intimacy.

In this chapter we will look at how to keep tabs on your rivals. But our main focus will be on how you can create competitive advantage in your own business, not on what others are doing. To create and sustain a competitive advantage, yours must be a truly customer-orientated business, where every aspect of product development and service is driven by the needs of customers.

We will also look at the issue of managing cash – a vital area for early stage growth businesses – and at dealing with the managerial problems you are likely to face.

1   Taking advantage

Big businesses devote multibillion-pound advertising budgets to trying to convince us that they have a competitive advantage. They tell us that their soap powder washes whiter, or their shampoo will give you shinier hair.

Growing businesses cannot normally afford this kind of advertising expenditure. But they can create competitive advantage by taking to heart Milton Hershey's axiom, and providing their customers with true quality in their products and services. Even very small businesses can create competitive advantage.

On my local high street, several small shops closed down when a big supermarket opened its doors – but not the butcher's shop. Instead, it has continued to thrive and has just moved to smarter, larger premises. How did it achieve this?

First, it knows its customers and has got its products right. Its customers are mainly middle-class 'foodie' types who are prepared to spend a bit more for good ingredients for their family table or dinner parties. So all the meat is high-quality, free-range or organic. In season, customers can buy venison, goose, pheasant and wood pigeon, and other game and poultry often not available in the supermarket. The shop also has a range of suppliers providing it with wonderful cheeses, Gascon delicacies and top-of-the-range condiments.

Second, the business displays a high standard of service and customer care. Each of the butchers chats with the customers and can provide immediate feedback to the boss on who they are and what they want. The staff are ready with advice on which cuts of meat to use, recipes and cooking tips. Upmarket cookery books are left open on the counters, to spark off ideas in the customers' minds and prompt them to buy the ingredients. Shopping there is a pleasurable experience, far removed from grabbing a piece of packaged meat from a soulless supermarket counter.

That is a very simple example. But it sums up the key points of creating competitive advantage – focus on your customers and products.

2 The edge

Growth businesses are constantly thinking about how to get the edge on competitors. You need to start building competitive advantage right from the earliest stages of your business's life and work hard at maintaining it as the business grows. Businesses can gain an edge by:

- *Offering innovative products and services.* Bear in mind that, although you may be able to protect some innovations with patents, competitors will be eager to copy your offerings if they prove successful. Also, remember that it is not enough to add new bells and whistles to your products – you must be able to demonstrate that they are of real benefit to your customers.
- *Providing better service.* You may be able to deliver faster, more reliably or more flexibly than your rivals. Perhaps, as a growing firm rather than a big company, you can provide friendlier, more personal service, closely tailored to customer needs. Remember, though, that you need to fulfil promises made to customers and that as you grow bigger, quality of service needs to be closely monitored.

- *Image and ethos.* A desirable brand or company image can be a strong weapon in building up competitive advantage. But your reputation can easily be damaged if your company ethos fails to live up to the image you are trying to project. Your image should not be viewed as a superficial or insubstantial thing, therefore, but as an outward expression of your company values. In this chapter we will look at image building through excellence in products, services and customer care.

3   Continuous improvement

Your product or service, and the customers who buy it, are at the core of your business. That is a truism. But a characteristic of growth businesses is that they are evaluating and improving their products all the time, and that they pay constant attention to keeping and attracting customers.

A key cause of stagnation and eventual failure in businesses is simply getting into a rut. Complacency sets in and, before they know it, their products are out of date, they are out of tune with customers and losing trade to sharper new rivals.

To build a competitive advantage, businesses must be prepared constantly to evolve and improve their products and services to fulfil customers' needs and to remain one step ahead of the competition. They must be prepared to anticipate market trends, not just to react to them.

4   The products

Without the right product or services, you have little chance of survival, let alone of building a competitive advantage. But many companies, even ones with some excellent products and services, fail to exploit them to the maximum. To check whether your business is making the most of its products, carry out the following simple exercises.

- *What are your products?* This may seem like a simple question, but many companies have a range of different products, being sold with various degrees of success. Do you know which products or services are the most profitable? Are you subsidising any loss-making products and, if so, is this part of a larger plan? Do you have sales and profits targets for each product line? Are these targets being met? Are there gaps in your product range? How do your products fit together – in other words, what are your core products, for which there is steady demand, and what are the new products for your future?

- *Promotion.* Each product or product group may need its own promotion and marketing in order to maximise its potential. To take an obvious example, banks now sell a vast array of financial services including school fee plans, pensions, mortgages and insurance. Instead of bombarding all their customers with information about products unlikely to be relevant to them, they use their existing data to target each product at those most likely to be interested. Ask yourself whether you are promoting your key products as effectively as you could.
- *What do your products represent?* This may sound odd, but when you sell a product you are not normally selling just the commodity itself, but a set of values associated with it – not just a function, but an image.

  To take a simple example, a Lotus Elise and a Volvo estate are both cars, but in the first case you are selling speed, freedom and sportiness, and in the second reliability, safety and plenty of room for a family and their clobber. Each car obviously appeals to a different market. Identifying your product values will help you develop the right marketing strategies and should inform the ethos of your whole company.

5 Who are your customers?

The key to creating and maintaining competitive advantage is to build lasting relationships with customers and to continue to give them the products they need. To do that, you need to know who they are: their tastes, their aspirations, their self-image, why they buy and what they will spend. Failure to know your customers and to keep in touch with their wants means that eventually a business will fall out of favour with them, atrophy and die. Some very successful businesses grow up because the founders share the same tastes as their customers. They spot a gap in the market for a product they would like to buy and rightly assume that others would like it too.

But this approach has its dangers. Consider the case of the Laura Ashley clothing and furnishings chain. Founder Laura Ashley built a multimillion-pound business, which thrived in the Seventies and early Eighties through her own seemingly intuitive grasp of customers' tastes. She was in tune with the fashion of the times and her tastes were in line with those of countless other women. But Laura died, leaving her husband in charge. At the same time, customers stopped wanting frilly florals, preferring sleek tailoring and smart workwear. The business lost its way and is still struggling to recover.

The moral here is that growth businesses need to have an eye constantly on customers and their changing tastes. Indeed, most highly successful growth entrepreneurs have achieved their success not merely by keeping up with their customers' needs, but by anticipating them and by spotting opportunities.

Be prepared to listen to others in the business and to undertake research into what customers want, rather than relying on preconceptions. It is not enough to repeat a formula that has worked in the past, however successfully.

6   Inside the customer's head

If you are selling to the public, think carefully about what type of customer you are attracting – male or female, young or old, mass market or upmarket, special-interest groups such as photographers or diving enthusiasts. What do you know about them? Market research, covered in a later chapter, can improve your knowledge of customers immeasurably, but simple methods such as talking to them can yield a hoard of valuable information. Consider who are your most valuable customers and think about whether there are potential groups that you have not yet attracted.

For instance, a business selling adventure holidays might envisage its main market as affluent young unattached people. But what about over-fifties empty nesters who are fit, well-off and possibly raring to go on safari? Be prepared to challenge any stereotypes in your thinking about customers and their behaviour.

Leading diamond company De Beers is a case in point. Most people think of diamonds as a romantic gift from a man to a woman, but De Beers realised that this attitude was a little old-fashioned. Marketing executives at the company reckoned that successful, well-off career women wanted to buy diamonds for themselves, to celebrate achievements such as a promotion, or simply because they did not see why they should wait for a man to present them with a sparkler. De Beers began advertising jewellery such as diamond pendants and earrings aimed specifically at this market, which now forms a significant part of its total sales.

Ask yourself whether the person who buys is the same as the end user. For instance, parents buy toys for their children, men buy jewellery for their wives and girlfriends, women tend to buy food for the whole family. If this is the case, your products have to appeal both to the purchaser and the end user.

Think also about whether you may be unwittingly alienating important customers and what to do about it. Auto-repair company Kwik-Fit, for instance, found that hiring female staff greatly increased the satisfaction of its women customers, who often felt intimidated and patronised by male fitters.

7 Business customers

If you are selling to other businesses, as opposed to the public, you need to understand how they decide which suppliers to use. You also need to find out which people do the buying, who influences their decision and who has the final say in purchases. Find out what your target business buys, how often and in what quantities. You will need to discover too how they go about making their decisions, for instance, through personal contacts, holding 'beauty parades', asking for tenders, or through approved supplier lists.

Another important point is to find out the best time to approach a potential client. He or she may have a decision-making process that starts a long time in advance, so there would be no point pitching in with your wares at the last minute. Equally, at the end of the financial year, spending budgets are likely to be low, so it might be better to target a pitch at the purchasing manager when he has a budget available. It is worth identifying the key people in your clients' businesses and meeting them, to find out what they want from you and how you can improve your service to them.

Subscribe to the relevant journals and magazines for your industry to gain a clearer picture about your market, your customers and your competitors. Make the effort to attend trade fairs, exhibitions, dinners or awards, which will give you a chance to get to know your customers socially. Consider joining a business club or your local Chamber of Commerce, which will also bring you into contact with potential customers.

Case Study 1: Don't be typecast

BLP Print Solutions, based in Newcastle-upon-Tyne, has built its success on finding a market niche and focusing totally on its customers. The company, which was joint winner of the customer orientation category award in the *Financial Mail*'s Enterprise Award in 1998, does not compete for large-scale contract printing, where it would face established rivals, but concentrates on small to medium production runs with a quick turnaround. It prints everything from promotional material and point-of-sale displays to leaflets for direct mail campaigns. Customers include household names such as Black & Decker, Procter & Gamble, Boots, Virgin, Northern Rock and Safeway. It has achieved its success through a willingness to listen to customers and to learn from its big company customers.

To make sure it meets customer needs, Sales and Marketing

Director Martin Wrightson draws up agreements that present a monthly picture of performance, including whether goods were delivered on time and whether they were of the right quality. 'Listening to customers is almost like receiving free consultancy,' he says. 'But it also means our customers find themselves dealing with a very flexible supplier.' The company also has a monthly customer satisfaction survey.

For complex products, BLP uses software to provide a schedule of key dates and to warn if anything is running late so that action can be taken. The aim is to create a long-term relationship with customers. To that end BLP has invested in the latest printing and design equipment, and has won several quality standards including ISO 9000 and Investors In People.

This focus on customers has given BLP a competitive advantage and has led to rapid growth in recent years, with turnover growing from £7.8 million when it won its Enterprise Award to £11.31 million in 1999, ahead of its forecasts. Martin Wrightson says, 'Since we have won the award, we have changed the focus of the business slightly. We now have three strands to the business: packaging, direct mail and a total print management service for companies that outsource.' He believes that BLP is unique because it designs and delivers customised solutions to solve customers' individual marketing and supply chain issues. He adds, 'Rather than just be a manufacturer we want to be a service provider, then to provide solutions, then customised solutions looking at the needs of every customer and finding ways to add value for them. We just don't lose customers unless they go bust or are taken over. The secret of our success is that we don't produce a bland service or product but a tangible solution for customers.'

8   Listening to customers

Setting up systems to get feedback from customers will help you establish goodwill, cut down on complaints and will also be an important mechanism to help you gain competitive advantage. Consider the following steps for encouraging feedback:

- *Train staff to talk to customers.* Find out about why they have come to your business, what you do well and where you could improve.
- *Set up a complaints policy.* Don't be defensive – a complaint is not a battle between you and the customer but a valuable learning opportunity.

  Dealing with complaints in a positive way will stop customers simply defecting – often people express higher degrees of satisfaction with a business if a gripe has been dealt with professionally than they did before their grievance arose. Make sure staff are properly trained to handle complaints, that they listen to disgruntled customers and that they never respond rudely. Staff should apologise, sympathise, listen, ascertain the facts, say what they will do and then do it. Try to set a timescale for dealing with the complaint and stick to it. For example, if the complaint is being passed to a more senior member of staff, tell the customer when he or she is likely to call back. Nothing increases frustration more than when a customer has to keep chasing you for responses.

  Keep a record of complaints. Analysing the problems that arise can give you an insight into where you can make your business better and thereby gain competitive advantage.
- *Consider setting up a customer telephone hotline.* This can provide you with feedback on your products and services, and any problems customers are experiencing.
- *Consider setting up a website, if you have not already done so.* Encourage customers to e-mail you with their comments. Make sure you monitor and analyse e-mails and hotline calls regularly.
- *Consider carrying out occasional surveys of your customers.* You may find this works better if you offer them an incentive to join in, such as a prize draw.
- *Analyse defections.* Contact customers who defect to the competition and find out why.

9   Customer care

Creating a loyal customer base will give you a strong competitive advantage. There are a number of straightforward steps you can take to care for customers and keep them coming back. Never neglect existing customers – it is far easier and cheaper to sell to them than it is to attract new ones, and satisfied customers will recommend you to others, a powerful and cheap, way of winning new business.

- *Train all staff in communication skills.* Make sure they know that they must be polite and courteous at all times, and concentrate on customers rather than their own agenda. If a customer needs serving, the lunch break should wait!
- *Anticipate problems.* Make sure all staff are trained to contact customers and keep them fully informed if a glitch has occurred, for example, if a delivery will not be made at the time originally set. Be honest about problems – trying to pull the wool over the customer's eyes is likely to create more trouble in the long run. Never put the customer in a position of having to chase after you – it is wasting his or her valuable time and creates a terrible impression of your company.
- *Set standards of customer care.* Make sure they are in operation at every point at which customers come into contact with your business, covering speed of response to telephone calls, deliveries and so on. Take particular care over monitoring how quickly telephone calls are dealt with. Untold business is lost when customers are left endlessly on hold and give up in frustration.
- *Make use of information technology to care for customers.* Keep key details on a database, which you can use to access information easily. A database is also invaluable in helping you to categorise customers and to analyse their behaviour, needs and buying patterns.
- *Communicate with customers.* Methods include a simple newsletter or mailshot, to keep them informed about new products and services.
- *Consider 'rewarding' customers with special events such as a*

Christmas party. Entertain valuable clients individually, but do not be too lavish or it may become embarrassing to them.

- *Consider loyalty schemes.* Big retail chains have introduced these to great effect and they can work for growing companies too, without having to cost a fortune. Retail businesses can produce cheap cardboard 'loyalty cards' giving customers one free item each time they make a set number of purchases, or spend a set amount. You may also consider giving regular customers discounts on purchases, or rewards. It may be possible for you to collaborate with other businesses on this. For instance, a hairdressing chain might reward loyal customers with vouchers for a beauty salon and vice versa.

The value of such schemes can often be justified on the basis of the information it enables you to collect about customers. But take care with discounting, because it does need to pay for itself.

10   The competition

Competitors want your customers, your product ideas and your best staff. As soon as you create a competitive advantage, they will try to erode it by copying you and by coming up with something better of their own.

So what can you do? Find out as much as you can about them to get a picture of their strengths and weaknesses. Who is the market leader and what can you learn from them?

You can obtain information from sources such as their advertising, their company report and accounts, their website and any promotional literature they produce. If applicable, visit rival stores or premises and try out what they are offering for yourself.

Make sure you keep abreast of developments in your industry by taking the relevant trade magazines. Industry trade fairs and exhibitions can also be valuable opportunities to size up the opposition.

11   Mind the gap

Having carried out an analysis of your products, your customers and your competitors, you should now be in a better position to identify opportunities to create competitive advantage.

Try to identify 'value gaps' – deficiencies in the existing products and services offered by your rivals, or indeed your own company – and then fill them. Value gaps exist because businesses become complacent and simply concentrate on what they have always offered, without thinking too hard about what would really suit the customer. Filling such a gap could give your business a valuable selling point over competitors. An example of this might be a department store that offers a personal shopping service for busy customers who want to put together a co-ordinated wardrobe without spending days trailing through the rails.

Alternatively, whole businesses can be built in a value gap. An example here might be the organic food shops and food delivery companies that have sprung up in response to the limited selections of such goods in most major supermarkets.

Ask yourself what your business could do to create innovative products and services to fill the gaps. Bear in mind that you should not just be thinking about what customers want today, but what they will want tomorrow and next year.

Case Study 2: In control

A company set up in a basement office in 1991 has raised millions for the National Health Service by turning hospital car parks into profitable businesses. Controlled Parking persuaded NHS trusts that they could make money by having their car parks managed professionally, charging visitors and staff to use them. Its success is founded on its total commitment to customers, and it won the customer orientation and financial management category awards in the *Financial Mail on Sunday*'s 1999 Enterprise competition. Since winning the award, the business has continued to expand and became fully accredited as a security company. It now provides security services for nine NHS trusts.

To reflect the new nature of the company, it underwent a

rebranding exercise and changed its name to CP Plus in March 2000. Based in Hampstead, north London, CP Plus was set up with only £13,000 capital and is now the largest hospital car park manager in the UK. Ian Langdon, Operations Executive, runs the company with Head of Development Ellis Green, though CP Plus was founded by Langdon's father Michael, now in his eighties, Barry Green and Susan Royston in 1991. Green and Royston remain shareholders but Langdon now has his father's holding. Its first deal, with the Queen Elizabeth II Hospital in Welwyn Garden City, Hertfordshire, was soon followed by another with St George's Hospital in Tooting, south London. In 2000, it was making just under £1 million a year in profits.

Controlled Parking guarantees its clients a negotiated fixed income over the term of a contract, usually three years. In return it installs payment machines and barriers, and manages the car park. Langdon says, 'Before we take on a car park we research the traffic flow carefully because we guarantee clients an income whether our projections are met or not. If our figures are wrong we lose money.'

In addition to its NHS car parks, CP Plus also has contracts with fifty Safeway stores and with Granada Motorway Services, Roadchef and First Motorway, giving it around 75% of the motorway market.

Langon says, 'I am a service industry and if I can't deliver I shouldn't be in the business. The company has never failed to have a contract renewed – and it is much harder to retain a contract than to win one,' he adds. 'When you re-tender you are tested on what you have delivered, not what you are promising.'

CP Plus maintains its focus on customers and its competitive advantage by holding monthly meetings with supervisors and clients so that it keeps closely up to date with issues on the ground. Langdon says, 'We ask clients what key point indicators they want from us at the outset of contract, so we can keep focused on delivery. Car parking used to be the proverbial man in a hut. The customers paid up, but they didn't expect much. We offer a very different deal. We provide a service so that women, or anyone who feels vulnerable, can be escorted to the car. We also have a "get you going kit" with jump leads and chargers, so if someone leaves the lights on, we can get them going. There is a free breakdown service through a tie-up with the RAC.'

The company also insists that staff appear smart and that car parks are kept clean and tidy. 'We are not the cheapest,' Langdon admits. 'But our customers are paying for a service.' He believes that staff play a key role in customer service and retaining competitive advantage. Since winning the Enterprise Award, the company has been accredited by Investors In People

Langdon continues, 'On the security side, which is a notoriously badly paid industry, we pay salaries of up to £25,000 a year. Overall, we have invested more as we grow in training and in retraining, so that all operatives are retrained every six months. If you train staff you retain staff. You get loyalty to the company, the customer gets better satisfaction and it is cost-effective because it is so expensive to hire new staff. Another way we retain the competitive edge is to have office discipline. We run the business on a tennis court approach, so that whatever communication we receive we try to lob back straight away. We have invested heavily in communication because we want to retain our role as an innovator in the marketplace and to extend our client base. I am passionate about this business. If you don't love your business, you cannot nurture it.'

12   Keeping an eye on cash flow

In the early stages of growth businesses often concentrate on creating competitive advantage and maximising sales but forget to pay enough attention to an essential commodity – cash. Cash is the lifeblood running through the veins of a business and, unless it keeps flowing, the company will die. It is no good winning a great new order if your cash kitty is empty and you cannot meet your promises to the customer.

Many essentially profitable businesses fail through problems managing cash. They do not get money in quickly enough from customers and become unable to pay suppliers, start breaching overdraft limits, are consequently unable to fulfil new orders and, before they know it, the business has collapsed. Even if matters do not get to this pitch, cash-flow problems take up valuable management time negotiating with the bank manager or fending off creditors. They also have a negative impact on profitability and growth. We will deal with this subject in more detail later in the book but at this point it is a good idea to be aware of the basics.

Cash flow is all the money that comes into and out of your business. It is concerned with actual payments, not sums owed to you or that you owe.

- *Inflows*. The main flow of money in is normally from sales. If you sell on credit, the flow of money in is delayed, so it is important to institute good credit management. Other inflows may come from sources such as bank loans or overdrafts.

- *Outflows*. Your expenditure may include accommodation costs, purchases, salaries, capital expenditure, tax, VAT, work in progress, financing costs such as bank interest and your own drawings.

- *Draw up a cash-flow forecast*. It will give you a clearer picture of how the outflows and inflows compare and will warn you of potential problems ahead. It will also be a valuable tool in negotiating finance with your bank manager or other backers. Unlike a profit and loss account, capital repayments to loans or purchases of assets count, whereas accruals and depreciation do not.

   There are some extremely useful accounting software packages on the market which you can use to prepare cash-flow forecasts and which will allow you to vary assumptions at the touch of a button, showing you possible scenarios if things work out worse – or better – than expected.

   Prepare monthly cash-flow forecasts looking at least one year ahead. Be realistic, not over-optimistic, or the forecasts will be useless.

- *Be covered*. Make sure you have enough cash to cover predictable major outgoings such as salary bills.

- *Watch out*. Be wary of payment problems with new

customers. Good credit checking procedures can help minimise these, however.

- *Don't grow too fast.* Before taking on any major new orders,
make sure you have enough cash flow or other finance to fulfil
them.
- *Be realistic.* Compare your actual performance against
forecasts and make any necessary modifications to your
assumptions. Investigate the cause to identify corrective
action.

13   Growing pains

In the early growth phase of your business you are likely to face a
number of issues. We have concentrated here on building a
competitive advantage through focusing on customers and products, and we have also looked briefly at cash flow, a vital area for
early growth businesses. But entrepreneurs are likely to face a host
of personal challenges at this stage. Early growth is a period of
rapid learning, often through mistakes.

The problems firms might face include: a key customer not
paying up, a computer systems breakdown, fewer than expected
customers, suppliers failing to deliver, unforeseen technical
problems, the departure of a key member of staff or demand
greater than the business can meet. Entrepreneurs may be
encountering many or all of these problems for the first time and
have no experience at all of how to deal with them.

We will not go into solutions to specific problems here,
though many will be dealt with in subsequent chapters of this
book. But it is well worth thinking about the potential problems
and how you might cope with them. The stress of dealing with
these growing pains can take its toll and create tensions both
within the business and at home.

Don't try to continue doing everything yourself. When a
business is first set up, the founder or top team normally handle
every aspect of its day-to-day running. Even when they have hired
staff from the start, the founder(s) usually oversee(s) everything

closely and make all the decisions. Some businesses carry on like this for long periods, or indeed indefinitely. But once a company starts to grow, this level of control and day-to-day involvement becomes untenable and you have to begin to delegate. You will probably find that you do not have all the skills needed to grow the business and that you might have to hire a professional sales manager, for instance, in order to progress.

In spite of the powerful arguments for delegation many, if not most, entrepreneurs find it difficult. This is understandable, because it involves surrendering control over the precious business they have worked so hard to create. But if you insist on keeping total control, either your business will be unable to grow, or you will eventually cave in under the weight of tasks you have set yourself. Carry out a 'You analysis' – what is it you do that is important to the business? How can those behaviours be replicated by others, or at least substituted?

In the next chapter we will look at how other people can contribute to your growth and your success.

3

People Power

You can have the world's safest jet flying 200 people but if one tiny cog fails those people will not come home. Business is like that too – all of us are vital to a company's success.

Sir Tom Farmer CBE, *Chairman and Chief Executive, Kwik-Fit Holdings*

So much of what we call management consists of making it difficult for people to work.

Peter F. Drucker, *management author*

The success of your business is closely bound up with the quality of the relationships it creates, with customers, suppliers and, as we examine in this chapter, with staff. Staff can seem a headache for growing firms, which often look on in envy at larger businesses with their well-staffed and professional human resources departments, devoted purely to dealing with personnel issues. But growing businesses often have the edge when it comes to exploring new ways of working, dispensing with unnecessary bureaucracy and creating a go-ahead culture from day one.

Growth businesses recognise that every member of staff has a role to play in their success, and realise the value of developing and getting the best out of their people. They concentrate on motivating and achieving positive results, rather than on imposing power structures or setting up rigid rules that make people's jobs harder. Good people, well motivated, will produce great results.

In this chapter, we will look at the all-important issues of leadership and creating entrepreneurial teams, and at the nitty-

gritty of hiring, motivating and rewarding staff. We will explore
how flexible working can give growing firms a competitive edge
and we will also look at possible difficulties, such as how to deal
with underperforming or problem employees.

1   The sharing crisis

The French author and philosopher Jean-Paul Sartre once wrote
that 'Hell is other people'. That is a fine enough sentiment for
Parisian philosophers sipping black coffee in the cafés of St
Germain, but not so great if you want to create a growth business.
Often, however, entrepreneurs do find it difficult to give other
people meaningful roles within their businesses. This is com-
pounded because in the early stages the business is often virtually
synonymous with its founder.

But as the business grows, the founder's ability to do things
him- or herself becomes less important, and what matters is his or
her ability to take a strategic view and to lead others. In many
businesses this creates a sharing crisis because the founder has a
psychological block about allowing others in. Understandably,
founders often do not want to give up control or cede decisions to
others, because the business is *their* baby. This does not just
happen where businesses have been set up by a solo entrepreneur.
Two or more founders can also become insular, self-reinforcing
and unwilling to admit others into their inner sanctum.

The transition from dominating to sharing is a very difficult
one because it involves relinquishing absolute power. But in order
for the business to grow, this must happen. In other words, the
business must be able to transcend the individual limitations of the
original entrepreneur. This process may be hindered by the
popular mythology surrounding entrepreneurs. When business
people succeed, most of the adulatory publicity they receive
concentrates on their seemingly heroic individual qualities.
However much these entrepreneurs stress the fact that their success
has been a team effort, no one seems to listen. In fact, research by
the BDO Stoy Hayward Centre for Growing Businesses at

Nottingham Business School[1] and other academics shows that entrepreneurial teams are most successful at building growth businesses, rather than individuals, however visionary or talented.

All growth businesses have to negotiate a transition where they move from a reactive, day-to-day operation, where management seems to consist of fire-fighting the latest crisis, to a more strategic, planning-based model. This will almost certainly involve a major change in the way you run the business, from doing it all yourself to sharing and delegating.

Many people find it difficult to delegate. The secret of successful delegation is trust. Begin by delegating small tasks to build confidence on both sides, then give responsibility for whole projects but agree clear objectives and the means of monitoring them. Be available to help if staff are struggling, but encourage them to find solutions themselves. Try to create a culture which is not blame-driven, and can tolerate and use failures in order to learn. Make it clear, however, that you expect high levels of motivation and performance.

2 Follow the leader

Most entrepreneurs think of 'people issues' as being concerned with how they deal with others. But what about yourself? Can you lead the business towards its strategic goals, or do you simply manage it day to day? You play a major role in setting the tone and creating the culture of the organisation, in motivating staff and driving everyone to achieve its aims. Of course, if you are the boss, people will do as you say because they want their pay packets. But do they believe in you? Are you someone to whom they want to give their best? In other words, are you a leader?

Business experts have recently devoted a great deal of thought to leadership, as opposed to management. In broad terms, whereas management is about dealing with complexity, controlling and problem solving, leadership is about developing a vision, motivating and inspiring. Not everyone is a born leader, but some leadership skills can be learned – and a leader can make an enormous difference to an organisation. You cannot become a leader simply by being the 'boss' or the owner. You only do so with the consent of others, who choose to give your leadership legitimacy. Effective leaders normally display a range of skills:

- *Setting goals.* You must decide the strategy and direction of the business, and be able to explain it to others so that they feel part of it and motivated to achieve it.
- *Motivating.* You must be able to help people see meaning and value in what they do.
- *Encouraging.* You must be able to persevere through problems and be orientated towards finding solutions.
- *Making ideas real.* You should be able to turn ideas into reality by motivating yourself and others to act on them.
- *Relating to people.* Honest, realistic discussions with staff will help win their commitment.
- *Learning.* Look for reasons why you have succeeded, so you can do it again. Learn from failures, so that mistakes are not repeated. Avoid creating a culture of blame where the business is held back because people are fearful of making a mistake.
- *Networking.* Try to be an ambassador to promote the business to the outside world.
- *Making decisions.* Others should be able to have faith in a leader's decisions. Consult on major decisions, and encourage others to use their initiative and make appropriate decisions for themselves. But make decisions firmly and promptly, and don't get into the habit of procrastinating.
- *Giving credit.* People often find it harder to give out praise than to mete out criticism. Make it a habit to give people the credit due for their successes. Show people that their ideas, comments and criticisms are treated with respect.
- *Self-criticism.* Be prepared to come to terms with your own strengths and weaknesses, and to learn and improve. Accept that others lower down the organisation may have valid criticisms about the way things are done.
- *Communicating.* This should be second nature. Nothing is

more demotivating to staff than feeling they do not know what is going on, that things are happening over which they have no say and no control, or that they do not know why things are happening.

- *Flexibility.* To grow is to change. If you are the leader of a growing business, you have to embrace change and work with others to help them see it as positive, not threatening.
- *Role modelling.* Others will follow your example and take on your behaviour. Make sure they can rely on your integrity and that you are seen to behave to customers and colleagues in a way that you would be happy for others to imitate.

3   Team spirit

One of the most striking observations to come out of the Enterprise 2000 programme is how many of the top-performing businesses were founded or run by teams. The importance of teams in business growth is borne out not only by the anecdotal evidence of the Enterprise 2000 programme, but also by academic research. It is not based on touchy-feely ideas about working with others, but on tangible differences to the bottom line. Studies in the US have shown that almost 60% of America's 500 fastest-growing private companies started with teams of two or more partners.[2] Team ventures have been found to be more profitable and longer-lived than businesses run by individual entrepreneurs, and quicker at pushing forward product development and marketing. Solo entrepreneurs are far more likely to find themselves at the helm of a low-growth or no-growth business.

Even if you founded a business by yourself, you are likely to want to create a top team to run it as it grows bigger. Teams are often also effective throughout a business, for instance, in sales or in production.

In our experience, winning Enterprise 2000 companies were often set up by small teams, which are interdependent, share a common vision and together make the most of each individual's skills. To a large extent this is common sense. A group can clearly bring more skills, experience, judgement and insight to a business than a single individual. Team-working can lead to fewer layers of bureaucracy, greater motivation and commitment from employees. In turn, this can produce lower overheads, greater productivity and better customer service.

Case Study 1: Designs on success

Design company Paper White began life in the early Nineties when its founders, Stephen Page and Jonathan Howkins, lost their jobs. With no capital at their disposal, the pair had little more than their credit cards, their design flair and some innovative ideas about people management to get the business started.

Now Paper White is one of the fastest growing and most profitable design companies in the UK, with clients such as fast food giant McDonald's, oil company Shell International and the Royal Academy of Arts, Abbey National Treasury Services and property management company Jones Lang Wootton. In 1998 it scooped the overall prize in the *Financial Mail*'s Enterprise competition and the category award for people investment. Teamwork and openness is at the heart of Paper White's business philosophy. There is constant communication, no secrets and staff know exactly what the two directors are doing and why. Staff are told of the decisions made at the monthly directors' meetings and encouraged to have an input into strategy. 'Teamwork is critical to us,' says Stephen Page. 'It is so much part of the ethos of the company. We, as directors, do not have all the skills necessary in the business and we could not bear the burden of working in a dictatorial way.'

The company invests heavily in training for staff, who need to be able to cope with dealing directly with clients. Employees are trained by a leading consultant in the design industry in negotiation skills, giving presentations, project management and public speaking. The consultant also interviews all employees in confidence at least once a year and reports back to directors on the culture of the company. The use of an outside third party means that employees are able to voice criticisms freely without fear of reprisals, which helps keep the feedback process objective, rather than descending into rows or personal attacks.

The company is also flexible about allowing staff to incorporate other goals and activities with their working lives. One member of staff works part-time in order that he can, at the same time, pursue a career as a stand-up comic. Page says, 'We are happy to let him do this because otherwise we would not have an employee of that calibre. It is important that people have a life outside work. His comedy also brings strengths to his work for us; for instance, it gives him more confidence in presentations.'

The directors of Paper White have been open to building up a mutually beneficial network of relationships with other consultants too, who supply expertise that is not available within the company. Page states, 'A huge amount of our business involves IT so we use consultants all the time. That leads to an informal exchange of skills and on-the-job training.'

The culture of openness even extends to competitors. Paper White freely exchanges non-sensitive information with rival design companies, a process which the directors believe helps them to learn. It also co-operates with competitors to improve the profile of the design industry as a whole. 'When you get down to it, it is all about relationships with people. Relationships are the most important part of our business. It is really important that people feel they are listened to and their opinion is valued.'

4   Building a winning team

As any football manager could tell us at length, building and maintaining a winning team is an extremely tough challenge. It raises some difficult questions about how a team is formed, who should be in it, who should lead it and how. Creating the top team can throw up particular difficulties because many entrepreneurs are often highly individualistic and even egocentric. These qualities can be virtues at the beginning, when a business must be driven forward, but can turn into vices as the company expands. Many business teams are formed rather randomly from friends, relatives and former colleagues. Normally the team will be made up of people who like each other, have similar outlooks and complementary skills and attributes, so each can bring something to the business.

Other issues such as money to invest, experience and expertise may also be important. Often, the founders are not conscious of the fact that they are creating an entrepreneurial team. They simply have a business idea and come together to work on it. But being aware of the power of the team can make a big difference to business growth. It can help push forward strategy, deal with conflict, communicate the company's vision and instil its values throughout the business.

At the start, the team is normally comprised of the founders. Each member should be committed to the shared vision, have the ability to fit in with the business culture being created and should be trustworthy. People should not be brought on to the team just because they are a friend or a relative, as this is likely to create resentment and conflict down the line. Care should be taken so that the top team itself does not become isolated and secretive, or inaccessible to others with a stake in the business, most importantly the rest of the employees.

As the founding team nurtures the business, it is vital for future success that they incorporate new entrants into their vision and values. The aim is not to form an exclusive founders' cabal, but to create an inclusive company where everyone has a stake in success.

Your top team can also benefit from drawing on outsiders such as a business adviser or an investor who can bring a fresh perspective, expertise and an objective eye. Try to avoid a situation where one person is allowed to dominate. If this happens, you have a team in name only. Acknowledge that, depending on the issue, different team members probably know best. Effective teams do not revolve around one dominant leader like soldiers obeying a general. They behave more like a soccer squad, where the captain directs others, but is also on the pitch playing a full role in the match.

At this stage your company may not be big enough to have a board of directors. But concentrating on setting up a top team will help the business grow and will pave the way for a productive and effective board.

5 Top team tips

- *Be clear about your vision and aims.* A common vision unifies people and encourages a sense of commitment. But you cannot all work towards a common vision or goal unless everyone knows what that is. A good exercise is to ask each team member what he or she thinks the vision of the business is. There may be a surprising variety of responses.
- *Spread the team ethos.* The team spirit should not be confined to the top of your business. Many successful companies try to create and foster teams throughout the company. Teams can work well in all sorts of disciplines from design to manufacturing to sales, where each member is working for the benefit of the whole and will make efforts to lift the performance of all the others.
- *Think consciously about the composition of the team.* Does it have the right number of people, the right balance of skills and the right set of attitudes?
- *Set measurable challenges and targets.* This should encourage the team to pull together and improve performance. Consider linking bonuses and rewards to team, rather than individual, achievement.
- *Create trust through open communication.* Accept that when something goes awry, it is more likely to be through error than conspiracy.
- *Be flexible over leadership.* Be a football captain not an army general.

6   Team meetings

Business meetings have a bad name. Too often they are seen as a waste of time or as an opportunity for indulging in office politics. Clear and frequent meetings, however, will help you create and improve business strategies, help iron out problems and are the key to communicating with the rest of the employees. Team meetings need not be formal – some businesses hold short meetings every day. But it is a good idea to have regular structured meetings to deal with the big issues facing the business, say once a month. A few simple tips will help make meetings more effective and less time-consuming.

- *Have an agenda.* Make sure you have an agenda for each meeting, which is circulated to everyone in advance. Typical items on an agenda might include: Agreeing and/or assessing strategy; changes in the industry or marketplace; monitoring financial performance; sounding out new ideas. Often, executives in charge of key areas give a report of how their side of the business is performing, highlighting the most important successes, failures and any issues to be addressed.

- *Don't fight.* Meetings should be kept as non-confrontational as possible. Disagreements are inevitable but participants should be encouraged to confine their comments to the business arena and never to stray into personal criticism or abuse. There is a big difference between saying to a colleague 'I'm not sure that idea would work because . . .' and 'Oh no, we're not doing that. You're always coming up with stupid suggestions'.

- *Have a strong chairman.* The chairman plays a crucial role. He or she should control the meeting, ensuring that it is not allowed to stray into irrelevancies and that everyone gets a chance to have their say. Where there are disputes, the chairman should work towards creating a consensus. The chairman need not be the founder or chief executive. The role can be rotated, or you may wish to emulate larger companies, which normally appoint an outside chairman who can be more objective.

- *Location, location.* A good setting for the meeting is important. Either set aside a room which is comfortable and where you can be assured of no interruptions on your premises or, if none is suitable, hire an outside venue.
- *Draw up minutes.* Follow up the meeting with written minutes and an action plan. These should be revisited and progress monitored at the next meeting. If applicable, staff should be informed of any decisions made.

Remember the golden rule: rows in private, solutions in public.

7   Barriers to teamwork

It would be pie in the sky to suggest that teams can run harmoniously at all times, leading the business to shared growth and success. As in any relationship with others, entrepreneurial teams are likely to face all sorts of tensions. One of the most common is the 'prima donna' syndrome, where one individual feels he or she has all the talent and is being held back by the others.

Problems may also arise if there are disagreements between members of the team which are allowed to grow into rifts.

Alternatively, people may feel insecure about being open and trusting of the group.

When you do hit conflict, there are a number of measures which can be taken to get back on track.

- *Take stock.* Reaffirm your original vision and aims.
- *Don't shout.* Listen to others and try to understand their viewpoints.
- *Be honest and direct.* Do not be vague or sarcastic when stating criticisms, but remain calm and clear. Do not leave others guessing or trying to read between the lines about what you really mean. Explain the reasoning behind your point of view rather than just making assertions or assuming your view is 'obviously' right.
- *Avoid personal attacks.* Remember that others on the team

are unlikely to have sinister motives or to be simply trying to 'get at you'. They almost certainly want the business to succeed just as much as you do.

- *Avoid ultimatums.* Forcing situations – 'It's him or me', 'We do this or I quit' – will only escalate conflicts. And you could end up being taken at your word.
- *Don't be Machiavellian.* Do not try to recruit people privately on to 'your side'. Air your views openly.
- *Look on the bright side.* Congratulate yourselves on what you have achieved instead of brooding on where you have fallen short.
- *Get help.* In the case of serious problems, consider using a 'facilitator', an impartial person who can help you recognise and defuse conflicts. Ideally, this should be a professional consultant with a mix of commercial and group dynamics skills.
- *Consider sessions with a business theatre group.* This may sound a bit outlandish, but several troupes of professional actors specialise in helping business teams deal with conflict through role play and performance, which can provide a safe environment to explore difficulties.
- *Don't be drastic.* Only expel a team member or break up the team as a last resort – it is very disruptive and destructive.

8   Hiring the right people

Having the right staff on board, and motivating and empowering them, cannot be underestimated as a factor in business growth. Staff supply the skills you need, and will often be the public face of your business with customers, suppliers and the wider world. On the other hand, high staff turnover or underperforming employees will prove very expensive and damaging to profitability. It is worth putting in plenty of thought and planning before taking on a new staff member.

First, be clear exactly what you are looking for. Prepare a specification for the job, and outline what qualities and skills the person will need. These will form the basis of your selection criteria. Be aware that some criteria will be more important than others, so you might want to rank them. Bear in mind also that your dream candidate may not exist, so be realistic.

Consider how you will attract the best candidates. This will determine where and how you advertise the job, whether in a local or national paper, a specialist trade journal, through the Employment Service or perhaps on the Internet. For certain senior positions, you might want to enlist the services of a headhunter. They should be experts in matching candidates to jobs but can be expensive.

9   Good interview and selection technique

- *Have more than one interviewer.* This is so that you can question the candidate over a range of topics and avoid relying on one person's impression alone.
- *Be prepared.* Make sure the interviewers are briefed on the job requirements and selection criteria.
- *Make time and space.* Hold interviews where you will not be disturbed. Allocate around forty-five minutes for each.
- *Take notes straight away.* Make time to discuss each candidate immediately after you have seen him or her, otherwise they will all become a blur. Do not try to see too many in one day.
- *Say who you are.* Introduce all the interviewers and their roles to the candidate and try to put the candidate at ease.
- *Work out questions in advance.* This will ensure you cover the most relevant and important ground with each applicant.
- *Don't discriminate unfairly.* Do not make personal remarks to interviewees. Remember that decisions must not be based on the grounds of race, sex, marital status, religion or nationality. It is illegal to discriminate against disabled candidates. This sounds a bit negative, but there is no need to become paranoid or 'hung up' about saying the wrong thing. It is simply a question of recognising the positive value of keeping an open mind when looking for the best person.

- *Be objective.* Score the candidates against your job criteria and also use your personal judgement. Try to be aware of, and discount, any prejudices you may have.
- *Look at candidates in the round.* Don't rely on the interview alone. Some people have great interview skills but are less convincing when they actually get the job. Take up references.
- *Take your time.* Don't rush into a decision based on first impressions.
- *Communicate.* Inform all candidates in writing of your decision as soon as possible.
- *Cover your legal obligations.* Be aware that, as soon as a candidate accepts your offer of employment, a contract exists, whether or not it is in writing. You are legally obliged to provide every employee with a written statement covering the terms and conditions of employment within the first two months of that employment.

10 Should you hire friends and family?

Many people successfully run a business with their husbands or wives, family members or friends, or bring them in at a later stage. Equally, it is very common for entrepreneurs to draw on formal or informal family 'help' in their business. The advantages of bringing family members into the business are that you may have a high level of mutual trust. In addition, since the fortunes of the business may be inextricably linked to their personal prosperity as well as your own, providing a powerful motivator. Working with friends may also seem attractive because of the trust and liking between you.

But do be aware of the issues involved. The values operating in the business world are often radically different from those which prevail in the arena of home and friendships. For instance, we are supposed to love our children, parents and siblings regardless of their ability, achievements or skills. In business, however, objective criteria about performance are supposed to prevail. The clash of the two value systems can lead to confusion over how family and friends are treated within the business. Sometimes they are treated with undue favouritism at work. More often, family members are expected by the entrepreneur to act as unpaid or underpaid helpers. The situation can be further complicated if family or friends have invested in the business and feel they have special rights as owners. These problems can prove very difficult, but clarity and openness from the outset can reduce the potential rows.

Some dos and don'ts include:

- *Don't* hire family members or friends if they would not have got the job on their own merits.
- *Do* link pay and promotion for family and friends to the same performance appraisals as everyone else.
- *Don't* overpay. By the same token, do not expect relatives or friends to help you out on a long-term basis for no pay or for a pittance.
- *Do* try to establish a market rate for the job by comparing it with similar posts in your area and use that as a guide.
- *Don't* use business funds for family purposes.
- *Do* be clear with family and friends who have invested in the business over what level of involvement they will have. Clearly, investors have an interest in the company's overall performance, but do not normally get involved in the day-to-day running of the business.
- *Don't* allow a family member who is not involved in the business to become the power behind the throne. Key decisions should be made by the top team in the business, not round the founder's kitchen table.
- *Do* be aware of the unsung contribution your family makes to your business. Many husbands and wives in particular play a major role in helping their spouse's business to succeed by providing moral support, home and childcare. Perhaps some shares would be a good anniversary present!

11 For richer . . .

Businesses run by married couples have performed strongly in the Enterprise Awards. Dart Valley Systems, a company making electronic water-saving devices in Paignton, Devon, is run by husband-and-wife team Neil and Wendy Allen. The couple have won a string of prizes including the Innovation and Technology category award and the Marketing Council special award in 1999, and a commendation in 1998.

Anne and Rafi Bechar run soft cheese producer Dan Dairies, based in Leeds, and won the Sales and Marketing award in 1998. Other husband-and-wife teams that have achieved success include Jo Hansford, the top Mayfair hair colourist, and her husband David, who is the financial brains behind the salon. Jo scooped the category award for Sales and Marketing in 1997.

These couples are good examples of how marriage can forge a strong business team. They have a bond of mutual trust and the fact that family prosperity depends on the business is a strong motivator.

But breakdown of a relationship could wreck a business. Experts recommend that husbands and wives draw up a charter for working together, that they do not try to use the business for personal ends or to attempt to bring romance back into a relationship. They also counsel maintaining a degree of separation between home and work, and that couples try to treat each other calmly at times of stress.

12   Motivation

Retaining and motivating staff will help improve productivity and profitability. Profit sharing and share option schemes can play a powerful role in motivation, but it is important that staff feel they have an emotional as well as a financial stake in the business. For staff to be motivated, they have to feel valued. This is not just about money, but about feeling that they are achieving personal aims, being treated with respect and that their contribution to the business is recognised. People are more likely to be motivated if they are allowed to use their own initiative, to participate in decisions affecting their daily working life, have access to information, and are accountable for their own successes and failures.

Communication, as ever, is the key. Employees need to understand clearly what is expected of them and to see how they are matching up against performance targets. Performance appraisals, carried out at regular intervals, say once a year or every six months, allow managers to recognise an employee's achievements and to identify and correct problems. Equally, an appraisal is an opportunity for employees to give feedback about the business, its management and their own aspirations. Simple measures such as suggestion schemes, perhaps offering a reward for any ideas taken up, can play a big part in increasing staff motivation and having them feel they are making a genuine difference to the business. Social events such as monthly staff lunches or dinners, or regular outings, can also foster a greater sense of involvement.

13 Training

Training is a key concern for growing businesses, which may find it hard to recruit high-calibre staff in competition with larger employers and have to train people to the level of skill and professionalism the business needs. Offering training can also be an important motivator for staff themselves, giving increased confidence and a sense of achievement.

The obvious drawback is the expense – both of the training itself and of the absences of the employee from the workplace. But training is often essential if a smaller business is to compete with larger rivals. The government has recognised that training is often a barrier to growth in small firms and is embarking on a major overhaul of vocational training. And in spring 2001 a new national Learning and Skills Council was set up along with a local network of agencies to implement training on the ground. There are already a host of sources of free or cheap training, including Business Links and Training and Enterprise Councils. There are also plenty of commercial training companies. National Vocational Qualifications or NVQs are based on standards of work performance and are available for most occupations, including customer service and small business management.

14   Investors In People

Growing businesses should consider committing themselves to achieving the Investors In People Standard. The Standard was developed in 1990 in collaboration with leading large and small businesses and was revised and relaunched ten years on. It provides a framework for improving business performance and competitiveness, through best practice in developing staff. More than 35,000 organisations are now recognised as meeting the Standard or are committed to achieving it. Investors In People organisations include household names such as BT and Boots but also growing businesses employing as few as three people.

The Standard is promoted by an organisation called Investors In People UK, a public body supported by the Department for Education and Employment, and is delivered locally through Training and Enterprise Councils in England and Wales, Local Enterprise Companies in Scotland and the Training and Employment Agency in Northern Ireland. The Standard has four basic principles: commitment to develop all employees to achieve business goals and targets; regularly reviewing training and development needs in the context of the business; taking relevant action to meet training and development throughout people's employment; and evaluating the outcomes of training and development for individuals and the organisation as a basis for continuous improvement. Research has proved that adopting the Standard has a positive impact both on how much employees enjoy their jobs and on business performance.

Investors In People companies were found to have double the return on sales and on capital, and eight times the profit per employee as those not using the Standard. Investors In People UK sponsors a special prize in the Enterprise 2000 awards to recognise the vital importance of people investment to business growth.

Case Study 2: MAD for it

Marketing agency Outside the Box is not afraid to use unconventional methods to motivate staff. MAD sessions, the Wow room and Funky Fridays may sound like a Seventies disco revival but, in fact, are some of the motivational techniques that helped win the business the people investment category award in 1999's Enterprise competition.

Part of their prize was a day spent with Sir Tom Farmer, founder of Kwik-Fit and a strong supporter of the Investors In People standard. The business, based in the commonsensical northern city of Leeds rather than the wilder reaches of fashionable advertising land in London's Soho, was founded in 1993 by Mark Davies and Tina Catling. Its clients include Boots and paint maker Dulux. Davies and Catling, who now employ fifty staff, built the business on lateral thinker Edward de Bono's idea of solutions that come from 'outside the box' in that they are not constrained by conventional thinking. Since winning the award, they have opened offices in Birmingham and London and, through the Enterprise Award, have continued to build a relationship with Sir Tom Farmer, who acts as a mentor. 'I listen to him for ages in awe,' says Catling.

Outside the Box's focus on staff begins at the recruitment stage, where the business is on the lookout for original thinkers. Staff are given quarterly performance reviews and are encouraged to be bold in their career aims. Catling says, 'Normally, if people want to do something outside the boundaries of their existing company, they would have to leave. But we want staff to believe they can achieve what they want with us. So if someone wants to work in New York, we'll talk about it.'

MAD sessions – it stands for More Amazing Developments – are held each month for staff to discuss ideas. The ideas aired should be ones that make people go 'Wow!', with more mundane ones dealt with at weekly meetings. The business has also set aside a Wow room for brainstorming with clients.

As for Funky Fridays, they take place on the last Friday of each month, when the firm treats staff to a restaurant meal. There are also two staff awaydays each year. Catling continues, 'Clients can see that our creative approach is not about being silly or having a good time. It produces good business ideas.'

Recently, the company launched a new scheme called Grow.

'It is a personal development plan for people, to give them tools and suggestions for how to develop their own career,' Catling stated. 'We keep saying that at our company it is like being at university, not at school – we expect people to be quite professional and we don't spoon-feed them. We gave everyone a primrose in a pot to launch the scheme, because it is about nurturing and growth. People have an assessment, where they are expected to be quite introspective, to analyse what their job is about, and to assess their strengths and weaknesses. They then have a counselling meeting where they can look at themselves and we take on the role of coaches. It has been very well received so far. People can feel quite patronised by old-fashioned performance reviews, but here they feel quite empowered, to use the horrible management jargon.'

Catling is convinced that such techniques do have a real effect on staff: 'We have very low staff turnover in comparison to the rest of the industry. We ask our people to benchmark us against the rest of the industry and the results have been very good.'

She and her fellow bosses are also keen for employees to have a balance between their career and life outside: 'It is difficult to get people to balance work and life, because we are a client-facing business and staff want to do the best for their clients. We directors all have children so we have a policy of not working at weekends and we try to make people go home at 4.30 on a Friday. I have worked in big agencies in the Eighties and I know about the culture of presenteeism. We certainly don't encourage it here. We are in a creative business and people cannot be creative if they are totally exhausted or very stressed.

'Big businesses are often not very nice places to work and we see it as one way that we can gain an edge when it comes to recruiting the best staff. Some people think, oh, all this stuff is OK in a creative industry, but we make widgets and so it doesn't apply to us. That's not true. It is about growing your brand from the inside out. Your people and your culture have to reflect your brand – if they don't, ultimately you will be in trouble.'

15   Incentive pay

Incentive pay schemes should be designed to help achieve a specific objective. The aim should be SMART – Specific, Measurable, Achievable, Relevant, Timed. Objectives could include increasing the company share price to a given level over a given period, hitting a particular sales target by a set time, or achieving set improvements in customer service. Business-wide incentive schemes can help raise general productivity and morale, and make the point that its success is dependent on everybody working there. You also need to decide how long the incentive scheme will run. It may be appropriate to run a scheme for a set period, to reflect the achievement of a particular goal. You may, of course, want to set up a scheme as a permanent feature.

For incentive schemes to work, employees must understand what they are and why they have been set up. It is a good idea to hold a presentation, explaining the scheme. Review the success of incentive schemes regularly, and adapt them if they are not working. Take advice from an accountant or management consultant as to the most appropriate schemes for your business and on how to set them up.

There are a variety of different incentives to consider:

- *Commission.* Commission payments are often used to motivate sales staff, who frequently receive a relatively low basic salary, topped up by commission payments based on a percentage of their sales. Commission is a clear motivator to get out and sell, but there are some dangers. Salespeople may be tempted to cut corners to clinch sales, which can lead to customer dissatisfaction or worse down the line. The pensions mis-selling scandal, where financial salespeople on commission sold thousands of inappropriate pension plans to the public, is perhaps the most dramatic example of this.

    Very high payments to sales staff can also create resentment in others, especially where sales depend on support staff as well. Manufacturing workers are sometimes paid according to how much they produce. This can lead to a reduction in standards unless quality targets are also imposed.

- *Bonuses.* Bonuses can be awarded on an individual or a team basis. They should be linked to specific performance targets and not just doled out for Christmas, otherwise they are likely to be seen as part of normal pay and not an incentive to improve performance. Consider carefully the level of bonus to be paid. Too little and it is likely to be ineffectual, too much and employees may slack off after it has been awarded or, worse, defect to another employer once they have pocketed the cash. It may be worth thinking about an incremental scheme, where bonuses are linked to performance improvements over several years.

- *Share schemes.* Share schemes can be an extremely effective way of giving employees a long-term commitment to the business. They can also offer some tax advantages. In dot.com or high-technology businesses, employees will normally expect to be given a share stake, perhaps in return for a lower salary, in the hope of profiting from the company's potential fast growth.

But traditional companies should consider share schemes too. Workers who hold shares in a growing company could make large gains if it floats on the stock market or is bought by another company – a strong incentive for them to work hard for it. Chancellor Gordon Brown introduced measures in the March 2000 and 2001 Budgets to increase the number of employees with a stake in the company they work for. There are a number of different types of scheme and the main ones are outlined below.

SAVE AS YOU EARN (SAYE) SHARESAVE requires employees to save between £5 and £250 per month out of their pre-tax pay. From the outset, they are awarded options to buy the company shares at a discount of up to 20% of the then market value. In the meantime the employee benefit trust borrows money to buy shares. At the end of a fixed term the employee can use the money saved, plus a tax-free bonus, to exercise options to buy shares in the company.

Employers like this scheme because participants are asked to show commitment to their company by signing regular savings contracts of three, five or seven years.

The benefit from employees' viewpoint is that if the shares go down in value they can simply take their savings plus interest and bonus instead. Employees do not have to pay any income tax on gains they make when they exercise their options, provided they are held until the contract matures.

APPROVED PROFIT SHARING SCHEME allows companies to make tax-deductible payments to a trust, which buys shares in the company and hands them out later to employees. So long as the shares are held in trust for three years, the employee pays no income tax on the value of the free shares, though capital gains tax is payable when the shares are sold. APSS is being abolished by Chancellor Gordon Brown in 2002 because some of its main features have been incorporated into his new All-Employee Share Ownership Plan (see below).

COMPANY SHARE OPTION PLAN (CSOP-approved version) allows companies to grant employees options to buy shares worth up to a maximum of £30,000 per head on the day of the grant, at a future date. These options can only be granted at the market price and there are rules governing when employees can exercise the options if they are to avoid tax.

Asda, the supermarket group, operates a CSOP covering more than 26,000 employees. The company can choose which individual employees may participate but it is common for employers to offer all employees in a unit or a group of stores participation rights provided they have at least one year's service.

There are also non-approved share option schemes, which are subject to income tax, but these are usually only offered to senior executives.

ENTERPRISE MANAGEMENT INCENTIVES were introduced by the Finance Act 2000 which received Royal Assent in July of that year. The idea is that they should act as an incentive for high flyers to work at fast-growth, high-tech smaller companies. EMI involves new tax-shielded share options. Initially, only fifteen key employees could each be granted options over shares of up to

£100,000. Under changes announced in the 2001 Budget, however, companies will be able to grant options of up to £3 million shares to any number of employees. To qualify for EMI a company must have gross assets of less than £15 million and it must be an independent trading company. To qualify for EMI the key employees must spend twenty-five hours per week on the business or 75% of their working time.

The tax reliefs are more generous than CSOPs, deliberately so, since the government is keen to help high-tech and other young go-getter companies to do well by attracting, motivating and retaining the best employees. If workers hold on to their options for at least four years after they were granted then the effective rate of gains tax will be only 10%. Normally there will be no income tax or National Insurance Contributions charged on exercise of the options.

ALL-EMPLOYEE SHARE OWNERSHIP PLAN OR AESOP is Chancellor Gordon Brown's flagship employee share ownership initiative, designed partly to encourage long-term employee share ownership and savings in the UK and also because he believes the AESOP will help close the productivity gap between the UK and some of its main post-industrialised rivals, such as the USA and Germany. It is the first approved UK plan to permit the award of free shares to all or certain employees on the grounds of their productivity. The employer can set a qualifying period of up to one year to enable employees to participate.

The AESOP is really three share plans in one:

(i) *Partnership shares:* employees can buy from pre-tax salary up to £125 per month or £1500 a year's worth of their company shares, or 10% of salary, whichever is the smaller. Shares must be purchased at market price but are free of tax and National Insurance Contributions at the purchase point.

(ii) *Matching shares:* employers can award 'partnership shares' to employees participating in the scheme up to a maximum of twice the number purchased by the worker,

with an overall ceiling of £3000 per year – also free of tax
and National Insurance Contributions.

(iii) *Free shares:* employers may award up to £3000's worth
of 'free' shares in the company to all employees, again
free of tax and National Insurance Contributions at that
point. These allocations could be subject to performance
conditions. For example, at least 20% of the shares could
be given to all employees on similar terms and the 80%
balance given according to performance, with different
targets for each of the various work units.

All types of shares awarded under an AESOP are free of income
tax and National Insurance Contributions for the employee,
provided they are held for five years. If they are cashed in between
three and five years, the employee will pay income tax and
National Insurance Contributions on their initial value, and if they
are sold within the first three years, tax and National Insurance
Contributions will be levied at the shares' full market value.

Many companies operate more than one type of approved
employee share scheme simultaneously.

- *Other incentives.* You may consider other incentives such as a
company car (though the tax advantages are rapidly
diminishing), foreign trips, vouchers for shops and so on.

   The benefits offered to employees can be a big selling
point in attracting and retaining the best people.

   A company pension scheme is a valuable benefit and,
under the government's planned pension reforms, small
companies with five or more employees will in future have to
offer employees access to a new stakeholder pension plan.

   Other benefits you may consider include private medical
cover, death benefits and so on. Consider offering a flexible
benefits package, where employees can pick the benefits most
attractive to them.

   Dot.com companies are offering staff anything from
concierge services to sort out the practicalities of their lives, to

a few 'duvet days' every year – days when one can simply hide under the covers for no particular reason.

16   Get Flexible

One great advantage of being a smaller business is the ability to be flexible and to organise the company to the best effect without having to deal with the legacy of established work practices, which might be outmoded. Flexible working has been one of the fashions of the past few years, but it is often not clear what is meant by the term, or why it might benefit a business and its employees. In addition, there is a preconception among some growing businesses that only big companies can afford to allow their employees to work flexibly. But flexible working can not only help a growing business to hire and retain top quality staff, it can also help build competitive advantage. Incorporating flexibility can enable a business to reduce costs, improve productivity, quality and service, meet the needs of customers and cope with the peaks and troughs of demand.

- *Flexible roles.* In the bad old days, employees' tasks were strictly defined by employers or by trades unions. People had one skill and they stuck to it, and woe betide them if they attempted to do anything else. Particularly in growing businesses, however, multi-skilled employees who can carry out a range of tasks are much more valuable. Flexible roles are also likely to produce fulfilled and committed employees. It is worth considering training measures and possibly job rotation to give staff varied work and enable them to function in different roles.

- *Flexible numbers.* Many growing businesses want flexible staff numbers to reflect the staffing needs of the company at different times of the year or the business cycle. It is important that this is undertaken as part of a well-thought-out employment strategy, however, not just as a way of keeping costs down. Remember that temporary staff have no incentive to display the same level of loyalty to your business as permanent employees. There may also be quality or training problems associated with temporary or casual labour.

A number of options are open to businesses, including:

(i)   *Fixed-term contracts*. Where an employee is taken on for the duration of a specific project or to cover a specific need such as maternity leave.

(ii) *Temporary staff*. To cover busy periods, seasonal work or staff holidays.

(iii) *Consultants and freelance workers*. To supply specific expertise that the business lacks, or to carry out one-off or sporadic tasks.

(iv) *Staff supplied by an employment agency*. To supply short-term cover. Bear in mind that these staff are employed by the agency, not your company, and the agency will normally charge a premium.

- *Flexible hours*. Perhaps when most people think about the term 'flexible working', they understand it to mean a varying of working hours away from the traditional nine-to-five, Monday-to-Friday working week. This is often seen as an option taken up only or mainly by female employees wishing to combine work with bringing up a family and is sometimes not considered an option to be taken up by staff who are 'serious' about their careers. In fact, flexible hours can be a good solution for all types of worker and there is no reason why it should be seen as a bar to ambition.

  The benefits to the employer include the prospect of being able to attract and keep good people, who might otherwise be unable to reconcile work with their other life commitments. Staff who are able to organise their work so that they have a better balance in their own lives may also make happier, more motivated employees. More tangibly, flexibility over hours can enable a business to have staff on hand when they are needed, and not hanging around with little to do when times are slack, thereby reducing costs and improving productivity.

The downside is that flexible hours may involve more administration checking hours, rotas and holiday entitlement. Possible flexible working arrangements include:

(i)   *Overtime.* The traditional form of flexible working hours. In growing businesses, long hours are sometimes inevitable to fulfil that crucial order and, ideally, employees should be ready and willing to pitch in.

        But employers should take care to manage overtime, which can prove costly if it is allowed to run unchecked. They should also be aware of the provisions of the European Working Time Directive which, broadly speaking, limits workers' hours to a maximum of forty-eight a week. Employees can choose to opt out of the directive and the forty-eight hours can be averaged over a period to address the issue of fluctuating business demands.

(ii)   *Flexitime.* This normally means that employees have some control over when they start and finish work provided they put in a given number of hours within a set period of, say, a month. Often, though, employees are expected to be present during 'core' hours. An example might be that workers may start work at any time between 8 a.m. and 10 a.m. and may finish between 4 p.m. and 6 p.m.

(iii)   *Annual hours contracts.* Here, employees are contracted to work a set number of hours over a year. This can be organised to meet the needs of staff and of employers in, for instance, a seasonal business where more help may be needed at particular times of the year.

(iv)   *Zero hours contracts.* No actual hours are specified in the contract so the employee only works when asked to by the employer. This can be a useful way of keeping costs low but the downside is that employees on such contracts may not display a high level of commitment.

17 Your place or mine?

Teleworking, or carrying out a job from home rather than the office, is a growing phenomenon, with an estimated one in eight employees working from home some of the time. Modern communications technology means that in theory, an employee equipped with a telephone, a modem and a fax machine could work virtually anywhere.

There are several potential advantages from the point of view of the employer and the employee. Teleworking can help the business to reduce office overheads and perhaps remove the need to relocate to larger premises before taking on more staff. It can also increase productivity through more efficient use of time, as employees will not need to commute and are likely to experience fewer interruptions from gossipy colleagues, for instance, during the working day.

Employees may find that teleworking improves their quality of life, enabling them to spend more time with their families or on other pursuits, and that their costs on items such as travel and office clothes are also reduced. In addition, it allows workers much more control over when they work. Teleworking may be done from home, on the road, at a local business centre or, if carrying out a major job for a customer, on the customer's premises. Most teleworkers will come into the office from time to time. Hot-desking is a technique for making the most of office space – instead of being given their own desk, teleworkers camp at whatever space is available.

Not all jobs are suitable for full or part-time teleworking. Those which may be include: sales, customer service, computer programming, consultancy, accountancy, law and other professional services, training and education, writing, research, editing, translating and some secretarial work.

Equally, not all employees want to telework, or are suitable candidates for working in this way. To be a successful teleworker, an employee needs to be self-disciplined and self-motivated, efficient at managing his or her time, a good communicator, comfortable with new technology and able to manage new boundaries between work and home. Employees will need a suitable home office. Preferably, this will be a separate room, with suitable office furniture. Depending on the nature and confidentiality of the work involved, employees may need a lockable desk or cupboard.

Although teleworking can cut overheads, it does require some investment in home office equipment on the part of the employer. Teleworkers will need a computer with a modem and possibly a fax machine. One or more business telephone lines will probably also be necessary. If the employee is likely to use the phone a lot, particularly to deal with customers, it is essential that the home office telephone systems are up to the job. Make sure facilities are installed to take messages when the employee is away from his or her desk or engaged on a different call.

Insurance is another area to consider. The employee's normal home contents insurance policy usually will not cover office equipment and additional insurance may be needed if the employee is to host business meetings at home.

Employers should also give staff guidance on health and safety requirements. In particular, pay attention to proper seating, and layout of computer work stations, lighting, safety of electrical equipment.

Teleworking should not be used as a way of getting staff off your payroll and making them 'self-employed' in order to save on tax and National Insurance. The Inland Revenue has tightened up on ruses such as this and is unlikely to accept that a person with only one client is genuinely self-employed. Consider introducing a new contract for teleworkers, setting out where they will be based, what hours they will work, who is supplying and insuring home office equipment, who is supplying and paying for telephone lines, that the employee will comply with health and safety guidelines, what contribution, if any, the company is making to domestic heating and lighting bills, and the rights of the employee or the employer to cease the teleworking arrangement. It is a good idea to experiment first with a small pilot scheme. This will reveal potential problems and give managers an idea of whether teleworking will be of significant benefit to the business. Keep in touch using the telephone and e-mail, and set out regular meetings in the office with teleworkers.

18   Teleworking tips

- *Results are what matter*. Measure employees' performance on results, not attendance or hours worked.
- *Evaluate the premises*. Encourage staff to evaluate the suitability of their own home for teleworking. For example, a young employee living in a shared house is unlikely to have access to a viable home office.
- *Explore childcare arrangements with employees*. Teleworking cannot normally be combined with looking after children and there is nothing more distracting for clients than hearing a screaming baby on the other end of the phone. A childminder, nanny or nursery arrangements will normally still be essential.
- *Be prepared to change the way you look at work – and home life*. Encourage employees to form a strategy for balancing teleworking with their home and social lives. Make sure they can cope if family or friends are tempted to treat them as available because they are working from home.
- *Define working hours clearly*. Do not take advantage of teleworkers and treat them as if they are on twenty-four-hour call. Behave to them just as you would an office-based employee and try not to telephone or e-mail them outside normal working hours unless it is urgent.

  Try to work out a policy on client calls made out of hours too. If customers know an employee is working from home, they may make demands on his or her 'free time'. Discuss your expectations of how out-of-hours calls are to be dealt with.

- *Do not impose teleworking on anyone.* Also be aware of the problems that teleworkers may face, including isolation and lack of motivation. Think about measures to address them, such as holding a monthly social event for teleworkers, or constant feedback on performance.
- *Do not overlook teleworkers for promotion.* It's not where they work but how good they are that counts.
- *Remember the social side.* Teleworkers might miss the office gossip – work hard to keep them in touch with the social side of the team.

19   Family-friendly working policies

Family-friendly working policies are often lumped together with flexible working, but they may or may not be the same thing. Employers need to ensure that they are familiar with legislation on maternity leave and parental leave to avoid falling foul of the law. Parents of either sex may benefit from flexible hours and other flexible working arrangements. In addition, employers may look at family-friendly arrangements. It is worth remembering that men as well as women may be interested in these options. Child-free workers, like men, are often overlooked in the debate on family-friendly working. However, they may have their own needs, such as caring for a spouse or elderly parents, or perhaps they have other projects, such as studying for an MBA.

Possible family-friendly working arrangements include:

- *Part-time working.* Part-time workers may be contracted to work either set or flexible hours. Employers should take care to familiarise themselves with the employment rights of part-timers in such areas as pensions, unfair dismissal and redundancy.
- *Term-time working.* Employees are contracted to work only during school or university terms. This can benefit employers, particularly if they experience lower levels of business during holiday periods. But efforts must be made to keep the employee in touch with developments during the long summer holiday.

- *Job-sharing.* A single job is split between two employees. This is often used by working mothers and others who want to work reduced hours. One advantage is that employees have operated successful job-shares at senior executive and management levels. But attention needs to be paid to the compatibility of the sharers, and to how they will communicate and divide work between them. Employers should also give some thought as to how job sharers' performance will be appraised – according to how well the role itself has been carried out, or on the basis of individual performance.
- *Career breaks.* Women having children are entitled by law to maternity leave. Many employers offer further time off in addition to the statutory requirements, in order to retain female staff. On extended career breaks it is vital that the business does not lose touch with the employee and it makes sense for them to undertake 'refreshers' during the break to make sure their skills are kept up to date. One area that needs careful consideration here is the fact that a replacement will need to be hired for the duration of the career break and employers will have to decide what to do with that person when the original member of staff returns to work.

20   Dealing with problems

Wherever you have people, you have potential problems. But setting up clear workplace policies can help minimise them and make issues easier to deal with when they arise. Being clear from the very beginning will set a new employee on the right track. It is a good idea to provide all employees with a contract setting out their terms and conditions of employment, and their job description.

Make sure new employees are properly welcomed, rather than just left to flounder in an unfamiliar environment, and that they are told as much as possible about the company. You might want to provide a written handbook – it need not be a lengthy document – explaining company policies.

Relatively small things can blow up into major disagreements so it is important to have clear guidelines. These include personal phone calls, e-mail and Internet use. It would often be unrealistic to ban personal calls altogether, but encourage staff to keep them to a minimum and always to prioritise business demands. It's worth pointing out that other staff as well as management frequently find lengthy personal phone calls extremely irritating.

Smoking is another potentially touchy area. It may be worth having a staff vote on whether or not lighting up should be allowed in the office. If you do ban smoking, consider setting up a room for smokers, but be clear about how often it is acceptable to take a cigarette break and for how long.

Set a policy on lateness and absence, including time off for compassionate reasons or domestic problems. Make sure everyone is treated equally.

Set up a simple procedure for booking holidays and decide on how you will allocate time if there is demand for the same dates. Usually, a first-come, first-served policy is fairest.

Be clear about what is considered acceptable office behaviour. Staff should dress appropriately and should observe basic rules of politeness. Habitual rudeness, swearing and dirty jokes should be outlawed.

Abuse of drink or drugs is usually considered grounds for dismissal. There can be some 'grey areas' regarding drink, such as whether it is considered acceptable to have a drink while entertaining a client or important contact, so try to clarify these. It is also worth clarifying the behaviour expected of staff at social events such as awards dinners or parties where people from outside the company will be present. Although staff should feel free to enjoy themselves, they should be clear that at such events they are acting as ambassadors for the company and should not behave in any way that will reflect badly on it.

Sexual harassment is a particularly fraught area, and can open up a legal minefield and expose your business to very adverse publicity. Be very clear that it will not be tolerated and that no employee should be intimidated at work. The same goes for bullying.

Office romances are possibly even more difficult to deal with. Many couples meet at work and go on to marry or have happy long-term relationships. But where extramarital affairs are involved the situation is much more touchy and it can be very disruptive if a relationship breaks up. Workplace couples can also cause tension among other staff members, who sometimes believe the two are 'ganging up'. Great sensitivity is needed in dealing with these sorts of issues, particularly when the couple concerned believe their affair is a secret – though of course it never is. As the boss, be very, very wary about embarking on a relationship with a staff member.

It is worth having clear policies over expenses and the acceptance of gifts or 'freebies'. Set out guidelines over how much it is acceptable to spend on corporate entertaining, travel and accommodation.

Talk to staff about confidentiality, explaining the need to be discreet, otherwise they could unwittingly leak damaging information. Consider restricting sensitive information on a 'need to know' basis.

21 Disciplinary procedures

It is worth taking legal advice when setting up a disciplinary procedure. Have it in place before problems arise. Your procedure should be clear and reasonable, setting out disciplinary offences, what offences can lead to instant dismissal, what the procedures are when an offence is committed and what rights employees have. Give each employee a copy of the rules and explain them verbally. A constructive talk with a manager can sort out most issues without the need to become embroiled in formal disciplinary proceedings.

In most cases, employees will be given verbal and written warnings before they are dismissed, so that they receive the opportunity to improve. Usually, they will receive an informal spoken warning first, followed by a formal spoken warning, and then a final written warning, explaining that a recurrence will lead to suspension or dismissal. Gross misconduct such as theft or fraud, drunkenness or drug taking, physical violence, wilful damage to company property or reckless disregard for safety can be grounds for instant dismissal, but it is often advisable to suspend an employee while investigating. It is worth taking legal advice before dismissing a member of staff to reduce the risk of being taken to an industrial tribunal for unfair dismissal.

Remember that disciplinary procedures should, whenever possible, be there to help resolve disputes amicably and that sacking is a last resort.

Regulation

There are a host of employment regulations to which firms must adhere. For example, all businesses employing more than five staff have to prepare a written Health and Safety policy and bring it to employees' attention. Other relevant laws include the Disability Discrimination Act, giving rights to disabled employees and setting in place provisions for serving disabled customers.

Under the European Working Time directive, employees, broadly speaking, must not be required to work more than a forty-eight-hour week and under National Minimum Wage regulations, introduced in May 1998, firms must pay a set minimum rate to all staff. From October 2001 it will be £4.20 an hour for adult workers and £3.20 an hour for eighteen- to twenty-one-year-olds and trainees.

There have been a number of recent changes to the law that will affect growing firms. The 1999 Employment Relations Act did much to alter the face of the workplace and employment law. One of the most significant provisions under the Act is that the qualifying period for protection against unfair dismissal was brought down from two years to one year. In addition, the ceiling for unfair dismissal awards was raised from £12,000 to £50,000. The Employment Relations Act also provides that from 4 September 2000 employees should have the right to be accompanied by a fellow employee or trade union representative of their choice in disciplinary and grievance procedures. This applies even if businesses are exempted from the union recognition provisions under the Act.

The 2001 Budget introduced improved maternity leave provisions and paternity leave. Growing firms must also administer the Working Families Tax Credit (WFTC) and the new stakeholder pensions.

In October 2000, the Human Rights Act came into force, where employers must advise staff if they carry out video surveillance or e-mail monitoring and check records they hold about staff. Business lobby groups have been very critical of the burden imposed by employment regulation on growing firms but it is important for businesses to comply, or they risk heavy penalties.

Local Business Links or their equivalent can provide help and advice. The relevant government bodies can also provide information and leaflets about regulation, and it is worth consulting your accountant or a professional payroll bureau for wage-related issues.

Notes

1   The Impact of Entrepreneurial Teams, BDO Stoy Hayward Centre for Growing Business, Nottingham Business School, Nottingham Trent University, by Professor Shailendra Vyakarnam, Dr Robin Jacobs and Jari Handelberg, Helsinki School of Economics.

2   Mangelsdorf, M. E., 'The Inc. 500: America's fastest growing private companies,' Inc. (1992), 14(10), 71–80.

CHAPTER 4

E-nterprising for Beginners

> Five years from now there will be no e-businesses and no dot.com companies. There will only be those companies that have learned how to change their business model and survived – and those that have fallen by the wayside.
> Matthew Barrett, *Chief Executive, Barclays Bank, 2000*

> Nine in ten net firms will go bankrupt. Many who are paper millionaires after three years will not survive if they don't add real long-term value.
> Stelios Haji-Ioannou, *Founder of easyJet and Internet entrepreneur*

Perhaps there is no single subject that inspires more fear, incomprehension and hype in the business world than that of e-commerce. Dot.com fever hit the UK in a big way in 1999 and early 2000. For a while, it seemed as though the old rules of entrepreneurship had been overturned and that any bright young thing with a trendy idea could make millions overnight. A host of minor celebrities from bad boy chef Gordon Ramsay to ageing former It girl Susannah Constantine rushed into e-commerce ventures. Martha Lane Fox and Brent Hoberman, Britain's most famous e-preneurs so far, floated their company Lastminute.com on the stock market for more than £700 million.

The boom was, of course, followed by a backlash – but the impact of the dot.com frenzy was to make many entrepreneurs aged over twenty-five and involved in traditional businesses feel as if they were dinosaurs. E-commerce was viewed by many as a twenty-first-century form of alchemy, turning base metal into gold, with some of the biggest dot.com names valued in multimillions, even though they appeared to have no prospect of making a profit.

It did not quite turn out like that. At the time of writing, the stock market valuations of Internet companies had dropped back significantly and there was a growing climate of scepticism about the dot.coms.

Of the 60% of small businesses which now have access to the Internet, half have their own websites, according to software company Microsoft. Most use the Internet as another means of advertising their business rather than to trade electronically. This does not mean that the Internet is just a fad that can be ignored; rather, it just needs to be kept in proportion.

The Internet will transform the way business is done – but then so did the telephone and the invention of motorised vehicles. Businesses cannot ignore it, any more than they can expect to function without a phone or a van. Virtually any business, no matter how traditional, can benefit from being on-line. It is not just a question of selling to consumers – known in the jargon as 'B2C' or business to consumer. Experts now believe that business to business – B2B – on-line will have a much more powerful effect on most firms. The Internet can transform sales, supply chain management, communications with the outside world, recruitment and other key aspects of your business. It can also give you access to information – the lifeblood of a business – at the click of a mouse, to government departments, expert researchers and fellow business people, not to mention newspapers and magazines worldwide. Most of the action on the Internet will not be from virtual start-ups, but from 'traditional' businesses bringing themselves into the e-commerce age.

The arrival of the Internet, however, emphatically does not mean that solid business principles – such as the need to make a profit – have been suspended. To succeed, an e-business must behave in exactly the same way as a good 'bricks and mortar' business, in other words it must be customer-focused, competitive, financially sound and profitable. Indeed, as the chief executive of Barclays Bank observed, in future there will be no such thing as an e-business.

1 The Internet for innocents

In essence, the Internet is the world's biggest computer network – an enormous, rapidly growing global communications system. It can be used to send messages, display and access information in words and pictures, and to trade electronically. To get on to the Internet you need a Personal Computer (PC) with a modem, which is simply a communications device that links your PC to an Internet Service Provider over the telephone lines. It is also possible to link up to the Internet from some mobile phones, personal organisers and interactive television sets, or by dropping into an Internet café or kiosk. Growth in usage of the Internet is phenomenal. According to estimates compiled by Barclays Bank, in 2000 there were up to 275 million users, compared with just 20 million in 1995.

- *E-mail.* This is the electronic equivalent of the ordinary old-fashioned post, known to Internet aficionados as 'snail mail'. With a few computer clicks you can type a message into your computer, then despatch it to the e-mail address of the recipient, who should receive it shortly afterwards. It is a cheap and convenient alternative to telephone, fax and conventional 'snail mail' – two big advantages are that the recipient does not need to open it straight away if he or she is busy and, unlike letters or faxes, e-mails are difficult to lose because they are stored on computer unless you delete them.
- *The World Wide Web.* The World Wide Web, or the Web for short, was invented by British scientist Tim Berners-Lee in the early Nineties. The Web is rather like a giant noticeboard on which anyone can post information. You can use it to find information about absolutely anything from the private lives of pop stars to nuclear physics. The Web also hosts the world's fastest-growing marketplace, with products for sale

ranging from books, travel tickets, financial services, fashion and much more. It is interactive, meaning that users can move from one site to another, following links or icons, according to their interests.

- *E-commerce*. E-commerce, or electronic commerce, is commercial activity on-line. The most common use of the term refers to selling on-line to customers, for instance, as in the case of Internet bookseller Amazon.com, but it also includes trading with suppliers and distributors.

2   What does it all mean to me?

In simple terms, the Internet will bring you three major business benefits that can be summarised by the acronym ICE: access to a huge range of *Information* from government bodies, universities, competitors, news media and others on the World Wide Web; effective, cheap *Communication* by e-mail and by setting up a website giving information about your business; and the potential for *Expansion* by using the Internet to promote your business and to sell products and services on-line.

3   How will the Internet affect my business?

To some degree the answer to this question depends on what sort of business you run. In the short term, certain types of business such as travel agencies, estate agents, computer retailers, CD sellers and financial services companies are being forced to embrace e-commerce or be put out of business by competitors. Others, such as a small hotel, for instance, may not appear to be affected by the Internet – but it still makes sense for a hotel in Cornwall, say, to be advertised in on-line guides to the area and the business may be able to use the Internet for recruitment or to reduce purchasing costs.

To take a broader view, the Internet is having some profound effects on all businesses. These include:

- *Empowering customers*. The Internet allows customers to

gain access to unprecedented amounts of information. They can easily compare prices on-line and are likely to use the supplier giving the best deal. Customers are no longer restricted to their local high street – in essence, the Internet is one big global souk. At the click of a mouse, customers can see prices worldwide and, although there are logistical barriers to purchasing cheaper jeans, say, from the US, the sheer visibility means that the Web is imposing downward pressure on prices.

- *Expanding markets.* The Internet gives companies access to a global market at very little cost – there is no need to set up new premises, hire armies of new staff, or even to visit new markets. This can be of particular benefit to certain niche smaller businesses, such as smoked salmon companies situated in remote parts of Scotland.

- *Supply chain management.* The Internet is empowering businesses in their dealings with suppliers. It is making it easier for companies to source the best deals for supplies and it can streamline supply chains, saving enormous amounts of money in administrative costs. The benefits can include: eliminating the need for paper-based orders and invoices; a reduction in staff time spent on administration and telephone calls; and better stock management, as suppliers can be given access to a company's manufacturing schedule and arrange to supply on a 'just-in-time' basis.

- *Virtuality.* The Internet can enable businesses to save on office overhead costs by having staff work from home or in the field. Professional services companies such as management consultants, designers, architects and lawyers, for example, where staff are often out working at clients' premises, are creating virtual offices, with staff linked up by the Internet.

- *Bringing down barriers to entry.* In many fields the Internet is making it easier and cheaper to set up in business, and to expand into new markets. Entrepreneurs can set up shop in a new market without having to invest in bricks and mortar or sales forces. An example is Internet Financial Services company egg, which offers mortgages, savings and credit cards despite having no branches.

- *Access to information.* The Internet is an extremely valuable information source for small firms. It is possible to find information and advice on all aspects of your business on-line, supplied by government agencies, commercial organisations, magazines and the like. You can also keep up to date with general business news and trends in your industry by tapping into newspapers and magazines on-line. The Internet gives you access not just to UK publications, but also to those from the US and elsewhere, which might otherwise be hard to obtain.

   One benefit of the Web is that it makes it easier and quicker to get your hands on competitor information, industry news, and statistics and financial data. It can also save you money in areas such as recruitment and business travel, where you can economise by booking hotels and tickets on-line.

Who Is on the Internet?

Worldwide. By 2005 there are predicted to be 230 million Internet users in North America, 202 million users in Western Europe and 171 million users in the Asia Pacific region. The number of adults on-line in South and Central America is expected to increase to 43 million, and the Middle East and Africa are expected to account for just under 24 million users. Source: The Computer Industry Almanac

The UK. More than 10 million people in the UK already use the Internet. A further 20 million people currently have no intention of going on-line, because they feel it is irrelevant to them or too expensive. Of those already using the Internet, 10% are regular users. Books and travel are the most popular items for shopping on-line. Women account for 43% of British users and 9% of over fifty-fives are on-line. People do harbour worries about the Internet, with pornography a major concern for 56% and 51% worried about fraud. Source: MORI

4   Web wisdom

Before setting up a website ask yourself why you are doing it. If the reason is because 'everyone else has one', then you need to give the matter a little more thought. Most businesses progress up a ladder in terms of sophistication and use of the Internet from simply using the Web to e-mail, followed by setting up a website, then trading on-line, then creating a fully fledged e-business.

Remember that a bad website is worse than no website at all, so do not rush, and determine clearly what you want the site to achieve. This is important because the Internet can affect almost every aspect of a business. It can increase revenues, cut costs and improve customer service and efficiency – but it can also waste time and money, and ruin a company's reputation. The key is to come up with a strategy and implement it professionally.

- *Brainstorm.* Set up a brainstorming team from all the divisions of the business that might be affected. Prompt the team to consider how the Internet might affect the business and what you need to do about it. An excellent source of information is a book, *The Electronic Business Manual: How to make the Internet work for your Business*, published by electronic business publisher Net Profit.

- *Identify opportunities and threats.* Focus on the main opportunities and the main risks. The opportunities might include gaining access to overseas markets, improving relationships with customers, recruiting the best staff, particularly graduates and computer specialists, and providing customers, shareholders and other interest groups with instant information on your company.

  The threats might include failing to keep pace with your on-line competitors, losing customers through technical or delivery problems and security breaches.

- *Selling on-line.* Selling on-line is a big decision. Factors that will influence your view will include the suitability of your product for Internet selling. For example, books, computer products and air tickets are all sold very effectively on-line. However, items such as wedding frocks are less likely to shift

– at least at full price – as in this sort of instance customers want the full shopping experience in person.

Consider also the demographics of Internet use. There is a preconception that the Internet is mainly used by young male computer nerds – but, in fact, one of the fastest-growing groups of users are retired people. Women now use the Internet in almost equal numbers to men.

- *Using an Internet consultancy.* At this stage you may decide to hand the project to an Internet consultancy. But you cannot simply hand over all the responsibility – you know the business, its aims and its values, better than any consultant, so it is you who must decide the outline of a strategy.

  The Electronic Business Manual has a listing of new media consultancies web design agencies and a constantly updated listing on its website, www.netprofit.co.uk

- *Focus on business goals, not technology.* Do not be seduced by wonderful innovative technology for the sake of it – profit is what matters in the end. Many entrepreneurs are still somewhat intimidated by technology and may be inclined to defer to IT specialists, or 'techies'. While IT specialists can advise on technical areas, they should not be put in charge of strategy – that is a matter for senior managers across all the departments likely to be affected. Allowing the techies to run the show would be like putting actors in charge of a theatre.

- *Assessing the costs.* The cost of setting up and maintaining a website varies from next to nothing to many thousands of pounds. The more work done in-house, the cheaper it will be. Registering a domain name, which denotes your territory in cyberspace, can be done through one of several registration sites that can be called up on the Internet and should not cost more than a few hundred pounds. You can employ a professional designer to create your website, or you can build your own by learning HTML programming code.

  Design software packages are available, such as Micro-soft Frontpage at www.microsoft.com/frontpage.

Hype vs Reality

It is easy to be swept away by the hype about dot.com businesses and perhaps to believe that you are being left behind. But the reality of Internet usage among growing firms is more muted. Research by the *Financial Mail on Sunday* and growing business experts BDO Stoy Hayward in early 2000 found that just over 25% of firms trade over the Net. Those making most use of it are companies based in the south-west and Wales, with businesses in Scotland and the North using it least.

Smaller firms with turnover of between £1 million and £5 million are less likely to use the Net, as are those with a managing director aged fifty-five or more.

As yet, the Internet has not made a great impact on profits for most firms, perhaps because much of the population is not yet on-line. It may also be because many businesses have not realised the full potential of the Internet as a business tool. Four out of five of those who trade over the Net say it accounts for a small percentage of their business, with the majority of customers still coming through conventional channels. A third of e-trading firms say it has increased business a little, with just 6% saying it has increased significantly. More than 60% say it has made no difference.

Most companies report increases in the region of up to 3%, though a few have claimed rises of up to 20%.

Of those firms not yet on-line, just over four in ten say they do plan to start trading over the Internet, but one in three admit they have no plans to do so.

Case Study 1: An e-dram – Isle of Arran Distillers

The Internet has enabled Isle of Arran Distillers, which in 1997 won the *Financial Mail* Enterprise Award for vision, business planning and clear objectives, to grow through export.

Isle of Arran Distillers are Scotland's newest whisky distillers, selling products such as Loch Ranza rare old blended whisky, presented in a distinctive blue bottle. It was set up by honorary president Harold Currie, now retired, who was previously managing director of Chivas. The company uses only traditional methods of distilling with wooden washbacks and copper stills. Its location by Loch Panza on Arran provides excellent water for producing whisky, which the company claims is cleansed by granite and softened by peat as it flows down from the mountains. Harold Currie states that he has revived the old traditions of whisky making on the island, once done at illegal stills, by producing the first new Arran Malt for 150 years. But the company has combined traditional production methods with modern marketing and has harnessed the power of e-commerce.

It set up an award-winning visitor centre in 1997 and has also won a prize for Scottish Exporter of the Year in 1998. Recent marketing initiatives include a new series of whisky bottles for collectors inspired by Scottish painters in conjunction with the Glasgow School of Art. Isle of Arran Distillers will produce a limited edition of up to 3000 bottles of single malt every year for the next seven years with a label inspired by a painting of the island. A limited-edition print of each painting will be included in the box encasing the whisky.

The company is also an example of how a traditional business can use e-commerce to expand and how the Internet can open up global markets to small firms, even those in remote locations. Its website provides information on the history of the company, the visitor centre, an electronic newsletter and an on-line whisky shop, which displays whiskies and their prices on a virtual 'shelf' so that browsers can see what is on offer. Customers can click on an icon to put a bottle in their on-line 'shopping basket' and can check the contents at any time. To make a purchase, customers simply enter their personal, delivery and credit card details on to a form on the screen and a confirmatory invoice is displayed on the screen. Kevin Ramsden, export sales director, says, 'We set up the website to heighten awareness of the company and to give us an additional sales outlet. There are still large areas today where we may not have distribution arrangements.'

At the moment, Isle of Arran sells only relatively small amounts over the Internet but believes that e-commerce will grow in importance in the future. 'People tend to buy single bottles over the Internet. Sales from the website are not yet a core part of the business, but they will become so in future. It is more important as a profile-raising exercise than for selling right now. Our website is being updated and we hope to continue to develop it.'

The site was developed with the help of consultants, who had contacts with one of Isle of Arran's shareholders. One advantage is that it can be linked with the websites of distributors overseas. Kevin adds, 'Our French distributor has an on-line shop, and if people want to know more about our products they can click on to a hyperlink and get into our website. It is working quite effectively. It is still at an early stage, however, and we are a long way off a situation where we and our distributors are using the Internet as our main business tool. But we do expect the distributors to develop their usage in future.'

Kevin points out that the Internet in itself does not mean that companies can escape from 'real world' snags and bureaucracy: 'We haven't got away from the real world. We still have to deal with practicalities that get in the way of selling our products overseas. One issue is the legalities of shipping whisky outside the European Union. In the USA, for example, you can't just send whisky to an individual and if we attempt to do so it will most likely be confiscated. So we are trying to address that by appointing a distributor.'

Another problem, Kevin says, is that the Internet makes it harder for Isle of Arran to control its own brand image: 'There is nothing to stop anyone around Europe offering our products on their own website. They can make all sorts of claims about the product that may not follow our pricing guidelines. It is a problem for us because we have a position and a price that we want for our brand. I think the Net will increase in importance to us. But we envisage operating a combination of traditional and new sales channels. It is a bit of a balancing act and there are dangers as well as opportunities for companies, if you are not on the alert.'

5 How to plan a website

A website can be as ambitious and expensive as you like. The first step is to decide what sort of site you want, what it should contain and whether you can do all the work in-house or need to hire a consultancy.

- *The costs.* A small site can be set up for less than £5000, but larger companies may spend millions on their sites. Experts at Net Profit suggest that if you hire consultants, you should expect to spend around £8500 for a medium-sized, above-average-quality site with graphics and some animation features. Adding a full e-commerce facility is likely to cost around another £1000.
- *Can you build a site in-house?* It is certainly possible and some growing firms have successfully done so. But remember that Sharon from the computer department is unlikely to build a world-beating site in her spare time.

  You can buy cheap e-commerce solutions off the shelf or use allegedly 'instant' idiot-proof on-line templates. Many packages guide users through the process of designing and setting up a store on-line, such as Microsoft Frontpage at www.microsoft.com/frontpage. They enable users to set up a store with an on-line catalogue in a matter of hours. They will also host sites, provide tools for credit card processing and even help with marketing.
- *A home for your website.* Your website is located on something called a 'server', a computer with enormous disk space and fail-safe systems. The server can be at your Internet service provider or ISP, that is, the company that provides you with access to the Internet. Alternatively, it may be at a specialist web hosting company, or at your web consultant's office. If your website is a large and important part of your business, it may be on your own server. If you have an account

with an Internet service provider, you will be entitled to free web space that will probably be enough for a small site but is not really intended for business use.

You can also use a web hosting company – these keep customers' websites safe and handle their e-mails. This may be a good option if your website is not yet a major part of your business. Netlink at www.netlink.co.uk claims to be the biggest web space provider in Europe. Some ISPs also offer hosting services.

If your website becomes a significant part of your business, you will probably want to invest a few thousand pounds on your own server, which will give you almost limitless space and complete control.

- *Domain names.* You will need an address in cyberspace, known as a domain name, a web address or a URL, standing for Uniform Resource Locator. It is important to pick the right name – one that tells potential customers about the nature of your business and that conveys the image you desire. Many companies simply put www in front of their company name and .co.uk after it. If you set up your site on an ISP or host server, your web address will indicate this – for instance, www.smith.demon.co.uk though you can register your own name and ask the ISP to rename your site.

  If you are an exporter, or want to convey the international dimension of your company, then choose a .com address rather than the more parochial sounding .co.uk. Check whether the name you want is already taken – 'stealing' the domain name of a rival can land you in court.

6   Getting help

Many growing firms will want to hire a web design agency to help with their site. Obviously, this is an important decision and the quality of advice you receive will have a big effect on the success or otherwise of your Internet strategy. All the usual rules for taking on consultants apply here, but in the realm of the Internet the task of choosing is made harder because the industry is so new. Some consultancies are excellent, but there are also plenty of low-quality people trying to make a fast buck. Be careful not to take client lists at face value – if a fresh-faced twenty-year-old claims to have worked for Marks & Spencer, it probably means she or he carried out some tiny task.

Some larger agencies will define your entire e-commerce strategy – most of their clients are big companies and they set their charges accordingly. There is no shortage of smaller local agencies, but their skills and quality are variable. It can be a good idea, however, to choose a local agency to help facilitate regular personal contact. Ask to see examples of their previous work and that of any freelancers they intend to use. Try to find people with commercial sense, who are capable of understanding your business, its values and philosophy. Check that the consultancy has the skills you need and take up references.

7   How to attract visitors to your website

One of the problems with the Internet is that it is a vast, baggy beast, containing millions of websites. The very nature of the medium means that people tend to meander around from one site to another, swiftly clicking out of any site that bores them or fails to provide what they want. The challenge, therefore, is getting potential customers and other interested parties to come to your website in the first place, keeping them there and, ultimately, persuading them to make a purchase.

- *Building an Internet brand.* Some Internet businesses such as Amazon.com or lastminute.com are so well known that customers will simply type in their address, click and be on the site, but to get to that level requires an enormous outlay on television, press and poster advertising. However, growing businesses should not underestimate the importance of using conventional means to get customers on to their websites. Print your website address on all stationery, display it on your signage and vans, and consider promoting it on local buses and taxis, for example.

- *Finding a way to your site.* If a customer does not know your address, finding his or her way to your site will be more haphazard. When looking for information on the Web, people normally consult a search engine or a directory for a list of possibly relevant sites. This means that you need to try to get your site listed – just as you would have your business listed in the telephone directory.

  Unfortunately, it is not quite so simple, because different search engines work in different ways. With directories such as Yahoo!, you have to register and your site is not guaranteed to be included. With search engines, robots are used to visit sites, looking for key words for indexing. A useful website is www.searchenginewatch.com which gives information on popular search engines. Submit-It! at www.submit-it.com will submit your site to a number of search engines and is also a useful source of information too. It is also worth submitting your site to local or regional directories.

- *Links to other websites.* Try to encourage people to come from other websites to yours by setting up links. This can be done by banner advertising, or by co-operating with others. For instance, to take a simple example, if you are selling wedding cakes, you might set up a reciprocal link with a jeweller or wedding attire shop. Companies in the same industry may set up affinity sites, and there are a number of local sites covering towns and cities. Some are run by local papers, while others host local businesses.

- *Making your site attractive.* Your site will be an attractive one to customers if it improves service; for instance, an estate agency site might allow customers to save time and aggravation by enabling them to view potential properties on-line, cutting out the amount of legwork they have to put in. It will also attract if it provides genuinely useful information and is fun to visit. Your site should be simple to navigate, look attractive and read well.

Do not overload the site with gimmicks and flashy graphics, which take ages to appear on the customer's computer screen – these are more likely to irritate than to impress. Do not ask customers to submit lengthy and complicated information, as this is likely to provoke them into quitting the site too. Make sure your website creates trust and establishes your credentials in your industry. Another good tip is to offer an e-mail 'contact us' facility to get customer feedback.

8   E-marketing

Your website can play an important role in the marketing of your company. Even if it does not generate huge amounts of extra sales, a well-designed site can help build a positive image of your company, and supply customers with information about your products and your industry. You can, too, use e-mail to market your company. Done properly, e-mail marketing can be very effective: because it is cheap it can be targeted at the customers you want and it can be personalised.

Unsolicited e-mail can be intensely irritating, however, so be discriminating. You can usefully e-mail existing customers and those who have expressed an interest in your company, perhaps via your website. One idea is to set up an Internet newsletter to be sent out to existing customers.

Case Study 2: Optimum Design

Rugby League player Pete Moran is hoping to become an e-millionaire with the help of his pensioner mother Cath. Pete, in his early thirties, lives in Wigan, Lancashire and played for Wigan, Leigh and England under nineteens. But when he realised he would not be able to achieve full adult international status, his attention turned to another career.

He went back to school to take A levels before going on to Liverpool University, intending to become a teacher. But instead, his big business idea came in 1996 when Rugby League was first played in the summer and he saw a need for lightweight protective gear. Cath helped out by experimenting with sewing foam and rubber pads in T-shirts and by lending Pete £2000 to get started.

A stroke of luck for the mother-and-son team came when Rugby Union became a professional sport. Pete had sold his padded shirts to some of the British Lions team touring South Africa in June 1997, and a torn shirt pictured on TV revealed his company's logo, Optimum Design, to millions of viewers. 'Suddenly we had hundreds of orders,' he says. With help from the local Business Link, he decided to set up a website to sell his gear.

The result was explosive and within months, business soared. 'We got on to the Internet with the help of a start-up package from our local Business Link,' says Pete. 'It was fairly simple and we paid 50% of the costs ourselves.'

In early 2000 Pete decided to upgrade the site to a fifty-page secure website, again with a subsidy. 'When I started I hadn't the foggiest idea about the Internet. I didn't understand it at all,' he says. 'I only learned to use a computer in 1994. But when you start your own business you just have to get on with it.'

Pete teamed up with Internet consultant Julian Parkinson of Analogue, a graphic design agency also based in Wigan. 'I met him at the Wigan business centre and he showed me what he did,' says Pete. 'I picked him because his designs were very trendy and he was into snowboarding, which I thought was great because our market is aged between thirteen to thirty. We went for Rugby League, but also middle-class Rugby Union players, who are just the type to be into skiing and snowboarding. He has a real understanding of our market.'

Optimum's website has a news section, and information about physiotherapy and exercise as well as an on-line shop. In 2000 it won a prestigious award as Regional Website of the Year, sponsored by computer company Compaq. The company has signed Lawrence Dallaglio, who plays for Wasps, England and the British Lions, to endorse its products. He joins others such as Welsh player David Young and Frenchman Christophe Lamaison. It has recently moved into bigger premises to cope with the large increase in orders. 'People's impression on the Web is that you are a massive company,' says Pete. 'In fact, we have just moved into 5000-square-foot warehouse and distribution centre, which is a bit of a change from me and mum sitting at home running the business from the bedroom.'

The Internet represents around 20% of total turnover and Optimum is expanding into other sportswear. It exports to America, Canada and France, and is appointing distributors in Chile, Latvia, Italy, South Africa, Japan and Australia. Pete is confident that he can match a well-run website with efficient delivery: 'We have been in mail order for the past five years so it is second nature to us.'

Julian Parkinson says, 'We were also a new small company and we gave them a good deal so that we could move forward and learn. Both our companies gained immeasurably. To get an on-line store only costs a few thousand pounds but you need to have the infrastructure behind it. At the moment a lot of people are talking about e-commerce. In the next twelve months people will really start to look at it more seriously. They have been scared off because of failures such as boo.com. When I go and see them I tell them the Internet is an extra channel. If your existing channels are not working you need to sort them out first. I tell them that they are unlikely to become instant millionaires.'

9   Your Internet shop

An on-line shop should enable customers to browse through your product range, pop goods into an electronic shopping basket, keep tabs on how much they are spending, including shipping and tax, and pay securely, possibly in a variety of currencies. There are a plethora of software packages around that will do the job, ranging from simple DIY options costing a few hundred pounds, to sophisticated systems costing tens of thousands.

Your Internet shop should make your customers feel as comfortable as a real shop, bearing in mind that many may feel unsure of themselves buying on-line. It should also be convenient and not subject customers to unnecessary delay. Make sure navigation is simple and leads visitors towards the 'till'. Try to build trust by giving information on delivery, security, refunds, payment policy and so on. Give an e-mail address and a telephone number so that customers can contact you if they need to.

A small personal experience: my first attempt at buying over the Internet was with some perfume unavailable in the UK from a rather grand Paris 'Maison de Beauté'. Ordering was simple and the on-line shop was attractive, but no confirmation was given on-line that my order had been received correctly. Rather disconcerted, I felt I ought to check the order by telephone, which not only involved airing my rusty French, but also negated the point of buying on-line. I was left feeling a little doubtful until the perfume actually arrived a few days later.

So the moral is, try to give customers as much reassurance as you can. Offer a choice of payment options and bear in mind that some customers may be uncomfortable giving out their credit card numbers over the Internet.

On-line traders need to consult their banks – if you are dealing with relatively small volumes, credit card payments can be treated in the same way as orders taken over the phone, but banks will want to know you are trading on-line and will probably provide a special Internet merchant number. For higher volumes an on-line clearance system is needed. To handle transactions, sign up with a service such as DataCash at www.datacash.co.uk, Worldpay at www.worldpay.com or Barclays ePDQ at www.epdq.co.uk.

10 Security

Security is a major concern on the Internet and many experts believe that e-commerce will not truly take off until customers become reassured that it is safe to buy on-line. The importance of security cannot be underestimated – imagine the damage to your business if customers' credit card details were divulged or obtained by hackers.

There is no real reason why credit card payments over the Internet should be any more risky than any other form of credit card payments, which are, of course, perennially vulnerable to fraud. Be aware that security breaches may come from staff purloining information and if you do store customers' credit card details, do so on a computer off the company network, protected by passwords and for the minimum amount of time. Offer customers the option of paying by credit card over the phone, or by cheque in the post.

Although most of the publicity about Internet security has focused on customer worries, the reality is that businesses are more likely to be the target of fraud. One growing area, according to credit card companies, is 'repudiation' where customers deny they have done a deal and the credit card company takes the money back from the seller. Disputes are much more common in on-line transactions than in others where the cardholder is not physically present. This may not be for entirely suspicious reasons – for instance, it may be too easy to 'click' on a purchase without meaning to, or the customer may not recognise the company details on his or her credit card statement. However, the scope for this to become a huge problem with Internet selling, particularly overseas, is obvious – and it could be very damaging to a business if a customer claims, truthfully or not, that a valuable order has never arrived.

At the time of writing the government was attempting to improve matters by pushing through a new Electronic Communications Bill, which will give electronic signatures the same status in law as handwritten signatures. The British Chambers of Commerce is offering a Chamber Sign system enabling a firm to transact business with a customer who has signed documents electronically and be confident that the signature is genuine. Banks, led by Barclays and NatWest, plan to introduce a similar system for customers, called Identrus. Electronic signatures have been developed through a technique called public key cryptography. Two cryptographic keys are needed for a digital signature. A private key, which is kept secret, is used to generate the signature and a public key is used by others to verify it.

11   Stand and deliver

The Internet offers instant, twenty-four-hours-a-day shopping. Unfortunately, however, it often all falls down when it comes to old-fashioned practicality – the delivery. No matter how wonderful your website is, you will not keep customers if they have to wait weeks for their goods. It is, therefore, vital that orders are efficiently processed and delivered.

One of the advantages of the Internet is that it enables you to minimise a potent source of customer dissatisfaction – not knowing what is going on. Confirm the details of an order to customers as soon as it is received, then e-mail them when the goods have been despatched. Make sure you have staff who can answer complaints and queries, and train them to respond both to calls and e-mails within a set time. Take precautions to prevent orders from getting lost in the computer system by backing them up on disk and by printing off copies.

Consider using a courier company to speed up your delivery times. Parcelforce at www.parcelforce.co.uk is heavily involved in e-commerce. It has won awards for its website and, along with IBM, has produced HomePage Creator, an on-line selling package for smaller companies.

Courier companies such as Federal Express at www.fedex.com, DHL at www.dhl.co.uk, TNT at www.tnt.co.uk and UPS at www.ups.co.uk will warehouse, handle tax and carry out a range of other services. In addition, they will allow customers to track deliveries on-line and you can incorporate this into your website so people can see when their product will arrive.

12   Streamlining your business

Most of the publicity about the Internet and business has focused on the exciting world of selling on-line. But it also has enormous potential to improve the internal functioning of your business in areas such as customer service, your supply chain, recruitment and new ways of working.

- *Customer service*. You can use e-mail instead of the telephone to deal with customer enquiries. Preparing a set of standard replies can cut down on time spent dealing with routine enquiries.

You can also keep in touch with customers with e-mail newsletters. In addition, you can improve customer service by, for example, offering a question-and-answer page on your website, back-up literature on-line, or an e-mail suggestion box where customers can let you know their ideas for possible improvements. Some companies can offer 'self-service' on-line, saving customers time and inconvenience. Examples include looking up train times and ordering a ticket on-line, rather than going to the station or enduring a long telephone queue.

- *Supply chain*. The Internet is a source of information on new suppliers, who can be asked for quotes by e-mail. Firms can post requests for tenders on the Internet, and use trading communities that team up buyers and sellers. Companies that have done so claim they can shave large sums from their expenditure in this way.

  Companies can also use the Internet to integrate their supply chain, so that invoices and orders can pass up and down the chain automatically. The advantage of this is that documents do not have to be processed by hand – they flow straight into the recipient's system, saving time, costs and reducing the scope for error.

  Integrated supply chains can also help stock control. For instance, suppliers could be given access to a customer's system so that they could automatically supply goods needed on a just-in-time basis. The benefit to suppliers is that they can see more easily how well an item is selling and organise their production accordingly. Electronically linked supply chains have been developing since the 1980s, but with the advent of the Internet they are likely to become more prevalent.

  The Internet is providing a low-cost route to link-up chains and appears to be leading to a culture of greater collaboration.

- *Recruitment.* The Internet is fast becoming a key recruiting tool. Job-seekers, particularly the young, graduates and those who are computer literate will increasingly turn to the Internet as a source of information about potential employers.

  You can include a special recruitment section on your website for new staff, with the advantage that people on the site are already likely to be interested in your business. There are many on-line recruitment agencies, too, with rates ranging from a few pounds for a one-line text advertisement, to several thousands to set up your own area on a recruitment site.

  The Internet also allows you to be much more flexible in your working practices, so that staff can work at home or on the road, rather than being chained to the office.

13   Jargon busting

One of the worst aspects of the Internet is the amount of impenetrable acronyms and jargon it has spawned. Here is a quick translation of some of the most common:

Address   The equivalent of a postal address. A web address is typically www.mycompany.co.uk; an e-mail address is typically myname@mycompany.co.uk.

Bandwidth   The capacity of a telephone link. Useful to facilitate the creation of pages directly from text, rather than via code.

Bookmark   A feature of web browsers, marking a web page so you can return straight to it in future.

Bot   A computer that does something intelligent.

Broadband   Very high bandwidth.

Browser   Software that enables you to view a web page, such as Netscape or Microsoft Explorer.

Chatroom   An electronic 'room' where people can talk to each other live, in 'real time'.

Digital   Processing sound, video, text and graphics by

breaking it down into a series of ones and noughts, or 'digits'.

Domain   A site's main address. Domain names are unique and must be registered.

Download   To import a file or program on to your computer.

E-mail   An electronic message system over the Internet.

Encryption   Coding of information for security purposes.

Extranet   An *intranet* that gives outsiders limited access.

Firewall   A security system protecting an internal network.

Geek   An archetypal computer user, said to wear anoraks and to have limited social skills.

Hit   A visit to a web page.

HTML   Hypertext Mark-up Language, or the computer language used to create web pages.

Hypertext   Highlighted words that allow you to jump from one site to another, or from one part of a site to another part by clicking on the word.

Identrus   A network formed by banks around the world to increase security in e-commerce.

Internet   A network linking computers across the world. The most common aspects are e-mail, the World Wide Web and newsgroups.

Internet Service Provider   A company that will connect you to the Internet.

Intranet   A private computer network used within a company or organisation.

ISDN   Integrated Services Digital Network. A high-bandwidth phone line giving fast access to the Web.

M-commerce   Carrying out transactions on the Internet using a mobile phone.

Modem   A device that allows information to be conveyed to and from computers down traditional telephone lines.

Portal   A website offering a range of services such as on-line shopping and e-mails.

Search engine   Used for finding useful information on the Internet.

Server A computer where a website is situated.

URL Uniform Resource Locator. The address of a web page.

Virtual Something that exists in computer form, for instance a 'virtual shopping mall'.

Virus A programme that can damage or wipe out other programmes.

WAP Wireless Application Protocol allows mobile phones and palmtop computers to access the Internet.

World Wide Web A giant noticeboard. Millions of websites on the Internet.

5
Marketing Magic

A sweet, brown, fizzy beverage . . . Coca-Cola is one of the world's truly non-essential products brilliantly marketed.

Wall Street Journal

I watch where the cosmetics industry is going then walk in the opposite direction.

Anita Roddick

The term 'marketing' is the source of seemingly endless confusion. It is often used to mean the same thing as selling and unfortunately it is often dismissed by business people as 'soft' or an inessential element grafted on to the 'real' business of producing things. But as the anonymous commentator in the *Wall Street Journal* recognised, marketing is what turned Coca-Cola from just another sweet drink into an almost all-powerful global brand.

Most successful entrepreneurs have an instinctive under-standing of marketing, even if they do not label it as such. The Chartered Institute of Marketing defines it as 'The management process responsible for identifying, anticipating and satisfying customer requirements profitably'. This involves market research, customer care, pricing, promotion, selling, distribution and other elements. In simple terms, you might think of marketing as the link between you and your customers.

Why do you need marketing? The glib answer is that you need it to stay in business. You certainly need it if your business is to grow, to continue satisfying existing customers and attracting new ones, and to retain its competitive edge. In practical terms, marketing ought to help you keep profitable customers, persuade them to buy more, or more profitable products, or to win new customers. You need marketing, in short, if you are to maximise your business's profitability.

Many growing firms now recognise the importance of marketing and appoint a professional to oversee their activities in this field. However, it is well worth entrepreneurs being versed in the basic principles, even if they delegate responsibility to another director or manager, and at first a business may not be able to afford to hire a marketing professional, making it a case of 'Do It Yourself'.

In this chapter we will look at how to develop a marketing plan, and take a peek into the seemingly black arts of advertising and public relations.

1   A marketing audit

A proper marketing strategy, rather than a scatter-gun approach, should be at the heart of your marketing effort. Help with drawing up a strategy can be obtained from your local Business Link or its equivalent in Scotland, Wales or Northern Ireland. Other useful organisations are the Chartered Institute of Marketing, a professional body for marketing and sales. It provides in-company training and open courses leading to recognised qualifications and with a library service for members including market research reports, statistics and databases. The Marketing Council is an organisation aiming to help UK business increase wealth creation and competitiveness through marketing. It organises a programme of seminars, road shows, publications, workshops and conferences. Full contact details are provided in Appendix 2, Useful Contacts.

In order to develop a marketing plan for the future, you need to know where you are now. The first step in this process is to gain a clear understanding of your market. It is worth devoting time and effort to researching the market in some depth. If you do not have the resources or the expertise to carry out the research internally, it may make sense to commission a market research agency. The Market Research Society is a professional body which publishes a guide to choosing a market research agency and provides a list of agencies working within its code of conduct. You can also use a local consultant, or local libraries, the Internet and your Business Link or equivalent.

One really important fact is that most businesses have absolutely loads of valuable market and customer information trapped within them: the good and bad payers, the most profitable products, which sectors tend to purchase your products, which combinations of products tend to be bought either together or over time, when customers buy. It is also really useful to contact past customers to find out why they don't buy from you any more, and existing customers to find out why they stay with you and what more could be done. This can be very small-scale, cost-effective market research and pay dividends for future marketing planning. You can then start to predict which customers will buy which products and when.

When conducting your research, the questions you need to answer include:

- *Your market.* How large is it? Is it growing or shrinking? What are the main trends influencing it? Who are your competition? Are there any government or regulatory issues affecting your business, now or in future?

- *Your customers.* Who are your customers? Why do they buy from you – or why do they buy from the competition? Who are your most valuable customers? How do customers buy your products; for example, from a shop, mail order or on the Internet? Use this information to draw up a marketing audit, which should give you a clear understanding of your market and your position in it. In the audit:

    (i)   analyse the market segments that you sell to;

    (ii)   determine which customers are the most profitable, or will be in future;

(iii) identify opportunities to sell customers additional, or higher-value products;

(iv) pinpoint the reasons that customers buy from you and from the competition;

(v) assess the effectiveness of previous marketing initiatives.

The marketing audit should provide you with a SWOT (Strengths, Weaknesses, Opportunities, Threats) analysis of your existing marketing and supply the basis from which you can develop a marketing strategy.

Simple Marketing Tips

● Find out your customers' buying patterns. With business customers, for example, if their new budgets start in April they may be planning their expenditure some months before, meaning that you need to contact them prior to that time. Or they may be keen to push spending through before their year end. If you are selling directly to consumers, be aware of factors affecting their buying behaviour such as Christmas or the end of the tax year.

● Keep in touch with customers and constantly ask them for feedback and ideas to improve your performance.

● Maintain a high profile with your most valuable customers, by arranging personal meetings, telephone calls, lunches or corporate hospitality. Less important customers can be kept in touch by mail, e-mail or fax.

Case Study 1: All systems go for Sagitta

Sagitta Performance Systems was set up in 1997 by Andy Norman, Managing Director, and Dave Leyland the Sales Director, as a management buyout from a company called Xyratex, itself a management buyout from computer giant IBM. Marketing has been at the very heart of its growth strategy. Sagitta has focused on providing a totally individual tailor-made system for each of its customers. Its marketing effort has also concentrated on forging alliances with others, including computer giant IBM. To achieve this, the company has had to acquire a detailed understanding of its customers and their needs, and also to display persistence and effort in creating relationships.

Its business is 'storage area networking' which, in simple terms, provides faster and more efficient networks connecting computer servers. Once a system is in place, it can help clients to reduce costs and improve productivity. Norman says, 'One of our customers is *AutoTrade* magazine, which every week must produce a publication with pictures of cars, so they have to use heaps of computer files. We built them a storage area network where a team of editors can all access material and work on it together. Their productivity has improved enormously.'

Sagitta's customers also include broadcaster BSkyB, which uses its systems to edit graphics for *Sky News* and *Sky Sport*, and several universities. Norman says, 'Storage area networking is like children's building bricks. You are designing systems differently for everyone. We turn technology into solutions for customers.'

He and Dave Leyland were inspired by a book called *Crossing the Chasm* by technology and communications guru Geoffrey A. Moore, published in the UK by Capstone, which addresses the issue of marketing for technology companies. Norman says, 'Moore suggests that as a new business you will never get into the mainstream and be wildly successful unless you cross the chasm. Crossing the chasm means you have to get yourself hitched to big-brand companies. We started off getting into niche markets where we could make a big difference. We do what I call parasitic marketing. We went to IBM to try to become a business partner. We spent a year canvassing and lobbying within IBM, so it was very hard work. But it has been worth it because now they take us into lots of accounts. Marketing is at the heart of what we do. We don't have a separate marketing budget or spend thousands on adverts or trade shows. We invest time, energy and effort in hooking up with the right people.'

2   Marketing objectives

The next step is to determine where you would like to be – in other words, your marketing objectives. When setting objectives, remember that it is not satisfactory simply to state an aim, such as increasing sales. Rather, you need to set a target to be achieved over a particular time-span so that you can measure performance. Remember also that your marketing aims should flow from the overall aims of the business.

Focus on a limited set of well-defined objectives and take a logical, step-by-step approach, concentrating on the following areas:

- *Target markets*. Decide which market segments and customers you wish to target, bearing in mind that it is sensible to reinforce your position in existing segments before entering new ones.
- *Product improvements*. Determine adjustments that you want to make to your products. Identify any products or services that need updating. Look at repackaging and resizing, and identifying new uses for existing products. Bear in mind, again, that evolving existing products is cheaper and less risky than launching new ones.
- *Pricing and distribution*. Consider how you will price and distribute each product or service in order to satisfy customers and maximise profitability.
- *Promotion*. Examine the various options for promoting your products and services, including advertising, PR, direct mail, telesales, exhibitions and personal recommendation.
- *Selling*. Review your sales terms and conditions – for example credit terms – to ascertain whether they could be made more attractive without compromising credit control.
- *Fulfilment*. Examine how you will fulfil new orders, which may require additional production capacity, new staff or new delivery mechanisms.
- *Service*. Ask how you can improve customer service, which can have a big effect on customer loyalty and sales at a relatively low cost.

- *Effectiveness*. Decide how you will measure the impact of the marketing activities you are undertaking.
- *Cost*. To be viable, your marketing activity must obviously be cost-effective. It can be difficult to decide exactly which costs to include under the heading of marketing, but at least apportion the main direct costs such as advertising bills.

3 Marketing strategy

Once you have defined your marketing objectives, you need to make some decisions on strategy in order to fulfil these aims. To choose the right strategy, you need to be able to identify the types of customer to whom you should be selling your products and services. Your strategy should ensure that your business will make it on to those customers' radar when they are buying. It should also cover how you will find new customers to replace ones that defect, and to fuel growth.

Before deciding on a strategy, it is worth carrying out an analysis of your position in the market, as this will have a major bearing on your marketing strategy and the methods of promotion you use. This involves identifying the key criteria that customers use when judging your products against those of the competition. What images come to mind when they think about you and your products? Who is your target audience?

It is also worth considering what segments of the total potential target market you wish to aim for. In the case of a clothes retailer, for instance, the potential target market is everyone who buys clothes. But this can be broken down into segments such as menswear, womenswear and children's wear. Womenswear divides into further segments such as fast-moving high-street fashion, business wear, designer fashion, bridal, evening wear and so on. Define your targets clearly and prioritise market segments in terms of how attractive they are to you.

Consider also whether you wish to adopt a market-led or a product-led approach to strategy. A market-led strategy identifies groups of customers to whom products and services can be sold;

for example, affluent single women who might buy a range of goods from scented candles to handbags. A product-led strategy concentrates on providing a product or service and then finding ways of selling it to a range of customers.

One model frequently used to define strategies for growth is Igor Ansoff's Growth Vector Matrix.[1] It sets out four basic strategies:

- *Market development.* This means selling existing products into new markets; for example, new countries or regions, or new groups of customers. For instance, you might think that your expensive bath oils sold in the affluent South-East would also sell well in better-off parts of the North. Or you might be selling sportswear to the young, but also see an opening for selling it to active older people.

- *Product development.* This means improving existing products or launching new ones to existing customers. The cosmetics industry is a good example of this – e.g. it frequently launches new face creams with added fruit acids, or liposomes, or UV filters. Lipsticks and eyeshadows not only come in new colours, but with new, supposedly improving ingredients or fragrances.

- *Market penetration.* This means selling more of your products to your existing customers, or attracting new ones. 'Two for the price of one' offers are a common technique for increasing market penetration. But businesses should be careful of trying to increase market share by lowering prices, as this can produce short-lived benefits at a high cost.

- *Diversification.* You may opt for this strategy if a current product or line is producing declining profits, or you believe it may do so in future. It may involve using existing equipment to make new products, or buying or starting new businesses. For instance, many traditional newspapers are diversifying into Internet and TV, because they believe these new media will gain in importance over the coming years.

Other strategies include:

- *Finding a niche.* This involves concentrating on one particular segment of the market, perhaps, say, holidays for single parents. Ask yourself whether the segment is big enough to assure long-term profitability.

- *Cost leadership.* Winning customers on the basis of cost leadership involves aggressive pricing, which in turn means you must be able to buy raw materials at favourable prices and have the technology to produce at low cost. For example, on-line savings and mortgage banks in the late 1990s won market share by offering 'best-buy' rates, a strategy they were able to pursue because of their low-cost telephone and Internet operations.

    It is a strategy often used to build market share quickly. But it can leave your business vulnerable to even lower-cost competitors, perhaps from overseas countries where labour costs are cheaper. It may also devalue the image of your products or services and you may attract only 'promiscuous' customers who will defect if you are unable to sustain your low-cost position.

- *Differentiation.* A strategy of differentiation is based on raising the quality or desirability of your product compared with others on the market. This may involve differentiating the product, customer service, or sales outlets. For instance, upmarket perfumes are only available in selected department stores and pharmacies in order to maintain their supposed exclusivity – and their premium price. Bear in mind that if you are making improvements, these must be ones that are valued by customers. Weigh up the costs against any likely increase in sales and profits.

These strategies are not mutually exclusive. Over a period, you may need to use a series of strategies, or you may have to employ different strategies for different parts of your business.

4   Monitoring your products and services

During your marketing audit you will probably have identified several areas within the marketing mix that need attention. One that can never escape scrutiny is your range of products and services. Products have a life cycle from launch, through growth to maturity and then decline, which might be as ephemeral as last season's fashion trend, or as long-lasting as a food such as baked beans. At launch, sales may be slow and profits are likely to be sketchy because of the launch costs. Promotions normally focus on increasing awareness of the product or service. Many products die shortly after birth. But some go on to the growth phase, where sales and profits are increasing. Promotions shift from raising awareness to stimulating customers to buy. Mature products are normally the most popular and provide a stable income. At this stage the focus is on improving the product or service quality to prolong the product's life. Once it enters the decline phase, a product will begin to sell less and to show falling profit margins. This is the stage at which entrepreneurs must decide whether to axe it, or to embark on a promotional push in an attempt to boost sales.

A recent example of the life of a product can be seen in the case of the pashmina shawl, which first began adorning the shoulders of metropolitan fashionistas in 1995 – the launch stage. By 1997 and 1998, the pashmina had entered its growth phase, when it was being featured in glossy magazines and had become a sought-after item in top London stores. In 1999 the pashmina entered the mature stage, with high-street stores having produced their own, cheaper versions, and features appearing in mid-market magazines and newspapers. At this point no self-respecting fashionista would have bought one – they had moved on to embroidered tea shawls instead. By 2000 the pashmina was well into decline, with shawls tucked away in the less glamorous store aisles.

The moral is that you need to keep an eye on where your products are in their life cycle and make sure you have new products coming on stream to counteract decline in older ones.

5   Meeting the targets

Take each element of your marketing objectives and set out detailed budgets, responsibilities and targets for them all.

Make sure that you communicate your aims to staff.

Draw up a sales and profit forecast based on last year's figures, if appropriate, and adjust it for changes in the market and the hoped-for impact of your marketing strategy.

Use three separate forecasts – an optimistic one, a pessimistic one and a moderate one – and plan how you will handle each.

Track progress monthly for every member of your sales staff and for each product line. Simple techniques for monitoring the effectiveness of different strands of marketing activity include:

- *Recording how customers heard of you.* Either use a standard sales enquiry form or, in the case of telesales, have operators ask customers the question each time they call. Use codes to identify sources, for example: MOS/A/1/6/00 for an advertisement in the *Mail on Sunday* on 1 June 2000.
- *Track the 'conversion rates' for each type of marketing.* In other words find out how many leads or enquiries turn into actual sales, in order to identify the most productive methods of marketing.
- *Keep track of the cost of acquiring a new customer.* Map the cost against both the initial sale and the expected lifetime revenue from that customer.
- *Track how many customers you have gained and lost.* Try to find out why customers have chosen to buy from you, or to switch to a competitor.
- *Calculate the average value of transactions.* Concentrate on chasing the most profitable business.
- *Take account of external factors.* These might include events such as a cold spell in summer affecting the sales of swimwear.

Lapsed/ex-customers are often an excellent source of new business, especially if you know why they're not current customers.

6   Building a brand

Brands are all-powerful nowadays. The brand is primarily what makes the difference between a pot of moisturising cream priced at £3 and one priced at £300. Some brand names are so powerful that they have become almost synonymous with the product itself; for instance, Hoover, Coke and Levis are often used to mean any vacuum cleaner, sweet fizzy drink or pair of jeans, regardless of the true manufacturer. Other brands – Chanel, Rolls-Royce, Louis Vuitton – confer cachet on both the product and its purchaser. The Internet has thrown up a whole new set of hot brands – names such as Amazon.com and lastminute.com were unknown a few years ago.

Clearly, branding is a key competitive weapon and it can be a valuable one in the armoury of the growing business. Brands are normally associated with multibillion-pound advertisement campaigns and logo designs. However, they are still relevant to entrepreneurial businesses. Two of the UK's best-known brands, Body Shop and Virgin, both arose from initially small, entrepreneur-led companies.

It is really important to stress that brands are not just logos, however. They are more complex than that and their value is in communicating the mix of values that the logo represents. For instance, as Anita Roddick says in the quote at the start of this chapter, the Body Shop brand represents a set of values that are opposed to the glossy perfectionism of the traditional cosmetics industry and instead promotes a holistic, natural approach. Branding is essentially about communicating what is different about your business to customers, in order to foster their involvement.

Creating a distinctive brand that reflects the nature and values of your business at the outset could provide you with a valuable asset and business tool in the future. Growing firms can reinforce their brand by making sure it appears on company stationery, vehicles, business cards and packaging. Brands are at their most effective when they reflect the real philosophy and values of the company, for example, the Body Shop brand, with its natural ingredients and concern for the Third World, reflects not just care for the individual physical body, but also for the body politic.

One interesting development exploited by some entrepreneurs has been 'anti-branding', aimed at discerning customers who are disaffected with traditional brands. For example, cosmetics entrepreneur Nicky Kinnaird set up her chain of Space NK Apothecary shops in the mid-Nineties, stocked with beauty products previously unobtainable in this country, directly to appeal to women who disliked the big-brand cosmetic counters in department stores. Needless to say, many of the previously little-known names in her stores became cult brands among those in the know.

To begin with, think about your reputation and image, as these are among your big investments. Consider what values you wish people to know you by and make sure you are true to them.

7   Advertising

We all have opinions about advertising. Every day, we are bombarded with advertisements on television, radio, in newspapers, on posters ... Advertising is an essential for any business and, properly used, will contribute to growth and profitability. But ill-thought-out advertising can be costly and lose customers.

Many people feel that advertising is somehow a 'con' – that it is luring us into buying products that we neither need nor want, simply to line a company's pockets. On the other side, many small business owners resent spending money on advertising.

The reality is that advertising is a key method of com-municating with customers. It cannot, however, sell products on its own. To be effective, an advertising campaign must be backed up by good products, delivery, customer service and other sound business values. A glossy ad that induces a customer to buy a shoddy product, or to use your business only to be confronted with below-par service, will lead to a high degree of resentment and dissatisfaction. In early 2000, for example, Barclays Bank launched a multimillion-pound TV ad campaign using film stars including Sir Anthony Hopkins, extolling its virtues as a 'Big' organisation. At the same time, however, the bank had embarked on a programme of rural branch closures. The result: its ad campaign led to ridicule and anger on the part of customers at the seeming disparity between the bank's advertising and the reality.

Before embarking on an advertising campaign, consider what you hope to achieve and whom you perceive as your target audience. What message do you want to convey to potential customers and what medium will you use to convey it? How frequently do you want your advertisements to appear and how much are you prepared to spend?

8   The medium is the message

A key decision is whether to advertise. If you decide to do so, bear in mind that you will get the best value from an integrated advertising campaign with the most appropriate media mix. The possibilities for where to advertise are virtually endless, ranging from notices in shop windows to national television. Commonly used media include the national, local and trade press, commercial radio, television, cinema, posters and flyers. Which you choose will depend on your budget and the customers you hope to target.

- *Press Advertising.* In the UK, the press is the most widely used advertising medium. Publications themselves will usually provide details of their circulation and readership profile. A weighty tome known as *BRAD*, or *British Rate and Data*, which lists the rates and circulations for a large number of publications, is available in larger public libraries.

    Press advertising has a number of advantages – the range of publications available is so vast that it is possible to target specific groups on the basis of their location, gender, income group, age, race, business or hobby. A good press advertisement can exploit the power of the written word and convey your message very effectively.

    It is relatively easy to measure response, as you can

include coupons or response hotlines in the advertisement and, provided you identify the right publications, it can be highly effective.

A word of warning, however. Not all entrepreneurs understand that journalists, especially those on national newspapers and magazines, guard their editorial independence very jealously. Do not, therefore, assume that you have the right to telephone a journalist and demand that he or she writes a favourable article on your business because you have spent money on advertising. Good journalists aim to be objective and attempts to lean on them in this way will almost certainly have the opposite effect to the one you intended.

'Advertorial', or an advertisement presented in the form of an article – though it should be clearly labelled as a promotion – is paid-for material and you should not expect to receive this sort of exposure free of charge.

- *Radio*. You can advertise on local or national radio either through a sales house or a local station. Radio is most popular around breakfast time – 6 a.m. to 9 a.m. – and during 'drive-time' when people are heading home in their cars, between 5 p.m. and 7 p.m. Radio is a good medium for those wanting to create a sense of familiarity and accessibility in their customers. The impact of the human voice and music or other sound effects can be very effective in creating emotion and atmosphere. Radio advertising is normally quick and easy to produce and airtime can be purchased in relatively inexpensive packages.
- *Television*. TV is the most effective, and the most expensive, option available. The audience is enormous and the power of the medium can be gauged by the fact that some TV ads – for instance, the Gold Blend couple – become part of the culture. National TV advertising is likely to be inappropriate and too expensive for most growing businesses. However, it may be worth considering local or regional television, or specialist channels such as sports for certain types of company. Cable TV is increasingly becoming a new medium for small

businesses to gain exposure to large audiences at a fraction of the cost of normal broadcast media and some products can do phenomenally well on shopping channels.

- *Posters, bills and signs.* Another common form of advertising is posters on billboards, train stations, buses and taxis. The advantage of these is that if they are in high traffic areas, they are seen by large numbers of people. It can be extremely effective, as was seen in a recent poster campaign for a particular brand of push-up bra, alleged to have caused a number of accidents as male drivers took their eyes off the road to leer at the model.

  Ads on buses and taxi seats are other alternatives. But because people see posters as they are passing by, they cannot act on the message immediately and buy the product. For this reason, posters are more effective in building awareness and supporting other ads, such as a press campaign.

- *Direct Marketing.* Direct marketing can be an extremely cost-effective way of communicating with potential customers and generating market research information. It includes techniques such as direct mail, mail order and telemarketing. Direct mail is the third-largest advertising medium in the UK, and one advantage is that it is relatively cheap and so can be used by even smaller businesses. Its biggest advantage, however, is that it gives you the ability to target and tailor your message.

  You don't need to use the post for direct mail – fax and e-mail are also options. The downside, however, is that many people are irritated by junk mail, or its cyber equivalent, 'spam'.

  The Royal Mail produces a *Direct Mail Guide* with tips and advice, and a variety of organisations provide mailing lists.

  The Direct Marketing Association is the trade organisation for companies in direct marketing in the UK. It provides an on-line directory of its members and approved suppliers, gives guides on subjects such as renting business lists and maintains a Code of Practice. See Appendix 2, Useful Contacts, for more information.

New legislation requires companies making direct approaches to potential customers by fax and phone first to check out whether they have exercised the right to be excluded from cold contact of this nature. Failure to comply can result in a £50 fine per contact.

- *Directories*. There are around 4000 directories in the UK, about half of which are industrial or commercial. In addition, there are well-known consumer directories such as *Yellow Pages* and *Thomson*'s, which cover local areas. Directories tend to be used by customers who already want to buy and are simply seeking a supplier. The problem is that these publications contain listings from thousands of businesses, so the key is to make yours stand out. It may be worth paying for a display advertisement rather than a simple listing and to use the space effectively. Given the mass of information shown on each page, make maximum use of blank space, big, bold design and type, and separate your ad from the mass of the text by putting it in a box.

- *Sponsorship*. This is a form of advertising which can be used to position your company and its products. It can create enormous visibility and also an added 'feel-good' factor, if you support, say, a charity or local event. The idea is that your company is associated with the kudos of the event or sponsored organisation and that it is mentioned in media coverage.

  Large-scale sponsorships, such as the Nationwide Building Society's of the Football League, are obviously out of reach, but small businesses can sponsor local events to great effect. Depending on your business, you might consider sponsoring a local sports team, concert or arts event, conference or charity.

  Do not simply respond to approaches for sponsorship – instead, try to take an active stance and to determine what you want to achieve before committing yourself. The main benefits are access, or the ability to get your message over to a group of buyers, and association, or the credibility of associating your business with a laudable activity.

- *The Internet.* There has been a great deal of excitement recently about the marketing and advertising potential of the Internet. It certainly makes sense to look at it if your products are suitable and your target market will be reached that way. For instance, computers, books, financial products, travel, new and used cars are all successfully sold on-line. Even if you are not actually selling goods over the Internet, you might consider setting up a 'brochure' site informing web browsers about your business, as an adjunct to your other marketing and advertising activity.

  Just having a website will not necessarily bring 'hits' – you need to promote your site. Internet marketing is becoming more important as cyberspace becomes more crowded. It is also, of course, possible to take out an advertisement to appear on another website or portal. For example, an investment bank might decide to advertise on the *Financial Times* website, ft.com.

  Undoubtedly, this form of advertising will grow in the coming years but at the moment it is important to make a sober assessment of how well such ads will reach your target market and to monitor the response carefully.

- *Teaming up with others.* Marketing with other similar companies through a trade association can often be cost-effective, especially when it comes to exhibitions.

- *Export marketing.* If companies want to export then there's loads of help available from Trade Partners UK, the government agency that helps British firms build their export capability. It has links with overseas embassies/cultural attachés who have access to detailed information about overseas markets. Businesses can tap into this network of help through their local Business Link export development counsellor.

9 Choosing an advertising agency

An advertising agency should be able to help you to carry out market research, design advertisements, plan a campaign, choose the best medium and book space. As specialists, they certainly ought to be able to add value over and above what you would achieve by doing it yourself. However, it is important that you choose an agency that suits you and provides value for money. Fees will depend on the type and volume of work, and on the calibre of the agency and staff involved. But the idea is that the costs should be outweighed by the extra income they produce.

As a growing firm, there is probably not a great deal of point in approaching one of the big-name London ad agencies. Look instead at smaller, possibly local, agencies. Initial meetings are usually free and agencies should show you work they have done for existing clients.

If you cannot make a decision in this way, invite a selection of up to three agencies to pitch for your business. You should prepare a brief specifying what you wish to achieve and asking them to present an appropriate strategy and ideas. Ask them to state how they will monitor the effectiveness of the advertising and specify the budget involved. Some agencies will not present to you without a pitching fee – this is not unreasonable when you consider that preparing a pitch costs them time and money, and it is not unknown for ostensible clients simply to walk away with the ideas without hiring the agency.

Once you have taken on an agency, the importance of careful and well-crafted briefs cannot be overemphasised. You need to be clear about what you want.

Case Study 2: Good relations

'A business without marketing is like a boy winking at a girl in the dark. He knows he's doing it but nobody else does,' says Guyanese-born Yvonne Thompson, who set up the UK's first black-run PR, advertising and sponsorship agency, ASAP Communications. 'Marketing is the last thing people think about when writing a business plan and the first thing they think about when they have to cut costs. But if you don't market your business, you are like that boy winking at the girl – you might as well not bother.'

Yvonne set up ASAP, based in Brixton, south London, in 1995, after working for herself in PR since 1983. 'I spent time in America and met a number of black agencies that helped blue-chip companies and government departments to target ethnic minorities,' she says. 'Afro-Caribbean communities are reckoned to have an annual income after tax of £9–£15 billion. It seemed an excellent business opportunity because no one at that time was doing it in the UK. Our clients are mainstream companies who want to target ethnic communities but don't understand the cultural differences. We also have as clients ethnic-minority businesses which want to promote themselves. When we started, we had to educate ethnic-minority businesses that there is a tangible worth to marketing and public relations.' Clients include black radio station Choice FM, the Department for Education and Employment and the Millennium Dome. ASAP has also done a project with the Metropolitan Police.

Yvonne Thompson herself is achieving an increasingly high profile – in 2000 she was selected by the Department of Trade and Industry to chair its ethnic-minority business forum, she has become a member of the Small Business Council, advising that government-backed body and she has been recruited to the London Development Agency. In addition, she has been appointed Chair of the Central London Learning and Skills Council, one of the new bodies replacing the training function of Training and Enterprise Councils. In 1999, ASAP won a commendation in the *Financial Mail*'s Enterprise Awards.

Yvonne says, 'Forming a black consultancy has helped to address black issues, ensuring they receive the widest possible attention. My mission is to change the image, perception and credibility of ethnic communities.'

10   Public relations

It is somewhat ironic that the public relations profession does not itself enjoy the best of images. Many people imagine it is either the esoteric, rather sinister practice of 'spin', or that it is trivial and pretentious, as typified in the TV comedy *Absolutely Fabulous*. Practised properly, public relations is, however, a perfectly ethical – and very useful – tool for entrepreneurs. PR is essentially a communications campaign designed to create a favourable climate of opinion.

Small firms can use PR to help grow their businesses, either on their own, or by employing a PR consultant. People increasingly care about the values attached to the products they buy and the wrong climate of opinion surrounding your business can be seriously damaging. Similarly, failing to communicate your strengths will obviously hamper business growth. A couple of misconceptions must be disposed of early on, however.

First, a PR strategy cannot be achieved overnight – it is vital to take a long-term approach, having clearly identified the climate of opinion you want to create.

Second, PR is not about glossing away the faults or imperfections of your organisation. Still less is it about 'controlling the media'.

It is important to be realistic about what PR can achieve. Essentially, it can help make the most of what you have got, but no amount of PR will make people think your business is wonderful when it is not.

Basic PR exercises that can be undertaken by small businesses include local charity work, open days, speaking engagements at industry conferences and the like, and entering – and preferably winning – awards. Gaining positive exposure in the media will reap enormous PR dividends, but must be approached with care.

- *Is it news?* It may sound obvious, but do not contact journalists unless you have a genuine story to tell. Target the most suitable outlet(s) from among the national, local and trade press. For instance, the *Mail on Sunday* is unlikely to run a story about your amazing new widget – after all, would you read that over your cornflakes? – but *Widgets Weekly* might find it riveting.

- *Be considerate.* Bear in mind that journalists are extremely busy and work to tight deadlines. Exercise some common sense and try not to telephone at times likely to be inconvenient – for example, don't call a Sunday newspaper journalist on a Friday. Try to e-mail whenever possible, so the journalist can look at your offering at his or her convenience.

- *Pick the right level of contact.* Make sure that you contact the most appropriate journalist for your story. A senior business editor, for instance, is not likely to be keen to hear about your new dry-cleaning shop, because she or he will be busy writing about multibillion-pound mergers. Often, it makes sense to make contact with more junior reporters – and you may reap the benefit as they rise up the journalistic ladder.

- *Be realistic.* Bear in mind that journalists receive literally hundreds of press releases and speculative telephone calls each week. To have any chance of gaining exposure, yours must be a story of genuine interest, succinctly and clearly written, and contain a contact number. Even if your material is not published straight away, journalists may file it for future use provided it is interesting and well presented.

- *Don't pester.* Do not follow up press releases with telephone calls – if the journalist is interested, he or she will call you and pestering is likely to be counter-productive.

- *Don't fib.* It is unwise to try to pull the wool over a journalist's eyes. Most are generalists and do not have in-depth knowledge of particular industries. This does not, however, mean they are stupid and any hack worth his or her salt has a 'nose' for when a line is being spun.

Tips for getting material into the newspapers include: a celebrity connection, if, perhaps, a famous person is a customer or a backer, a good strong picture or interesting survey research material relating to your industry. Human interest, humour or conflict are also attractive elements in a story.

Make sure all staff are prepared to handle calls from journalists prompted by your press release or other contacts, and that relevant people are available to talk to journalists at short notice. If you cannot supply information and quotes quickly, your story won't be used.

11   Unsolicited contact with the media

If you receive an unsolicited call from a journalist, do not instantly react with hostility, whatever your private views on the media. You are not a film star or a member of the royal family and it is unlikely that she or he will want to probe into some major scandal in your private life – the contact is far more likely to lead to positive coverage for your business.

If there is a problem it is far better to be honest with the journalist and to make sure she understands your side of the story and the steps you are taking to put it right. Saying 'No comment' means the journalist will be suspicious of you, and will only write up the opposite side of the story. Lie and you are likely to be found out, making matters much worse.

Remember, if you have already built up a good relationship with the local press, they are far more likely to give you the benefit of the doubt if things go wrong. If your business really is behaving ethically you are unlikely to suffer a sustained bad press.

12   Hiring a PR consultant

As with choosing an advertising agency, approach the hiring of a PR consultant in measured fashion. Be clear about your objectives in hiring him or her and be aware of the limitations of what can be achieved. The major London-based agencies are often out of reach of small businesses, but there are some extremely effective smaller operators. Bear in mind, however, that unprofessional PR will at best be ineffective and at worst do you more harm than good in the eyes of opinion formers such as journalists.

How much you pay will depend on the seniority of the staff

on your account and how much time they devote to your business. Be clear as to what strategy the PR consultant will pursue and how he or she proposes to do so. Many big companies buy in specialist PR help for particular events, such as a takeover or to deal with a specific crisis. Bear in mind, however, that if you hire a PR consultant simply to deal with a crisis, that person will not have built up an in-depth knowledge or understanding of your company.

The Institute of Public Relations is a professional body for the industry and all its members operate within a Code of Professional Conduct. The Institute has a service, for a charge, to match your needs with suitable members, publishes a number of guides that give practical information and advice on different aspects of PR (including use of the Internet) and operates regional groups across the UK. Contact details can be found in Appendix 2, Useful Contacts.

Case Study 3: Kanda Systems – piggyback route to success
A small Welsh company run by two former college lecturers has become a world beater in electronic tools by astute marketing on the Internet. Kanda Systems (www.kanda.com) makes tools that help engineers working on silicon chips that control anything from a mobile phone to a washing machine. But instead of selling these tools under the company's own name it markets them on websites that carry the brand names of the world's major silicon chip manufacturers, such as the French-Italian ST Micro Electronics and US giant Atmel. These sites are also built by Kanda, for which it is paid a fee by the chip companies.

This 'piggyback' marketing has seen Kanda grow from a two-man firm operating from a garden shed to a leading company in its field worldwide, employing forty staff. Its marketing has to appeal both to its clients – the chip manufacturers – and the end users, who are engineers. This demands a close knowledge of the needs and preferences of both groups.

The company won the sales and marketing award in the *Financial Mail*'s 1999 Enterprise competition. Its success is founded on its creative marketing ability. Orders flood in daily from places as diverse as California and Cambodia, and 95% of the firm's sales are now exported.

The company, based in Aberystwyth, Dyfed, was formed in 1994 as an electronic solutions provider by Wallis and Kevin Kirk, the Chairman and Chief Executive. They received funding of £10,000 from the small firms loan guarantee scheme. Kirk says, 'It is proof that a small company in a remote part of Wales can build a global market by using the Internet and a parcel courier service.'

Kanda also designs hardware in the form of circuit boards so that engineers can test whether the codes they have installed using Kanda's tools work in the device. The company's websites, too, have been a big hit with the chip-making firms, which have seen an increase in their business as a result of engineers logging on. Initially the company used its customers' brands, but now is trying to build its own.

It has developed its marketing expertise with the help of consultants. Kirk says, 'The biggest advantage of using consultants is that they have been there and done that. The problem is that they are not there on a day-to-day basis, so you have to pin them down. We chose our consultants through the Welsh Development Agency. It is important to get the right consultant. If you get the wrong one it can be a disaster, particularly if you follow their advice.'

He adds, 'We produce tools that allow our customers to sell their products. Clients like Japanese corporation Mitsubishi cannot easily get to their engineering customers through their corporate website, so we run a separate site for them. We are helping customers with their marketing to the engineers, which is crucial for them. It was really difficult to get a hearing at some of these companies, taking about a year. But we are now in a position where we are getting approached by them. We made a deliberate decision to go for a niche market. It is a very fast-moving industry and it is huge so you have to work out where your niche is. Marketing is crucial for us, especially now that we are in an international marketplace. We need to let people in forty-six countries know that our product exists. We have to get at customers. Marketing is the biggest challenge facing companies today.'

13   Marketing on the Internet

Many smaller companies such as Kanda Systems have achieved significant sales growth by using the Internet. Most use a combination of traditional marketing and advertising alongside the new channel.

It might seem hard to see how a traditional business such as a plumber, hotel or hairdresser could benefit from the Internet, but even these can be listed in on-line classified directories. Even if you do not actually sell over the Internet, remember that many Internet users log on to carry out research into a potential purchase, so it may be worth setting up an information site for your business.

Ideas for marketing your business on the Internet include:

- *Listings in search engines and directories.* These catalogue and list your website information so that when someone searches the Web for information on your sort of products and services, they can locate your site. Start off by registering your site with some of the major search engines and directories.

- *Banner advertisements.* Banner ads – where the user clicks on the banner to be sent to your website – can be placed on sites where you believe you can attract customers. For example, if you sell diving gear, you might put a banner ad on the website of a specialist diving magazine.

- *Message boards, news groups and discussion groups.* You can make contact and gain information about groups who may have an interest in your product through message boards, news groups and discussion groups on the Web. Message boards can serve as listing facilities for products and services for special-interest groups. News groups are forums on every conceivable subject from the stock market to stargazing and can provide valuable insights into your customers. If you post information to a news group, however, it should be genuinely informative, not advertising. You can also subscribe to discussion groups to exchange information on subjects of interest.

- *Links to other websites.* Try to negotiate links with other websites that are of interest to your customers. For instance, if you are a wedding dress retailer, you might try to negotiate links with cake makers, florists and upmarket hotels.

- *E-mail.* Your website can be set up to offer you a list of customers giving their e-mail address so they can be notified of special offers and so on. This is a valuable resource for generating repeat sales, though avoid bombarding customers with irrelevant e-mail.

Notes

1 Igor Ansoff, 'Strategies for diversification', *Harvard Business Review*, 1957.

CHAPTER **6**
Cash
Management

Money is better than poverty, if only for financial reasons.
Woody Allen in 'Without Feathers', *The Early Essays*

Money. That one little word holds so much promise of happiness
– or misery.

Not all entrepreneurs go into business simply to get rich.
Some have different reasons, such as independence from corporate
structures, or bringing an innovation to market. But whatever your
motivation, the success of your business comes down to money.
You do not need to be a financial wizard to be a great entrepreneur
– indeed, many successful entrepreneurs would make no great
claim to a head for numbers. What you do need, however, is an
understanding of the basic principles of finance and a willingness
to accord hard cash its proper importance. Too often
entrepreneurs get carried away with enthusiasm about a project or
a sale, and fail to think about the crucial point – will it make
money?

Most growing businesses will hire a specialist finance director
and will also have the benefit of advice from their accountant or
bank. At times, the finance director might seem like a boring,
number-obsessed killjoy who seems intent on pouring cold water
on every great idea by bleating on about expense. But, most likely,
he or she isn't a nay sayer for its own sake – a good finance director

will fulfil the valuable function of stopping enthusiasts from embarking on unprofitable endeavours.

This chapter does not aim to cover the whole of this enormous subject, but to give non-financial managers an insight into the key issues of cash flow, profit, dealing with your bank and tax matters. In addition, special attention has been paid to one issue that bedevils the *Financial Mail*'s business readership and entrepreneurs in general – getting paid on time.

1   Learn to love your accountant

When cash is tight at the start, you might be tempted to save by dispensing with professional accountancy advice. But an accountant can save you time and money, because you can use his or her experience of other businesses, and professional expertise. An accountant will help you to fulfil your statutory obligations and should be able to give valuable tax advice to keep your bills to a minimum. Other areas in which an accountant can help include setting up record-keeping systems, which sound boring but are the source of valuable management information enabling you to track the progress of your business.

When choosing an accountant, bear in mind the following points:

- *Consider the needs of your business.* A big firm will offer a less personal service and will cost more than a small local firm, but will cope with a wide range of services and expertise. A smaller local firm may be appropriate if your needs are simpler.
- *Check credentials.* Make sure the accountant is a member of a recognised professional body such as the Institute of Chartered Accountants. You can also ask for references from the accountant's clients.
- *Take recommendations.* Your local Business Link or colleagues may be able to recommend a good local accountant.
- *Be clear about your needs.* Formulate a clear idea of the

services you need and discuss the likely costs with the accountant.

For more advice on finding a good accountant, see page 178.

2   Finance for absolute beginners

Accountancy is the language of business. As an entrepreneur, you do not need to be an expert, as you will most likely be using a professional accountant and you may have a finance specialist working in your business. But if you do not comprehend the basics you will be at a serious disadvantage in communicating about your business and even comprehending it fully. Understanding the fundamentals will give you an informed picture of how your business is performing and enable you to participate fully in directing its strategy.

Here, we shall outline the key elements of financial accounting for those who are not specialists: profit and loss accounts; your balance sheet, cash-flow statements and budgeting.

- *The profit and loss account.* Your profit and loss statement gives a picture of your trading performance over a period of time, usually the last accounting year. The statement usually follows a simple format showing *turnover*, that is income from sales net of VAT, less the *cost of sales*, i.e. direct costs such as raw materials. This produces a *gross profit* figure. *Indirect costs* such as rent, rates and salaries are then deducted, giving a figure for *operating profit*, or profit before interest and tax. Deduct tax and interest and you arrive at a *net profit* figure.

- *The balance sheet.* The balance sheet gives you a snapshot of the financial strength of the business at the end of an accounting period. It summarises what *assets* you own and what *liabilities* you owe. *Fixed assets* are things like plant and machinery, and have to be *depreciated* or written down over their useful life. *Current assets* are short-term assets such as stock, debtors and cash. *Current liabilities* are amounts that you owe in less than one year, such as trade creditors or a bank overdraft. *Long-term liabilities* are amounts due after more than one year such as longer-term bank loans. *Net assets* is the figure you arrive at when you deduct the liabilities from the assets – in other words, what the company is worth. This should be the same figure as *shareholders' funds*, which includes share capital and reserves. If you are unincorporated, it may be shown as capital and reserves or partnership capital. The total financing for the business is known as *capital employed*, which constitutes all borrowings including overdrafts plus shareholders' funds.

- *Cash flow*. A cash-flow statement shows the changes in cash allocations over the accounting period – what surplus has been generated, what borrowings have been made and how they have been employed. It includes not just notes and coins, but money in the bank, and should give you a sense of whether the business is generating cash, or just eating it up. We will return to the subject of maximising cash flow later in this chapter, as it is an important one where, unfortunately, many growing firms come unstuck.

- *Budgeting*. Annual financial accounts obviously are historical and do not come frequently enough to help you manage your business, so you need to prepare budgets setting financial targets. Produce a cash-flow forecast, and a forecast profit and loss and balance sheet. Be realistic – last year's figures, if available, may be a reasonable guide, but do take account of any relevant changes. Calculate a range of scenarios and the probability of achieving them – computer software makes this easier. Compare budgets to reality to identify problems and opportunities.

3   Knowledge is power
Your ability to make good decisions on the running of your business depends on the quality of the information you have at your disposal. You should try to focus on a few key indicators of

the financial health of the business. The most important areas to look at for all businesses are sales, costs and working capital. In addition, your business will probably have some key indicators of its own, for instance, sales per square foot in a retail business.

- *Sales.* The number of enquiries or leads should give you an indication of future sales, especially if you have built a good idea of the percentage of enquiries turning into orders. Your order book will give a guide to future cash flow. *Orderbook cover* compares the value of orders with the amount of sales you need to break even for one month. So if you have orderbook cover of twelve months, you could survive for a year without making another sale. Track which products or services are selling well, how well each salesperson is doing and any changes in the conversion rates of leads or enquiries to sales.

- *Costs.* Monitor costs carefully so you can identify the most important *variable costs*, that is, costs that go up and down. Keep a weather eye on any increases in costs as these can have a drastic effect on your gross profit margins. Try to identify ways of keeping key variable costs down and to reduce their volatility. For example, can you use alternative suppliers?

- *Working capital.* This is basically the capital you need to have to keep your business going. All businesses need working capital, though the amount varies from business to business, according to how quickly you need to pay creditors, how quickly debtors pay you and how much stock you need to hold. So, for example, a retailer with a high stock turnover, whose customers pay instantly in the shop, is likely to have a far lower working capital requirement than, say, a car manufacturer. Controlling working capital – debtors, creditors, stock and work in progress – effectively means you are controlling cash.

  If you are looking to grow your turnover, determine how much more working capital you would need to fund an increase in sales. A key ratio is net working assets over sales: *debtors + stock – creditors.* Apply this to an anticipated increase in sales to determine the extra working assets needed. It also serves as a measure of productivity.

Delay or reject new large orders if you cannot finance them, or talk to your bank if you feel it appropriate. Keep control of debtors and creditors – how to do this is covered later in this chapter. Concentrate also on good stock control. The *stock turn* is the ratio of the cost of sales to stock. If the figure goes down, it may indicate that you are buying in stock that you cannot shift. Break down the stock figure into separate categories to identify where the problems are.

- *Other key indicators*. Try to monitor the other key drivers behind the performance of your business. These will vary – for instance, they could include staff turnover in an estate agency or financial services firm, or machine down-time in a factory. For most businesses, cost-efficiency is a key driver. Non-financial drivers such as employee morale can be extremely important – you can keep tabs on these by tracking absenteeism and staff turnover.

4   How profitable are you?

You may be making a lot of sales, but the key information you need is how profitable you are. Your *profit margin* will tell you how much leeway you have on pricing and what sales you need to achieve to break even.

You can calculate your gross profit margin by working out gross profit as a percentage of sales. For instance, if your turnover is £100,000 and your gross profit is £30,000, your gross profit margin is 30%. Your net or operating profit margin is calculated by taking operating profit as a percentage of turnover. So, for example, if your sales are £100,000 and your operating profit is £15,000, your net profit margin is 15%. So long as you are achieving a positive gross profit margin, every sale is making a contribution to covering your overhead costs.

You can work out your break-even point by dividing your total overhead costs by your gross profit margin. For example, if your overheads are £100,000 and your gross profit margin is 25%, you need to make sales of £400,000 to break even. You can compare your profit margins to those of other companies in the same sort of business to see how well you are doing, and to previous periods, to track your performance over time. Also compare profit margins on individual products or services to see which are the most worthwhile for your business.

Another measure of profitability is *return on capital employed*. This shows how efficiently you are using the capital employed in the business. You calculate it by taking operating profit as a percentage of shareholders' funds. For instance, if operating profit is £20,000 and shareholders' funds are £200,000 then your ROCE is 10%. But bear in mind that this may be before you are taking money out for yourself. With generous directors' emoluments, perhaps little need to invest at present, or to service debt, the return might not be as good as it looks.

5   'Show me the money!' – Why cash flow is all-important

In the hit film *Jerry Maguire*, starring Tom Cruise as an ebullient sports agent and Cuba Gooding Jr as an American football star nearing the end of his career, Gooding responds to all of Cruise's lavish promises of contracts and sportswear endorsements by yelling: 'Show me the money!' Growing businesses should take that motto to heart and make it their own. Wonderful products, great ideas, an impressive new customer, a big order – none of it means anything until and unless you see the money.

Think of cash as being like the petrol in a car. The car might be a fabulous Ferrari, but without gas, it isn't going anywhere. And though you might be able to cruise along on 'empty' for a short while, you will soon grind to a shuddering halt. You need cash to pay the bills, to buy materials, to cover wages – in short, without cash your business will go under. All this sounds obvious. Nonetheless, bankers and other business advisers continually report on the numbers of inherently profitable businesses that go bust because they have failed to attend to their cash flow.

Entrepreneurs are sometimes so mesmerised by winning a new order from a prestigious client, for example, that they get carried away by their own enthusiasm and forget their motto: 'Show me the money.' If you end up spending a fortune meeting the costs of that order, with no cash coming in from the customer, you have a crisis on your hands.

Cash flow is simply the money flowing into and out of your business. It is real money, not amounts you are owed or that you owe. Bear the following points in mind:

- *Cash inflows.* The money you receive from sales is normally the major component of your cash inflows. Bank loans, overdrafts and other finance can give a one-off boost to your cash flow.
- *Cash outflows.* These are any money you spend, including stock, investing in new machinery, salaries, utility bills and so on. VAT and tax, too, are major outflows. You may also have to provide shareholders with dividends, or to pay interest and make repayments on bank borrowings.
- *Cash-flow forecasting.* The further in advance you know about any cash-flow crises, the easier it will be to deal with them. Prepare weekly or monthly cash-flow forecasts looking ahead for a year. These will give you early warning signals of crises, if there are any. Monitor your performance against the forecast to identify any problem areas.
- *Don't overreach.* Check that your cash flow can sustain any major new financial commitment such as a large new order before taking it on. It is sensible to limit the growth of the business to a level that you can finance comfortably, rather than overstretching yourself. Over-trading – an ill-defined syndrome where a business is trading at a level beyond that which it has the resources to sustain – is a major cause of problems. The symptoms are running up to and over arranged overdrafts, delaying paying creditors and so on.
- *Pay very close attention to credit control.* Getting paid on

time is a major issue for growing firms. This topic is dealt with in detail later in this chapter.

- *Set up warning systems.* Make sure managers inform you if sales or profit margins fall below a pre-set limit, as this indicates a cash-flow problem could be brewing.
- *Keep a weather eye on expenses.* Put in place cost controls and shop around for the best deals on utility bills and other outgoings. Consider computerising labour-intensive administration where possible and try to instil staff with a culture of thrift – switch that light off! Implement good stock controls so that money is not tied up unproductively in stock.
- *Review financing.* Make sure your business is financed in the most appropriate manner from the options available. The various options such as bank loans, venture capital and business angels are dealt with in more detail in the chapter on Finance for Growth.

Case Study 1: Adam Associates

Adam Associates, an IT disaster-recovery service based at the former Greenham Common airbase in Berkshire, has enjoyed dramatic growth since winning the 1999 Enterprise Award for financial performance. In that year it was listed as Britain's sixteenth-fastest growth business, according to research by Dun & Bradstreet. Behind its success lies its concentration on financial planning, control and the constructive use of management information to monitor progress.

Richard Pursey, Chief Executive, says, 'Financial performance is a key to our success. It is a question not just of satisfying our clients' needs, but keeping up with their future requirements. And that requires investment.' Adam Associates provides the hardware and technical support to make sure companies can carry on as usual if they suffer a disaster such as a fire, flood, systems failure or even a terrorist attack.

Since launching in 1994, Adam has now signed up as clients more than 50% of the UK's top hundred companies. After making a loss in its first year, it managed to top the £1-million profit mark four years later. Pursey believes that the company's strong financial strategy gives it confidence in its projections. It has successfully managed rapid growth and ensures healthy cash flow because its clients sign contracts that run for three to five years and pay subscriptions annually in advance. 'That means we know our income levels,' says Pursey. 'We have to invest all the time in hardware and software, and we have the cash flow to do it.'

Adam Associates is constantly evolving its own services and is expanding overseas. It operates in France, Belgium, Germany, the US and South Africa.

Common Pitfalls

Inexperienced entrepreneurs often fall into cash-flow traps such as:

- ploughing large sums of money into a new project with little idea of who – if anyone – will buy the product or service;
- failing to set money aside for major known bills such as tax or VAT;
- poor credit control leading to late payment or no payment at all;
- chasing sales with little idea whether they will be profitable or not;
- hanging on to obsolete or hard to shift stock;
- giving discounts for prompt payment or cash payment without doing their sums. For instance, is getting paid thirty days early ever worth 10%?

6   Dealing with the bank and other creditors

Being presented with a bill you cannot pay is never pleasant. Managing your cash flow and credit control well should make it less likely that you are in a position of not being able to pay your debts. Nonetheless, many businesses occasionally find themselves unable to pay a bill on time. In this case, it helps if you already have a good relationship with your creditors and that you manage the situation well.

- *The bank is not a bogeyman.* Banks are often cast as the villains of the piece when firms run into trouble. Sometimes this is true – but it is worth remembering that it is not in the bank's own interest to send viable businesses to the wall.

    There is a great deal of misunderstanding between banks and businesses. Bank managers often have no personal experience of running a business and may seem to the entrepreneur to lack any understanding of what they are going through, to be rule-bound and inflexible. Business people often also complain that their affairs are handled mainly by computer, or that they never see the same manager twice.

    The banks have, after receiving bad publicity and making losses on their small business loans in the early Nineties, made great efforts to address these issues. In addition, although the bank manager may not be an entrepreneur, he or she may well have experience of dealing with hundreds of small businesses and that is a knowledge bank that you can draw on.

    You can set about building a good relationship with your bank by trying to understand the manager's point of view and by keeping him or her informed. Remember that the bank is not a charity, and is under no obligation to lend you money unless it has a reasonable expectation of getting it back and of making a profit on that lending. To do otherwise would be both irresponsible of the bank, and unfair to its other customers and its shareholders.

    Try to build a track record so that the bank has confidence in you and in the information you provide. If you are normally reliable, then there is far less chance of the bank getting stroppy over one cash-flow glitch. Keep the bank informed of any anticipated cash needs. The more notice and explanation you give, the happier they will be. Show them proof that the cash shortage is temporary – let them see an order form, or whatever – if you can. Don't lie to the bank – it may seem tempting to gloss over problems, but you can hardly blame them for taking a dim view when your dishonesty becomes apparent later, as it almost inevitably will.

Keep track of other banks' offerings so that you can negotiate with your own bank from an informed position. Remember that if you do hit a cash shortage, your relationship with your bank becomes vitally important. Make every effort not to alienate them and to keep them informed.

- *Set up a payment policy.* A payment policy, well-thought-out and adhered to by everyone in your organisation, is a big help in creating good relationships with suppliers and creditors. Shop around for the best deal, bearing in mind quality and service as well as price. Bear in mind that if you drive suppliers to rock bottom on price, they are unlikely to harbour much goodwill towards you. Make sure suppliers understand your terms of payment; for instance, you might pay within thirty days of receiving an invoice.

  Evaluate whether you can pay bills early in return for discounts or price rebates, where these are offered. Overhaul your systems to make sure you are not failing to pay invoices because of administrative glitches.

- *Concentrate on important creditors.* Try to create a sound understanding with your most important creditors. These will include your financial backers, in many cases the bank, and key suppliers without whom you cannot function. Her Majesty's Customs and Excise and the Inland Revenue have the power to surcharge you automatically if you pay them late and local authorities can sue you for non-payment of business rates. Utility companies are not good creditors to cross as they can cut off your heat, light and telephone.

- *Creating co-operative relationships.* In the old days, firms tried to beat their suppliers down to the lowest possible price and that was as far as the 'relationship' went. That culture is changing, partly because firms and suppliers have had to co-operate over major issues such as the single currency and the year 2000 computer change. The other big factor leading to a more open and co-operative relationship is the Internet. Thanks to the Internet, more businesses are building integrated supply chains, leading to more openness with suppliers.

It is worth negotiating agreements with suppliers at the start and making sure you stick with them. Try to get suppliers involved in your business, so that they know your needs and understand your problems. If there is a dispute, address it quickly and honestly, though without being hostile. Problems tend to grow through mutual lack of understanding.

If you do all of these things, you should be in a better position to have suppliers who will help you out when you are in a hole, whether it be with extended credit or in some other way.

Ten Tips for Getting the Best from Your Bank

These tips from the horse's mouth have been supplied by managers at Barclays Bank, but they apply equally well to dealing with any of the other banks.

1 Discuss your plans with your bank before setting up in business. The bank will be able to provide you with helpful information and assistance relating to the viability of your plans, the issues to consider and will be able signpost you to relevant business support organisations for more specialist advice.

2 Draw up a long-term business plan – this will help you test whether your idea will work and enable you to monitor your progress.

3 Be open and honest with your business banker. Your bank will only be able to provide the most appropriate service to meet your needs if it has all the facts.

4 Keep your bank informed of all important developments

in your business. If you do so, the bank will be in a better position to prevent problems arising.

5 Discuss the most suitable finance options for your specific needs. Banks have a range of loan finance products available – so be open-minded as to what product is most suitable to your requirements.

6 Use the information services provided by the banks. All have booklets available that cover key aspects of running a business to help you develop informed business plans that will benefit your business.

7 Prepare and have all relevant information to hand for meetings with your business banker. If you are not sure what will be required, ask beforehand.

8 Be confident and clear about your business aims – your long-term business plan should help you with this.

9 Seek training to improve the way you run your business. Investing in the skills of your staff can only benefit your business in the long run.

10 Use the assistance available from business support organisations such as Business Link and local Chambers of Commerce to improve your business.

Case Study 2: Zoom the Loom

Zoom the Loom is an example of how an enterprise can flourish if it bases its business around sound financial management. It has used solid financial planning as the foundation from which to grow bigger and more profitable. Under its old name of Nightingale Factory Seconds the company, based in Basildon, Essex, won the 1997 Enterprise Award for financial performance. It demonstrated that it had the acumen to develop a good idea – selling for a good margin seconds in quilts and linen – in the teeth of a recession.

After the competition win, Managing Director and Founder Alan Nightingale believed the firm needed a change. He decided it was time for a hard look at the situation. The reassessment started with the basics. He believed the business needed to alter its image, especially as the economy started to improve. His first move was to change the name to Zoom the Loom, and to move part of the business upmarket, with some higher-end shops. He is now considering splitting off the two sides of the business totally in order to maximise the profits from each. 'We still run the old format,' he says. 'It may not be pretty, but it is very profitable.'

Nightingale makes sure that he pays creditors promptly and that cash flow is under control. 'We are very good at paying bills on time,' he says. The formula has been successful and the company has grown dramatically, with a turnover of about £12 million compared with just £1 million when it won the *Financial Mail* award. The number of shops has increased from twelve in 1997 to thirty-one in 2000 and staff numbers have risen from fifty to 200.

Nightingale is no great believer in business theory, however. 'People try to make a science of it, but you rarely see accountants setting up businesses because it needs the spirit of adventure,' he says. 'All business is based on common sense. You need to be very pragmatic – just give customers what they want at the right price.'

7   How to get paid on time

Late payment is a problem that costs UK businesses literally billions of pounds a year. In extreme cases late payment or, even worse, non-payment of bills can force a business under. I make no apology for devoting a good deal of space to this subject, as it is a major issue for many growing businesses.

There is a great deal of talk about unscrupulous larger companies exploiting small firms by being laggardly payers. The reality, however, is that growing firms could and should help themselves by implementing good credit control practices. Late payment matters because it eats into your profit margins and can, in the end, threaten the future of your business. And the longer a debt remains unpaid the greater the risk that it will not be paid at all.

The Better Payment Practice Group (BPPG) was formed in 1997 as a partnership between the public and private sectors. Its aim is to improve the payment culture of the UK business community and reduce the incidence of late payment of commercial debt. The BPPG is campaigning to raise awareness of the issue of late payment and the government is trying to help small firms, which can now claim interest on overdue invoices, thanks to the Late Payment of Commercial Debts (Interest) Act 1998.

8   Granting credit to new customers

The natural impulse on winning a new customer is delight at making the sale. But as frustrated finance directors never tire of telling their gung-ho counterparts in sales, that means nothing if you do not get paid – indeed, far from being a cause for rejoicing, that new customer will lose you money. It is amazing how many small companies still fail to grasp that reality, however. The truth is simple: credit control might sound boring, but what it really means is maximising your cash flow and minimising bad debts – and that will make a major difference to your bottom line, keeping the finance director happy. The sales director should be happy too, for if you have good credit control procedures, your future sales will be more reliable.

The best opportunity to turn a customer into a good payer is when you first begin to do business with them. Ask each customer to complete a credit application form with the correct name, payment address, the person for payments, phone and fax numbers, e-mail address, and acceptance of your terms. Request at least two trade references from regular suppliers as to credit worthiness and ask for consent to obtain a bank reference. Decide on the maximum credit amount you will allocate to that customer and set up an account for her or him.

At this stage it is a nice touch to send a 'welcome letter' to make contact with the person in charge of payments at your new customer, stating how and where payment should be made. For the first three months or so, keep a close eye on the customer to make sure she or he will be a decent payer. Explain your payment terms when the customer makes an order, and have them printed on the credit application form. The terms should include the credit period, any discounts or rebates you offer for prompt payment, whether your prices include carriage and the interest, if any, you charge on overdue accounts.

9 How creditworthy is the customer?

A great deal of grief could be saved if more companies checked on the credit status of their customers. The old adage, better safe than sorry, really applies here. There are a number of credit checks that you can make relatively quickly and simply. They do cost money, but much less than the potential loss of incurring a bad debt. Reputable customers should not resent you wanting to check on them, so credit checking should not cause you to lose out on business. However, checking can take time and, if you are anxious to start a new account quickly, you can adopt a policy of granting a small amount of credit without a check, while setting the vetting procedure in motion for further orders.

It makes sense to check up on existing customers as well. Even if there have been no problems in the past, the situation can change. A major customer running into financial trouble could have a serious impact on your business. Identify your biggest customers by listing all the accounts in descending order of value until they add up to 80% of the total. You should give the largest ones a full credit check, though you can carry out briefer checks on the smaller ones. It is worth listing customers by the size of their debt, rather than alphabetically, so you can identify major amounts outstanding at a glance. Also do an aged list of debts outstanding for thirty, sixty, ninety and more than ninety days.

- *Trade references*. Make sure the referee is a genuine supplier to the customer. Ask referees to supply details of how long they have traded with the customer, the credit terms they offer, whether the customer settles bills within these terms and the customer's average monthly spend. Ask also whether there is any other connection between the two businesses than that of customer and supplier. Provide a postage-paid envelope or ask for the form to be faxed back to you for a quick response.

- *Credit reference agencies.* Credit reference agencies will supply you with a report on potential customers, for a fee. They should give full customer details, financial results, payment experience of other suppliers, any County Court judgements and a recommended credit rating. Agencies may deliver instant reports on-line as well as by post or fax. Use an agency with a comprehensive database and a fast response. The disadvantage of using a credit reference agency is that the information is based on historical data and may be out of date. Dun & Bradstreet and Experian are two big, well-known agencies.

- *Bank references.* Bank references cost around £8–10 and are often written in vague terms. You need the customer's consent and remember that the bank's loyalty is to its customer, not to you. Ask specific questions such as 'Do you consider XYZ Ltd good for £5000 per month on thirty-day terms?' not general ones.

   Bear in mind that banks use only standard phrases. Examples range from 'Undoubted', which means the customer is almost certainly good for the money, to 'We are unable to speak for your figure', which, in plain English, means don't touch them with a bargepole. Anything less than 'good for your figure' is a guarded warning. Bank references should be used only for small-value decisions or to support other reports.

   You may also wish to consider requesting references from other professional advisers to a potential customer, for instance, the accountant, though again the customer will need to give permission.

- *County Court judgements.* You can write to the Registry of County Court Judgements for details of all judgements registered in the past three years. A lot of judgements is a definite warning sign, as it indicates customers are loath to pay up, or that they involve themselves in payment disputes.

- *The customer's payment policy.* If a customer has signed up to a voluntary code, such as that of the Better Payment Practice Group, it should indicate an intention to pay on time.

10   Reducing the risks

There are a number of possible steps you can take to reduce the risks of late or non-payment. These include:

- *Part payment.* Asking customers you consider risky for a payment in advance, while granting normal credit on the balance.
- *Stakeholder accounts.* Using an independent body such as a bank to hold funds from the customer until he or she is satisfied with the goods or services. These can be particularly appropriate for building work or similar, where the contractor needs funds to carry out the work.
- *Reduced payment terms.* The credit period for customers considered risky can be limited to one or two weeks instead of the normal thirty days.
- *Credit insurance.* You can take out trade credit insurance to reduce the risk of bad debts. Most cover is tailor-made and you will need to take advice from a specialist broker. Information on appropriate brokers can be provided by the United Kingdom Credit Insurance Brokers Committee, which operates under the auspices of the British Insurance and Investment Brokers' Association, (BIIBA.) See Appendix 2, Useful Contacts, for how to get in touch.
- *Incentives.* Sometimes the carrot works better than the stick and there are a number of measures you can employ to encourage reliable customers to settle their bills early, including discounts or rebates. Take care how you use these, however, as they can be expensive. Make sure that incentives are offered to good customers as a reward for paying promptly or to speed up payments further, rather than to bad payers simply to persuade them to pay on time.

11   Invoicing and paperwork

Invoice within twenty-four hours. Remember, nothing happens until your bill gets into the customer's payment process. Include payment terms and due date, delivery date and method, description, price and total payable, and the customer order number or payment authorisation. Send the invoice to a named individual and use first-class post or a courier for very large sums.

You cannot expect customers to pay against incorrect invoices – make sure yours are accurate. Be certain you have order details right, otherwise the customer has good reason to delay payment. Ask customers to confirm orders in writing and obtain proof of delivery of the goods. Try to ensure that the customer is satisfied with the order and to sort out any problems as soon as you can.

Send out statements of account every month, as early as you can, including details of all current transactions and any amounts outstanding. Make your credit terms clear in sales negotiations, on acknowledgements of orders, on account application forms, and on invoices and statements. If your goods – not services – are easily identifiable as supplied by you, you should have a condition of sale known as 'Retention of Title' which makes the goods your property until paid for. An 'All Sums Due' clause allows you to recover your goods against any cash the customer owes you, not just the outstanding sum relating to those goods. Make sure the customer knows about the clause and seek legal advice on drafting it.

12   Setting credit limits

You are not legally obliged to give anyone credit, nor do you need to explain the reason for your refusal. If you do decide to give credit, however, you will have to make a decision about how much. Put in place a policy of reviewing credit limits regularly, particularly for larger customers. Ways of setting credit limits include giving a limit of twice the monthly sales figure for that customer, if the references are good enough. With new customers, set a low credit limit to begin with, until they have established a good payment record. Alternatively, you may set a maximum amount you are prepared to be owed, regardless of current sales levels. A popular calculation is the lower of 10% of net worth or 20% of working capital.

You could also allocate customers a 'risk code' indicating how closely you believe the account should be watched. If you identify good payers, you can then put extra effort into trying to persuade them to buy more, so that your sales are on a sounder footing. Remember to review these codes regularly and make sure your staff are aware of customer credit limits. With major accounts, use good credit agency reports to indicate the right level of credit and get to know customers' payments staff.

13   How to collect your debts

A key part of your credit control policy is having clear procedures for collecting what you are owed. Allocate enough staff to the task, and make sure you have a timetable to follow for debt collection, showing when procedures should be set in motion. Make sure staff have access to the appropriate senior manager on serious-problem accounts.

- *Aged Debt reports*. The Aged Debt Analysis is the most important document for credit management. It should immediately set out the oldest and largest debts, and is a standard part of all good accounting software packages. It is a vital control document for senior management to monitor trends and weaknesses. Accounts should be listed in order of size, with the largest debt first. Disputed billings should be listed for action separately.
- *Collection letters*. Send out reminder letters seven to ten days after payment is due. Be short and to the point, and include details of the overdue amounts. The letter should be sent to a named person who has authority to approve the account for payment. Do not apologise for asking for payment, but do not be rude or hostile – it may be a genuine oversight. Do not send out a letter that looks like a circular, or the customer is likely to ignore it, and do not label your letter 'first reminder', as

that will encourage the customer to delay payment until another letter is sent.

- *Telephone.* Call customers four to five days after sending the reminder, if they have failed to make contact. Be firm and businesslike, but remain polite and friendly. Attempt to establish the reason for the delay without allowing the customer to deflect you with excuses. Keep a note of the conversation.
- *Final demands.* Send out a final demand around seven to ten days days after the reminder letter. A stop list can also be effective for products in short supply. The wording here depends on the action you intend to take; for instance, halting supplies or taking legal action.
- *Stop lists.* This is a list of customers to whom you do not wish to extend more credit. It should be updated regularly and circulated to staff. Inform customers that they have been put on the stop list.
- *Act on your threats.* If the final demand does not work, its threat must be carried out. Bluffs are soon seen as weakness. Faxes convey urgency and often beat defensive barriers when letters are being ignored or phone calls diverted. They should be sent to senior people.
- *Measure results.* Prepare a summary of debtors at the end of each month, and compare with the previous month and with any budget. You can monitor how well the system is working by calculating 'Debtor Days' or 'Days Sales Outstanding', in other words, how long customers are taking to pay up. A simple method is:

$$\frac{\text{Trade Debtors x 365}}{\text{Annual Sales}} = \text{Debtor Days}$$

Excuses, Excuses

The Better Payment Practice Group and factor Alex Lawrie compiled a list of the top ten excuses offered by late payers, and the most bizarre:

1   Waiting for the cheque to be signed: 23%.
2   Lost the invoice: 22%.
3   Cash-flow problems: 16%.
4   Account handler is off sick or is unavailable: 15%.
5   Cheque is in the post: 6%.
6   New computer system being installed or has failed: 6%.
7   Waiting for new chequebook or run of cheques: 5%.
8   Invoice in dispute: 3%.
9   We pay on sixty–ninety days, not thirty days: 2%.
10   You've missed the payment run: 2%.

The most bizarre excuses include:

'The chequebook has been destroyed in the flood.'
'The owner has been buried with his chequebook.'
'All names are put in a hat. If yours is pulled out you will get paid. If not, it will stay in the hat until next week.'
'The director went for an operation and never returned, as he went off with the nurse.'
'The tide is out and the director is unable to get in to pay cheques.'
'I do not speak English.'
'I cannot make payment until the planets are aligned, which is only twice a year.'
'We're in the middle of an armed robbery.'
'Not now, it's the office party.'

14   Dealing with evasive creditors

On a serious note, be sceptical of excuses, as they are often used as delaying tactics. Remain professional and friendly when encountering excuses, and bear in mind your past relationship with the customer. A previously good customer is far more likely to be telling the truth about a genuine mistake than one with a record of late payment.

- *Delaying tactics.* If someone tells you the cheque is in the post, ask for the cheque number and the posting date. If they say your invoice is on the next cheque run, ask when that run is and call a few days before that to check that your invoice is being processed. If they are waiting for the cheque to be signed, ask who the signatory is and then contact that person. In the case of an account handler being off sick, ask who is deputising – someone should be, if the person is going to be away for more than a day or two.

- *The person you need to speak to is never available.* Establish a time when he or she will be in the office/off the other line/out of the meeting and call back then. Ask for his or her mobile number and try that. If you still get no response, leave a clear voice message detailing the actions you want him or her to take. Follow up the message with a letter.

- *The case of the missing invoice.* If you are told that the customer cannot find your invoice, or that it is incomplete or incorrect, first of all check your own systems. Send a copy invoice if appropriate. If payment is still not forthcoming, use registered post. If you are told the computer system has crashed, try asking for a handwritten cheque.

- *Disputes over terms.* These should be avoided if you have followed the advice above on making your payment terms clear. It is a good idea to stress early in the sale that your own terms take precedence over theirs whenever possible. In the case of a large, big-company customer you may have to accept their terms or forgo the business – this may not be your ideal, but at least try to keep them to the terms they have imposed.

- *Rudeness and hostility.* Sadly, I have encountered this myself from a company that I knew to be having cash-flow problems. Stay calm and do not be deflected. Remember, if you are speaking to a junior member of staff, that he or she is unlikely to be responsible personally for the unpaid debt. Ask to speak to someone senior.

- *Can't pay, won't pay.* Pleading poverty is a sign of serious trouble with a customer. Confirm the debt and obtain a promise as to when payment will be made. If the customer is uncooperative, take a firm line (see below).

- *Factoring.* Factoring is an option to consider if you do not have the time or resources for your own credit management. Factors offer credit management and finance, which can enable you to improve your cash flow.

   Factoring companies normally advance you a percentage of your unpaid invoices of up to 80%. The balance, less the factor's commission, is paid to you when the customer settles. The advantage is that you do not have to wait for your money. The cost is normally around 0.3 to 0.5% of credit sales plus interest on the money advanced against invoices, usually at around 2-3% over base rates. There are a variety of factoring services available. For more information, contact the Factoring and Discounting Association (see Appendix 2, Useful Contacts).

15   Enforcement

Some recalcitrant customers ignore all reminders until they are faced with what they consider to be a real threat. If so, using a third party to collect debts can sting them into action.

- *Internal sanctions against poor payers.* There are a variety of sanctions you can impose against late payers. You can insist on your statutory right to interest (see below). You can also withhold supplies, in many cases an effective way of protecting yourself while encouraging the customer to pay up. It is most effective when your customer is a regular who needs supplies, but is a persistent late payer. Give the customer warning of your intention and be careful of using this sanction, as it can cause resentment if deployed inappropriately.

   Another option is to withdraw credit and to demand payment in advance. But do not reinstate credit the minute the customer repays the debt. Instead, insist on a period of 'good behaviour'.

- *Debt collection agents.* These work on a 'no collection – no fee' basis and charge between 5 and 15% of the amounts collected. However, you should be careful not to hire unscrupulous agencies.

- *Action without going to court.* Non-court action – going to court is not the only way of resolving a dispute. There are other options such as negotiation, mediation, conciliation or arbitration. The Lord Chancellor's Department has produced a leaflet 'Resolving Disputes Without Going to Court'.

- *Solicitors.* Can issue letters quickly that can focus the customer's mind remarkably well, for a prearranged fee.

- *Statutory demands.* This is a threat to petition the court for a winding-up or bankruptcy order if payment has not been made within twenty-one days. It can be sent by the seller, collection agent or solicitor, but it is not a measure to be used lightly.

- *Legal action.* The threat of legal action is often enough in itself to persuade debtors to pay. But only consider the threat if you are prepared to carry it out and if all other routes have failed, as legal action is expensive and time-consuming. The Lord Chancellor's Department has produced a variety of helpful booklets.

Legal procedures in Scotland and Northern Ireland are different from those in England and Wales. Further information can be obtained from the appropriate Sheriff Court in Scotland or County Court in Northern Ireland.

16   Your statutory right to claim interest

The government has introduced legislation to give businesses a statutory right to claim interest on overdue bills under the Late Payment of Commercial Debts (Interest) Act 1998. The Better Payment Practice Group has published a guide to the legislation (see Appendix 2, Useful Contacts). The legislation at the time of writing allows small companies with fewer than fifty employees to claim interest on overdue debts incurred by large companies with more than fifty employees. Small businesses are able to claim interest on late payments from other small firms from 1 November 2000. All businesses and the public sector will be able to claim from 1 November 2002. The law gives firms the right to charge a rate of interest of base rate plus 8%, far more than the overdraft rates charged by commercial banks. Payments are classed as late if they are made after the end of the agreed credit period. If there is no agreed period, the law sets a period of thirty days.

Before seeking to claim interest, bear in mind the effect it will have on your relationship with customers and ask yourself whether you can deal with late-payment issues by less confrontational measures. Even if you do not normally intend to claim interest, customers may be encouraged to start paying more promptly if you draw attention to your rights under the legislation in your terms and conditions. If you are going to claim interest, notify customers in writing and inform them when interest begins to accumulate.

You can pursue your claim through the County Court, or you could pass the debt and interest to a collecting agency.

17   Getting paid by overseas customers

Conventional wisdom is that extending credit to overseas customers is more of a risk than granting it to domestic buyers. You are further away from your customer, you may know less about him, and in some countries there are political and economic risks that can mean you do not get paid. But there are steps you can take to minimise the potential problems:

- *Assess country risks.* You can obtain data on the political and economic situation from the press, credit and business research agencies such as Dun & Bradstreet or Experian, reports from the high-street banks, or government departments such as Trade Partners UK and the Export Credits Guarantee Department.
- *Assess the customer risk.* Try to ascertain the customer's

solvency by consulting your agents or representatives overseas, or overseas credit agencies, or your bank.

- *Credit insurance*. The Export Credits Guarantee Service is the leading supplier of credit insurance, issuing policies on average worth over £3 billion a year to help UK exporters win contracts overseas, from £25,000 to £100 million.

- *Contracts*. Export contracts should contain a full description of the goods or services and should stipulate the currency in which the customer will be invoiced. Establish the period and method of payment. Insisting on payment in advance is the least risky option, but in practice is not used that frequently.

- *Letter of credit*. These are agreements between the overseas customer's bank and a UK bank to guarantee payment to an exporter, provided key documents are supplied on time. In theory, the system should be extremely safe, but in practice even a tiny snag in the documents can cause it to break down and this is often exploited by customers to drive down prices. A high proportion of letters of credit are rejected for payment when they are first presented at a UK bank so they must be handled with extreme care. High-street banks can offer guidance.

- *Cash against documents*. Under this method, the bill of lading and other documents required by the customer are available from a specified bank, which will release them only against payment.

- *Open account*. With established customers in non-problem countries, business is normally conducted on open-account terms, that is, the goods are despatched and then payment is sent on receipt or after an agreed period, frequently of one month.

- *Collecting debts*. Legal action can be difficult and expensive overseas because an export order may be governed by more than one country's laws. Major debt collection agencies offer recovery services in many countries but the costs can be high.

18   The taxman and the VAT-man

There are probably no two words more calculated to strike fear and loathing into the heart of the entrepreneur.

It is tempting for businesses in the early stages of growth to 'forget' about paying the Inland Revenue or the VAT-man. But this will soon attract official attention and hefty penalties, so it is not an option to be pursued by anyone with any sense. Most entrepreneurs will hand the nitty-gritty of their tax affairs to an accountant. That's fine, but it makes sense to have an understanding of your responsibilities.

- *PAYE and National Insurance.* If you have employees, you need to get to grips with the Pay As You Earn or PAYE system. In essence, this involves the employer deducting tax from staff wages and handing the money over to the Inland Revenue. You also have a statutory duty to deduct employees' National Insurance Contributions, which must be paid together with PAYE and employer's NICs. As soon as you register with the Revenue as an employer, you will be provided with various booklets explaining different aspects of the system. Your accountant and the Revenue will be able to give advice, but rather than doing it yourself, in all but the very smallest businesses it is worth hiring a competent person to administer your payroll, or outsourcing the job to a payroll bureau.

  Normally, the net tax deducted under PAYE and National Insurance Contributions must be handed over each month, though small amounts can be paid over quarterly. Keep your payroll records carefully, because mistakes can result in additional tax liabilities and penalties. At the end of each year employers have to fill in returns within certain deadlines. No later than 19 May, employers must complete a P35 declaration and provide each employee with a P60, giving details of gross pay and tax deducted. A copy, P14, must be submitted to the Inland Revenue.

  No later than 6 July, form P11D, showing expenses and benefits, must be submitted to the Inland Revenue in respect of all 'higher-paid' employees – that is those with earnings of more than £8500, including benefits and reimbursed expenses. Normally a P11D must be submitted for all directors. Employees must be informed of the details declared on the P11D within the same deadline.

- *VAT.* Value Added Tax is payable to Her Majesty's Customs and Excise, and is based on your turnover and costs, rather than your profits. The amount of VAT payable is the total of all the *output tax* charged to customers on goods and services during the period, minus *input tax* you have paid on your business expenses. If the input tax exceeds the output tax, HMCE will refund the difference.

  At the moment goods and services are divided into four categories for VAT purposes: *exempt*, on which no VAT is payable, such as the services of a doctor; *standard-rated*, on which VAT is chargeable at the standard rate; *reduced-rated*, on which VAT is charged at a cut rate – at the moment this applies mainly to domestic fuel at 5%; and *zero-rated*, goods on which in theory VAT is payable, though in practice none is paid because the tax rate is 0%.

  In the tax year 2000–1 the standard rate of VAT is 17.5% and businesses must register if their taxable turnover is in excess of £52,000. In 2001 the registration threshold was raised to £54,000. In addition, a new provision was introduced so that firms with a turnover of £100,000 or less may be able to opt for a new 'flat rate' scheme where VAT is calculated as a percentage of turnover. This saves on red tape as it means firms do not need to account for every individual sale and purchase. Failure to register will result in financial penalties if your turnover is above this level. It is possible to apply for voluntary VAT registration if you can convince HMCE that it is applicable. The advantage of this is that you can reclaim input VAT – particularly useful if your goods and services are 'zero-rated', such as children's clothing or newspapers.

  It is worth taking professional advice from an accountant on when to register. Once you have registered, you need to keep a separate VAT account to record the amounts of VAT you are adding to sales and the VAT charged to you on business expenses. You cannot reclaim VAT on a supply unless it is supported by an invoice which includes the supplier's VAT number and a description of the goods and services. If your business is registered for VAT, all invoices must contain specified information, including the date of supply and your VAT registration number. VAT returns must normally be submitted quarterly.

- *Income tax*. You will pay income tax under the self-assessment system if you are a sole trader. The taxman treats partnerships as if each person were running his or her own business and the tax bill is worked out in much the same way as if you were a sole trader. Profits are divided between the partners according to their profit-sharing agreement in the relevant tax year.
- *Capital taxes*. Capital taxes include such things as capital gains tax, which kicks in when you sell or dispose of your business, and inheritance tax, which can bite if you die or give away the business. Although these do not normally affect entrepreneurs starting up a business, there are all kinds of reliefs available so it makes sense to start talking to your accountant about planning for these taxes at an early stage. Entrepreneurs should pay more attention as they approach retirement.
- *Corporation tax*. Limited companies pay corporation tax, not income tax. Corporation tax covers all the company's profits – there is no distinction between income and capital gains, as there is with individuals. Self-assessment for corporation tax has now been introduced, so the burden of proof is on companies to justify the figures shown in their tax computations. Smaller companies benefit from lower rates of corporation tax. In the 2001–2 tax year, the rate for companies with taxable profits of up to £300,000 is 20%, with a special 10% rate for those making profits of under £10,000. The main rate of corporation tax is 30%.

7
Finance for Growth

You have a great idea, a team of people, you are utterly convinced you are on to a winner – now all you have to do is convince someone else to give you some money so you can make your plans a reality.

Entrepreneurs can be extraordinarily inventive about funding. I have come across some people who have started highly successful businesses by 'maxing out' their credit cards, or by raising money from family and friends. If you are serious about growth, however, these informal means of financing are unlikely to suffice for very long. Getting the right type of finance is important and so is an understanding of what your backers will want from you in return for advancing you their money.

Many entrepreneurs fall at this hurdle through lack of advice, or a failure to present themselves well enough, so I have included in this chapter guidance from leading experts. We will look at the different types of finance available and at how to get advice. We will also take a look at the dream for many ambitious entrepreneurs – a stock market float.

1 Yourself, family and friends

Financial backers will expect you to put your own money on the line in your new venture. After all, if you won't invest in it, why should they? You may be able to raise capital yourself from sources such as a lump sum redundancy payment, a pension lump sum, an inheritance or some other windfall.

Entrepreneurs, particularly in the Asian community, often turn to their families or friends for help. This can be a cheap form of finance and you may be able to convince your family and friends to back you more readily than outsiders. But be aware that borrowing from them can cause enormous problems if things go wrong and they lose their money. Make sure you spell out the risks and consider setting out a plan of what you will do if the business fails; for instance, moving to a smaller house to repay your relatives. Think also about how you will meet outgoings that you might consider essential, such as school fees.

Another option is to use your personal assets to raise funds, for instance by taking out a second mortgage on your home. The disadvantage is that if the business fails, you have lost everything: – your business, your income and the roof over your head. Before going down this route, make absolutely sure you have the unqualified support of your husband, wife or partner. At this stage the entrepreneur's mind should become concentrated on the seriousness of the whole project. Unless you are free and single, it is vital to have the backing of your family.

2   Grants and special loans

If you have a good business idea but cannot meet the criteria for a conventional bank loan, you may be able to obtain grants or cheap loans from a number of sources.

- *The Small Firms Loan Guarantee Scheme.* The government runs a Small Firms Loan Guarantee Scheme through the Small Business Service which guarantees loans from banks and other financial institutions for small businesses with viable business proposals, which have tried and failed to obtain a conventional loan because of a lack of security. The idea is that you take out a loan from a bank, on terms determined by the lender, but the bank has additional security because it is backed by the Department of Trade and Industry.

Loans are available for periods of between two and ten years on sums from £5000 to £100,000, or £250,000 in the case of businesses that have been trading for more than two years. The scheme guarantees 70% of the loan, or 85% in the case of businesses trading for more than two years. You must pay the lender as usual and, in addition, you must pay the DTI a premium of 1.5% each year on the outstanding amount of the loan, or 0.5% if the loan is taken at a fixed rate of interest. To qualify, your turnover must be £1.5 million or less, or £3 million in the case of manufacturers. There are restrictions on the uses to which the loans can be put and not all businesses are eligible. You need to make an application direct to one of the scheme lenders.

Small Firms Loan Guarantee Scheme Lenders

There are currently twenty lenders:

First Trust (Allied Irish)	Lloyds TSB Group
Bank of Ireland	London Enterprise Agency (LEnta)
Bank of Scotland	National Westminster Bank
Barclays Bank	Northern Bank
British Steel (Industry) Ltd	Northern Investors Loan Finance Ltd
Clydesdale Bank	Royal Bank of Scotland
Co-operative Bank	Ulster Bank
Doncaster Business Advice Centre	Venture Finance plc
3i Group plc	Yorkshire Bank
HSBC	Yorkshire Enterprise Ltd

- *Local schemes.* Many of the larger cities have schemes that provide loans to small firms, normally of up to £10,000. There are also regional schemes run by the European Union and Development Agencies. Your local Business Link should be able to help you identify suitable schemes and to apply.

Businesses wishing to expand in Wales and Scotland can apply for support under the Welsh Development Agency, where you can borrow up to £750,000 or Scottish Enterprise, which will advance up to £500,000.

The schemes favour certain sectors including manufacturing industries, hotels and tourism, and to qualify you normally need to have a track record as a stable employer and demonstrate that you are creating employment.

- *The Phoenix Fund*. The government has created a new fund, the Phoenix Fund, worth £30 million, to encourage entrepreneurship in disadvantaged communities and groups. It is comprised of four elements: the Phoenix Fund will channel money to businesses through organisations called Community Finance Initiatives (CFIs), rather than to entrepreneurs directly. CFIs are locally run, not-for-profit organisations that lend small amounts to businesses which the banks consider too risky. They often operate in defined deprived geographic areas.

- *The Prince's Trust*. This offers support and advice to young people hoping to set up a business. To qualify, you must be aged eighteen to thirty, or thirty-one in Scotland and unemployed or 'underemployed' in an unfulfilling part-time or temporary job. The Trust can offer: low-interest loans of up to £5000; test marketing grants of up to £250; grants of up to £1500 in special circumstances; advice from a volunteer 'Business Mentor' during your first three years of trading and extra support including discounted exhibition space and specialist advice.

- *Shell LiveWIRE*. Shell LiveWIRE is a community investment programme funded by oil giant Shell, aiming to help stimulate young people aged sixteen to thirty to start or grow their own businesses. It offers start-up cash, training and advice, and runs a national competition for young entrepreneurs.

- *Former coal and steel areas*. Funding is available for businesses set up in former coal and steel areas. BCE Business Funding provides secured loans of up to £250,000 to businesses wishing to create jobs in former coal-mining areas.

British Steel (Industry) Ltd offers loans of between £10,000 and £150,000 in areas affected by the rationalisation of the steel industry.

- *Grants.* The Department of Trade and Industry and other organisations make grants to businesses. This is a complex field and you need to be wary of 'grant cowboys' purporting to be able to obtain grants, but really out to fleece you. The local Business Link or its equivalent should be able to give you a list of schemes in your area that are appropriate to your company.

3   Bank loans and overdrafts

Overdrafts and loans can be a simple and effective way of financing a business, but they should be used in the correct way. Before borrowing, bear in mind that your debts will soon become unmanageable unless you are generating enough cash to make the repayments. When thinking about your 'gearing' – the proportion of your finance in the form of debt – consider the risks involved. High gearing is not a good idea if you cannot predict future cash flows with any confidence.

Overdrafts are meant to cover short-term needs, while loans are more appropriate to cover development and start-up costs, and to finance long-term assets such as plant and machinery. It is a good idea to talk to the bank about arranging a package all at the same time.

- *Overdrafts.* These are meant to be for short-term financing only, not to cover the purchase of long-term assets. You should use overdrafts to finance ups and downs in your cash flow: for instance to cover seasonal troughs, or to cope with a drain on cash such as a surprise new order.

  The advantages of overdrafts are that they are flexible and relatively cheap if used properly, as you only pay interest on the amount overdrawn each day. In principle, however, the bank can demand repayment at any time. You will also need to renegotiate your facilities once or twice a year. Normally you will be charged an arrangement fee on the full overdraft limit and interest on the amount you borrow, but it is worth shopping around for the best deals. Make every effort not to go overdrawn without having arranged it in advance and try not to exceed agreed overdraft limits as the bank will exact heavy penalties.

- *Loans.* For longer-term funding needs it is more appropriate to arrange a loan. Once you have set up the loan, that financing is guaranteed to remain in place unless you fail to make payments or breach another condition of the loan agreement, unlike an overdraft, which in theory can be recalled by the bank at will.

You can match a loan to the life of an asset you want to buy; for instance, by taking out a five-year loan to buy a piece of equipment with an expected five-year lifespan. However, you pay interest on the full amount you owe for the whole lifetime of the loan and the bank may require you to sign legally binding conditions or 'covenants' before lending you the money.

The bank will look at a number of measures indicating your capacity to repay and will insist that you operate within constraints based on its assessment. You will normally be expected to provide security for larger amounts, giving the bank a legal charge over assets such as property or equipment if you default on the loan. The bank may ask for personal guarantees such as a charge over your home, life insurance policies or shares. You will normally be charged an arrangement fee and you will have to pay any costs the bank incurs such as legal advice or valuing security. The bank may also want you to take out life insurance or a critical-illness policy.

Interest is either charged at a set rate over base rate, or, for larger loans, you can opt for a fixed-rate loan, where the rate of interest is determined at the outset and does not change, no matter what happens to base rates. This makes it easier to budget, but you could lose out if base rates fall significantly below what you are paying. Having said that, the rates will reflect the market's expectations of future interest rates.

- *Foreign currency loans.* Exporters receiving income in a foreign currency may want to borrow in that currency to reduce their exposure to exchange rate risk. This can be organised at any high-street bank, but try to operate a 'matching' principle where liabilities in a foreign currency are offset by assets in that currency. Otherwise, if the exchange rate moves against you, foreign currency loans could spiral out of control.

4   Getting the best deal from your bank

Banks do not have to lend you money – after all, you would be unlikely to extend an IOU to a friend if you thought there was little chance of getting it back. Do not expect the bank to lend purely on your say-so. Lending managers are accountable to their own bosses and they will want to see hard evidence that your business is a good bet. Have a solid business plan to show the bank and be able to back it up with hard evidence as far as you can. You are more likely to impress if you have credible cash-flow forecasts, a good previous banking record and a strong balance sheet.

Shop around for the best deals and then haggle for lower interest rates and charges. It is also good policy to ask the bank to show you the total cost of the loan or overdraft, so you can compare deals more easily.

Case Study 1: Kallo Foods – growing organically and by acquisition

Kallo Foods (formerly Garma Foods International) was a double winner in the *Financial Mail*'s 2000 Enterprise Awards, scooping the prizes for financial management and strategy planning. The company was formed in 1997 with the merger of Garma Gourmet UK, part of one of Italy's largest privately owned companies, and the Orient Trading Company, which was owned by Chris Lane, who is now Managing Director of the merged company.

Kallo Foods supplies the major supermarket chains with breadsticks, crackers, snacks and confectionery, and customers include Tesco, Sainsbury and Marks & Spencer. Based near Guildford, Surrey, Kallo enjoys the advantages of being a small operation.

Lane, who is a principal shareholder, says that the company is very efficient and more flexible in making decisions than some of the giants. 'In a multinational firm it can take a year or more to launch a new product, while we can do it within two months.' The firm's objective is to sell healthy and organic food products to a broad range of blue-chip retailers, offering value for money, and to provide active support in selling the product through to the consumer. Lane says, 'People often ask us how we can penetrate such large markets, monopolised by the major manufacturers. We do not wait for the retailers to tell us what they require but go in with fresh ideas. We offer something different from that which is generally available.'

The firm uses the most up-to-date technology to include fast-order processing and the sales team has access to its offices via laptops and modems. Lane completely reorganised the company, its structure and its product portfolio when he took over. In August 1998 Garma Foods (as it was then called) made its first small acquisition, a confectionery business with the distribution rights to a range of Belgian chocolates being sold through Asda, Harrods and Waitrose.

In January 1999 Lane set out a clear strategy that the way forward for the company was through a more aggressive approach to acquisitions. He says, 'We retained a mergers and acquisitions specialist, who has had experience at Ernst & Young and HSBC. We went through a search looking at a hundred companies. We narrowed it down to thirty then came up with a shortlist of ten. In the end, we plumped for a company called Kallo, which had been trading for seventeen years as a small family business. It had recently shown growth because of the boom in organic food.' Lane entered into detailed discussions with the two brothers who owned Kallo and, over the next seven months, carried out 'due diligence', a full check on the company, its operations and its management.

In February 2000 the deal to buy Kallo was signed. Lane says, 'We have doubled turnover and we are incredibly profitable, about double the industry average. We have achieved this through niche marketing, careful cost control and financial and strategic planning.' The first thing he did when he took control of Kallo was to appoint Carolyn Robinson as Financial Director from consumer company United Biscuits, an accomplished finance expert with a great deal of a international experience. He says, 'Cash management is vital to a successful business. If you have cash-flow problems, that can take you down. We are just in the throes of completing a strategic review of business for the next three years with a consultant. We will look at the business in terms of finance, marketing and sales.'

The first result of the review has been to drop the company's previous name, Garma Foods International in favour of Kallo Foods, clearly identifying the company with its leading branded asset. Kallo Foods is aiming for £40–50 million of sales turnover within the next three years. Lane adds, 'The key to it all is profit. One of our options three years down the line is to float the company. If we achieve our three-year growth plan that would be the ideal time to look at the option of a flotation.'

5 Equity finance

The term equity finance is often used when a business issues shares to outside investors. It differs from loans in several respects. With a bank loan, you agree to pay interest and to repay the capital lent to you. The lender, naturally, runs the risk that you will not pay back the loan, and will set the rate of interest according to the perceived risk.

With equity finance, investors do not lend money. Instead, they take a stake in your business in the form of shares – essentially, they become part-owners. In return, they hope that your business will grow, meaning that their shares will increase in value and perhaps also pay them an income, known as a dividend.

Shareholders are therefore taking the risk that your business will fail to grow and that they will lose money.

Sources of equity finance include business angels, venture capitalists and the financial markets, such as the London Stock Exchange. Equity finance can provide your business with the funding it needs to grow. However, in return, you are ceding some of the ownership and control to outside investors.

6   Business angels

Business angels are well-to-do individuals who provide funds to small firms in return for a chunk of shares. Many of them are themselves successful entrepreneurs who want to take a stake in the next generation of start-ups. They can fill the funding gap for businesses that are too small for conventional venture capitalists (see below) to be interested in. In addition to providing money, angels can also be a valuable source of expertise and advice.

Angels may be an appropriate source of funding for businesses that want to raise £10,000 to £500,000 – some may even invest £1 million – and are prepared to hand over some shares in return. A typical angel will want to have hands-on involvement, so this type of financing means you have to be prepared to form a personal relationship with him or her.

- *Finding your angel.* You may get in touch with an angel informally through friends and family or wealthy business contacts. Business to business sections in newspapers may include advertisements for investors looking for ventures to finance, or, if you are operating in the e-commerce field, there are clubs such as First Tuesday that match entrepreneurs with investors.

    Alternatively, you could approach an angels' network, which is somewhat similar to a business dating agency in that it aims to bring together attractive businesses with interested investors. To register, you will have to supply a business plan and financial forecasts, then the network will pass on your details to angels. There may also be events where you can meet the angels.

A number of organisations can help, including the British Venture Capital Association, which produces a guide to angels' introduction agencies, Sources of Business Angel Capital. The National Business Angels Network acts as an umbrella for numerous national and local networks matching businesses and investors. Venture Capital Report also informs business angels about opportunities. You will pay a listing fee and a success fee if you meet your angel through the service. Remember that it is as much about chemistry as about a technical match (see the Appendix 2, Useful Contacts, for more information).

- *How to impress an angel.* Business angels are prepared to take risks, but it is important to appreciate that they are doing so in the hope of earning a high return. Normally, they will aim for an average annual return of at least 20% over the life of their investment. They will also be interested in how they might realise their hoped-for gains. Options include the business buying back the angel's shares, a stock market float or the sale of the business to a trade buyer. Even if they intend to stick with the business for the long term, it is worth discussing their possible exit routes at an early stage.

  To impress an angel you will need to demonstrate that you have a thorough understanding of your product or service and your market. It helps if you can point to a good track record. Angels also like to see a seasoned and highly professional management team, and they will look for commitment from the team in the form of personal investment in the business and rewards linked to its performance.

  As with Hollywood film directors, you will only be given a very short time to 'pitch' to an angel, so make sure you make the maximum impact in the minimum time. Explain what the business does, avoiding jargon and focusing instead on what makes it special. Tell the angel how you would use the money to grow the business and show him or her that you are offering the potential to make money. Detail how much money you want to raise and what proportion of your shares you are prepared to hand over.

- *How angelic is your angel?* It is not unknown for individuals to put themselves about as 'angels' when in reality they are simply looking for a job, or seeking inexperienced entrepreneurs to exploit. They may even be competitors seeking intelligence. Check angels' CVs, and take up references. Quiz them about their motivation, in other words, why they want to invest in your business and what they hope to get out of it. Find out also what skills they have to offer, and what worries and risks they perceive in your business.

- *The practicalities.* Once you think you can do a deal with an angel, confirm that he or she can offer the finance. You will need to provide the angel with a business plan as the basis for working out issues such as the dividends, fees and salaries paid to you and to the angel; your respective responsibilities within the business; how performance will be monitored; and how the angel will make an exit. Get advice from your accountant and solicitor on what form the investment should take and on negotiating the terms. Make sure everything is in writing.

Tips for Finding Your dot.com Angel

- Research your market well – know who the competition is, what their strengths and weaknesses are and how they are doing.
- Make sure you have a critical mass of potential clients willing to trade on-line.
- Ensure your management team has good business skills, or the potential to develop them.
- Make sure you have the potential to win a share of market by having concrete knowledge of what consumers want.
- Have a traditional fully thought-out business plan backed up by as much evidence as possible.

Insider's Tips on Finding a Good Accountant

Choosing the right accountant is not always easy. But if you are serious about growth, you need to find an accountant whose skills and knowledge match your ambitions. Making a good choice of accountant can make all the difference to how quickly and sustainably your business grows. So it is worth taking the selection process very seriously. I asked one of the UK's foremost experts, David Maxwell, a partner at leading accountants and business advisers RSM Robson Rhodes, for his advice. He suggests the following approach:

- *Draw up a strategy.* Not all firms of accountants and business advisers are the same and certainly not all are equally knowledgeable about the issues facing growing companies. To make the right choice for you and your business you need to invest some time and effort.

    Most companies choosing a firm of advisers go through a process which includes various stages. To give you the best chance of choosing wisely, take the following steps:
- *Prepare adequately in advance.* Contact the Institute of Chartered Accountants in England and Wales or the equivalent professional body in Scotland or Northern Ireland. Speak to people you know in companies with similar growth or industry characteristics. Do not include too many companies on your initial shortlist – about four ought to do the trick. Otherwise the process will be too time-consuming.
- *Be clear about your objectives.* From these devise a list of criteria. The criteria can then be used to make up a checklist, which will remind you of your priorities in relation to your business. This checklist will help you draw up a shortlist of firms and to evaluate their proposal documents, presentations and the people you meet. The checklist need not be elaborate, as in most cases the decision will rest on three or four issues.

- *Delegate the responsibility for managing the process to one person.* They should produce and circulate all the paperwork, co-ordinate and act as a first port of call for the firms you invite to tender.
- *Make 'scoping' meetings an integral part of the selection process.* These initial meetings allow the accountancy firms to ask all the questions which will allow them properly to price their services to you. Look for people who have made an effort to prepare for the meeting and are interested in your aspirations as well as the needs of the business. Be aware of the personal side – look for indications these are people you will 'gel' with. At this stage, ask whether the people visiting you to scope the job will actually form part of the team assigned to work with your company.
- *Watch for the sell.* At all stages of the exercise, bear in mind that the people you meet are likely to be in 'sales mode' and will try to steer you to their own agenda. Any proposals you receive should demonstrate that your prospective accountants listened to you. Beware of any documents you feel have been produced 'off the shelf'. Look for proposals which meet your requirements in terms of focus and style. If representatives of firms have listened to you they should be able to demonstrate an understanding of your needs. On fees, do the fees seem realistic and is the rationale for the fees explicit?

  Your checklist should cover:
- *Empathy.* Does the firm display empathy with growing companies and are they knowledgeable about them?
- *Orientation towards growth businesses.* Do the people you meet ask well-considered questions around the issues you face, on topics such as investors and funding? Do they have good relationships with a broad range of capital providers and access to relevant networks? Is the firm structured around serving growing, entrepreneurial companies and can they demonstrate a track record of providing a range of non audit-services relevant to growth companies?

- *Skills and experience.* Does the accountancy firm's balance of skills and experience appear a good fit? Do the people you meet demonstrate understanding of your business, your objectives and style? Do they have experience of working with companies experiencing similar 'growth pains'? Do they know enough about your sector and others which are relevant? This point is particularly important if you are in a volatile sector, or if you are seeking more than just a standard service from your accountants. Are the people who will be in your team sector specialists or can they draw upon that resource from within the firm?

- *Personal factors.* Can we work well with these people and is the firm offering the appropriate level of contact for each task/meeting? Ask yourself, 'Will these people challenge me, work with me and help me?' If senior level contact is important to you – and it is for most companies – ask about how much partner time your company is likely to be allocated throughout the year. Do the people seem to have the right attitude and are they of the right calibre? Are they excited about working with you? Ask yourself whether you would hire these people to work in your finance team.

- *Fees.* Have you been provided with an adequate breakdown on fees? Are they clear and comprehensible, or are numbers presented in a way which makes them appear as if they have been plucked out of thin air? Is the basis of any advisory fees clear? Are expenses and VAT included or excluded?

- *Value.* Will you get value from your interaction with these people? Try to determine what each firm will bring to their relationship with you. Firms may try to demonstrate during the selection process that they are keen to work with you. But review your experience of them to date and rate teams for speed of response, personality, originality of thought, accessibility of people at the right level, depth of support, what they will provide over and above what they 'have to'.

7   Venture capital

Venture capital is a source of funding specifically aimed at growing businesses. It is normally provided by specialist venture capitalists such as 3i plc, who raise their money from large pension funds and other investors. A number of companies that are now household names were formerly backed by venture capital; for instance, computer group Sage.

Typically, venture capitalists will provide unsecured financing, but in return they will want a proportion of your shares. Venture capitalists, or VCs, as they are nicknamed, are by nature demanding beasts. They are taking calculated risks and they want to see high rewards, sufficient to justify the costs of assessing and managing those risks. This is not an option for the faint-hearted.

- *Is venture capital suitable for you?* It may be, if you are seeking a minimum investment of £500,000. The reason for this high threshold is the fixed nature of 'due diligence' costs. Due diligence is the process of checking out you, your business and your plans. Venture capitalists will want to see the prospect of annual returns in the region of 25% or more. You will need to show that you have a seasoned and professional management team with a successful track record, who are prepared to risk their own assets. The venture capitalists will also want to see management pay and rewards tightly linked to performance.

  Most venture capital investment is in firms with a proven track record, rather than in start-ups, and venture capitalists often provide backing for management buyouts or buyins (see below), where management teams buy a division of an existing company and run it as an independent entrepreneurial business.

  The venture capitalists will be extremely interested in how they will realise the profits they hope to make. Normally they will want to exit within three to seven years either by a trade sale, a float on the stock market, or by being bought out by the management. The managers must be prepared for a stressful and hard-working time if they are to satisfy the venture capitalists.

- *What the venture capitalists will want from you.* Venture capitalists, as stated earlier, typically look for a compound annual return of 25% to 35%. They will normally take a big stake in the company of between 20% and 50%. VCs may want to have a representative on your board, usually as a non-executive director. They will normally limit themselves to strategic decisions, but expect them to start taking a hands-on role if things go wrong. You will be expected to provide the VCs with regular information, such as monthly management accounts.

- *Watch out.* Venture capital deals fairly frequently fail and they can fall apart even at the last minute. Usually, the reasons are because the performance of the business goes down during the negotiations, there are legal problems that cannot be resolved or, most common of all, an agreement on price and other key terms cannot be reached. Venture capital is expensive and takes a lot of time, often between six months and a year. Be careful that you do not take your eye off the ball and allow other aspects of the business to drift during that time.

  You will be expected to pay the venture capital firm's costs and you will have to pay your own specialist advisers, who do not come cheap. The total costs can easily be as much as 10% of the amount raised for smaller sums.

- *Finding a venture capitalist.* The British Venture Capital Association publishes a free directory of its members and a guide to raising venture capital. At this stage it is worth taking on a professional adviser to help prepare a business plan, and to identify and contact selected venture capital firms. Venture capitalists are deluged with proposals from hopeful companies, many of which are turned down without even a meeting. You will need to have a solid, credible business plan to persuade the VCs that yours is a worthwhile company for investment, and be able to back up assertions and forecasts with convincing evidence.

- *Negotiation.* Once a venture capital firm is interested, you face a long, stressful period of negotiation. During initial talks, you should get an indication of how much they will invest and what they want in return, but at this point nothing is firm. You should haggle over what costs you are expected to pay and these should only be payable if the investment actually goes ahead.

Before a firm agreement is made, there will be a long process called 'due diligence' where the venture capital firm checks out your business. They will give a thorough examination to your financial and legal details, and will probe into how well the business is run. The process normally takes between one and three months, and will be carried out by the venture capitalist's financial advisers. The main terms of the deal will be contained within an 'investment agreement' and the deal is not done until it has been signed. Obviously, you need a solicitor to help negotiate and draw up the agreement.

● *Choosing an adviser.* You really do need a specialist adviser. They do not come cheap, but their expertise is invaluable when dealing with hard-nosed venture capitalists. All the major accountancy firms have corporate finance experts and there are independent corporate finance specialists who can work alongside your existing accountants. It is important that you can strike up a good personal rapport with your adviser, as you are going to be seeing an awful lot of him or her over the coming months, in some highly stressful situations. Do not be impressed by the credentials of a big firm – the individual adviser is the one you will be dealing with. Ask for details of deals he or she has personally done over the past twelve months.

8   Management buyouts

Management buyouts are deals where a team of executives working in a big company buy their division from their employer and run it as an independent business. A management buyin is similar, but the management team comes from outside the business. MBOs and MBIs are popular with venture capitalists because they are viewed as being less risky than start-ups, as both the business and the management have a track record. They have also made millionaires of a few lucky former employees, including Gerry Robinson, boss of leisure group Granada and Nicola Foulston, Chief Executive of Brands Hatch.

To win backing, management teams must be credible and will typically be in their forties to early fifties, though age or youth is not always a barrier. As ever, a sound business plan is one of the keys in convincing potential backers. It will look at why the owners want to sell, and what you could do to reduce costs and boost growth. Multinationals often want to sell subsidiaries that no longer fit in with their global plans. But the parent company has to be satisfied that the deal represents best value for them. You and your family need to plan for the equivalent of six to twelve months' gross salary being invested in the buyout. And be prepared to work even longer hours than you do already. While the potential rewards may be considerable, they will typically take four to seven years to materialise.

Good moments for launching a buyout might include when:

- the parent has taken over another company, which shifts the focus away from your activity;
- head office would prefer the cash, knowing your division is a drain on central resources;
- the parent company has been taken over and your firm does not fit into the new plan;
- the owner of an entrepreneurial business is retiring and is not passing down the business to his or her family.

Be aware that mounting an approach at the wrong moment could mean that you lose your job as well as getting nowhere with your buyout plan. Even if the parent company wants to sell, you should prepare for several months of intense negotiations. Until the deal is signed and sealed, be prepared to contend with competitive bids from outsiders or even a rival external management buyin team.

If you do succeed, you and your colleagues will have to transform yourselves from executives in a corporation to being owners. Your the relationship with junior managers will change. You are still their boss, but they will view you in a different light and may be resentful if they think you are making millions from the buyout. A choice may have to be made between offering them incentives or seeing them leave.

It makes sense for you and your backers to have a good idea of how you will make an exit, preferably having made your profits. In most cases this is done through a trade sale, a float on the stock market or a secondary buyout, where the original backers sell their stake to another venture capitalist that will take the company through the next stage of its growth.

Attracting Potential Backers – an Insider's View

It is absolutely vital to go about attracting financial backers in the right way. This advice is provided by Graham Spooner, a director of Classic Fund Management.

Whether you have retained a professional adviser or are making contact directly with proposed investors, you must have a clear strategic focus as to what your business proposition is and to be able to communicate this clearly to potential backers. These may include venture capitalists, bankers, other funders and also private investors.

You must ensure that your business plan or information memorandum complies with section 57 of the 1986 Financial Services Act, which relates to Investment Advertisements, so seek professional advice. Don't 'chase too many rabbits' – try instead to identify the relevant sources of finance to approach.

- *Provide an executive summary of your business plan.* The executive summary is like your personal CV – it should be no longer than two pages – and its purpose is to obtain a meeting with your potential backers. Of every hundred business plans received by venture capitalists, only twenty will result in a meeting. The executive summary is the first

– and in 80% of cases the only – part of the plan to be read. It must whet the appetite of the reader to encourage her or him to read on and to have a meeting with you.

- *Prepare a presentation.* Prepare and rehearse your presentation to investors. Remember that different funders will have different requirements. Debt providers will want a greater emphasis on cash flow and headroom in working capital facilities, whereas equity investors may have a greater emphasis on capital upside and seeking a successful exit.
- *Personal chemistry.* Investors and bankers are looking to back people. You need to establish an empathy with them so that they become your champions within their own organisation. The key questions that you must address include:

   who you are and what is your relevant track-record;
   what does your business do and how does it work;
   why is your business successful (what are its strengths and weaknesses, its opportunities and threats; what are the barriers to entry and risk factors);
   what are your plans (both personal goals and corporate objectives) for the future.

- *Profile of your business.* Financial backers are seeking to assess the key attributes of your business and, in particular, will wish to focus on:

   your people, including the dynamics of the team and its potential in quality to deliver;
   your business plan (i.e. to make it happen);
   your product (or service) and process;
   your position in the market place;
   the ability of your business to generate a positive cash flow and achieve maintainable profits growth;
   your personal commitment, both financially and your motivational drivers;

the policing of the business: your controls and systems, your approach to corporate governance and the role of non-executive directors.

> • *Managing the process.* Aim for 'no surprises' and never forget that the purpose of raising capital is as a means to an end, rather than an end in itself. You must ensure that the day-to-day running of the business does not suffer throughout the process of raising capital and that you 'don't take your eye off the ball'. Be prepared for something going wrong (the 'wobble'). Project management is what some 80% of the process is about and at times it will feel like an 'emotional roller coaster'! Good luck and enjoy making it happen.

9   Floating on the stock market

Many entrepreneurs dream of floating their business on the stock market. A float can bring a number of benefits, including access to funds both when you float and in future, through later share issues. It can bring a wider shareholder base and a market for your shares. You can use listed shares to pay for acquisitions, if you want to expand by taking over another company, and to incentivise employees. A float will give your business a higher status in the eyes of customers, suppliers and the world at large, and will give your business a public profile.

Importantly, a stock market listing provides the owner with a way of crystallising financial rewards for hard work by selling a chunk of shares – though selling a large proportion of shares all at once when you float can send out the wrong signals and new investors may set a limit on the amount they will let you offload.

But many growing businesses steer clear of the stock markets for a variety of reasons, including the costs of flotation, loss of control and the fact that managers become accountable to shareholders and must comply with requirements to report information. In the past, stock market listings have been restricted to businesses that are already reasonably established. This still applies to a 'main market' listing on the London Stock Exchange. However, other markets have been set up to cater for newer and more speculative companies, particularly those in high technology.

- *The London Official List.* The main UK stock market is one of the biggest and best regarded in the world. However, there are stringent listing requirements and a float on the main market is very expensive.
- *The Alternative Investment Market.* The Alternative Investment Market or AIM was set up to cater for smaller, growing companies. Its listing requirements are less stringent, in accordance with the needs of relatively young companies.
- *NASDAQ and EASDAQ.* NASDAQ is a US market which has attracted many high-growth, high-technology companies. The regulations and listing requirements are strict, and the costs of listing are correspondingly high. EASDAQ is the European equivalent of NASDAQ.
- *Ofex.* This is not a formal market but a trading facility for the shares of unquoted companies. Those looking to raise small amounts of equity of, say, between £250,000 and £1.5 million, may do so through a broker who places shares with private clients. An Ofex facility allows investors to trade their shares more easily.

CHAPTER **8**

The Restless Company – Why Innovation Matters

> I believe in the idea of a 'restless company' where existing technologies are constantly challenged in a search for products that work better.
>
> James Dyson, *inventor of the Dyson dual cyclone technology and Chairman of Dyson Appliances Ltd*

Britain is a nation of inventors. According to Japan's Ministry of Trade and Industry, no less, Britain has been responsible for more than 40% of the inventions that have been significant to Japanese industry since the Second World War. But, unfortunately, our track record at innovation – the successful commercial exploitation of those new ideas – is not so good. There is a long list of successful products invented in Britain but developed overseas, including the hovercraft, brain tumour scanners, integrated circuits and the advanced microchip processor. Liquid crystal displays were developed at Hull University. But it is Japan, not Britain, which dominates the manufacture of LCD watches, calculators and other goods.

Those entrepreneurs who do successfully exploit their new ideas may, like Dyson and other inventors such as Trevor Baylis, who came up with the clockwork radio, make their fortunes.

But even if you are not in the business of inventing new products, growing companies must embrace innovation as a strategic necessity. Innovation is not just about inventing new products or technology – it comes in many forms. As well as product innovation, businesses may also be innovative when it comes to people, markets and processes.

In this chapter we will look at the secrets of success behind innovative companies, how to encourage innovation in your organisation, how to patent inventions, and where to get help with technology and finance.

1   Secrets of innovative success

Most people imagine inventors as slightly eccentric individuals designing Heath Robinson-style contraptions in their garages. In fact, a successful commercial innovation can be anything from a highly technical pharmaceutical breakthrough to putting a hole in a mint and calling it a Polo.

At first sight, successful innovations may seem to come about at random, or more thanks to good luck than to good judgement. But research into the factors that drive innovative companies has revealed that there are some ways in which companies can foster and nurture innovation.

As part of a campaign, 'Sharing Innovation', the Design Council and Consensus Research International surveyed more than 1000 companies that were awarded 'Millennium Product' status, see box on page 193, for their innovations. Key factors in creating an innovative company include:

- *Culture*. Corporate cultures that support innovation are characterised by openness. Information is not hoarded by those at the top, and communication is encouraged. Innovative cultures expect high performance but do not create a climate of blame or fear, where people are discouraged from innovating for fear of making mistakes. Responsibility is devolved down the management chain and there is a non-heirarchical culture.

- *The brainwave factory.* Innovation comes from a stable of product ideas, or an individual or group inspiration. Most innovative companies have a set of systems for capturing and developing ideas on a regular basis, such as product development meetings, informal team meetings, brain-storming sessions and formal R&D programmes. A perhaps surprising number of entrepreneurs claim that their Eureka moment came while drinking in the pub with colleagues.
- *Teamwork.* Two – or three or four – heads are invariably better than one when it comes to innovation. Team members are not just people working in the business – take ideas from suppliers, partners and customers and make them part of your innovation team.
- *Target your market.* The research shows that most innovative companies defined their target market at the very beginning of the development process. A fifth of successful companies that did not already have experience of their target market conducted market research to help them find out.

A characteristic of successful companies is that they have an in-depth understanding of the dynamics of the markets in which they operate and are in tune with the present and future needs of their customers. When a new product challenges the accepted market formula, successful innovative companies recognise that they may need to change the way they access their market. For example, new Internet banking products challenged the idea that most customers wanted to carry out transactions at their branch, prompting companies to look at reaching consumers through PCs, mobile phones and interactive TV.

- *Winning in the marketplace.* You need to understand how your innovation is positioned against the competition. Where possible, compete on the basis of quality, design and service rather than cost, and concentrate on adding value.

- *Managing innovation.* Managing innovation is no easy task. Command-and-control management tends to stifle innovation, but a laissez-faire attitude can lead to chaos and confusion. The best managers, according to the research, are very supportive of, and committed to, the project and offer their help at crucial moments rather than involving themselves on a day-to-day basis. The ideal management style is neither hands-on nor hands-off, but hands-ready, so that the project team feel supported and trusted, yet know that they have the freedom to get on with the job.

- *Managing risk.* Innovation is by nature risky. You are investing possibly a large amount of time, resources and money in an untried project, so understanding and managing risk is vital to success. Successful innovators take steps to understand the nature of the risks involved and to manage it actively so as to keep it within acceptable limits. Usually this involves reviews at each stage of the project.

- *Protecting your innovation.* The importance of securing your competitive advantage is absolutely crucial and successful innovators set out explicit strategies for protecting their products, patenting, trademarking and registering designs. The strategy should also address the issue of how to monitor and police infringements of patent, and what action your business is able to take. In some fast-moving industries, such as software and electronics, companies do not view patent as a relevant option and embark instead on a strategy of continuous innovation.

Beware the Innovation Cowboys

A number of 'innovations companies' have been set up claiming that they will help inventors launch new products. Take care before using their services. In some cases the company will ask for money up-front to provide a 'marketing report' or 'feasibility study' which turns out simply to be a rehash of publicly available material.

In one case a foreign-owned company was charging inventors hundreds of pounds for virtually identical reports and was failing to promote their ideas.

Better advice is usually available for free or for a fraction of the price that these companies charge.

Millennium Products

In September 1997, Prime Minister Tony Blair launched a Design Council initiative to identify the most innovative, well-designed products and services in the UK to mark the new millennium. More than 1000 innovations were recognised and announced as Millennium Products.

Millennium Products were selected on the basis that they opened up new opportunities, challenged existing conventions, demonstrated environmental responsibility, used new or existing technology and showed clear benefits for users.

They provided a showcase for the best of British innovation and a research base to analyse the main factors and pitfalls behind innovative success.

Since their selection, Millennium Products have toured the globe in a rolling programme of international exhibitions, and have been displayed in the 'Spiral of Innovation' next to the Greenwich Dome.

Case Study 1: Teamwork drives innovation at Sagitta

Sagitta Performance Systems, set up in 1997, spotted a niche in the market for 'storage area networking', which, in simple terms, provides faster and more efficient networks connecting computer servers. Once a system is in place, it can help clients reduce costs and improve productivity. It won the innovation and technology prize in the *Financial Mail*'s 2000 Enterprise Awards, as well as the prize for marketing.

From the outset, technical innovation is put into a commercial context, by setting up teams comprised of people with different skills and experience. That way, the company ensures that it is not taken over by technology for its own sake, without a profitable commercial outlet.

Managing director Andy Norman is convinced that creative productive teams are vital for innovation: 'We get people into multi-discipline teams focused on the type of market that we wanted them to go after. We have technical people working with sales people on projects. Teams are essential if you are going to innovate – you simply can't do without teamwork.'

Sagitta also places great emphasis on running an open organisation, where aims and visions are communicated to the staff. Norman adds, 'Innovation is all about change. Before you can have an innovation, you have to have the vision. And if you have not explained to each individual how they slot into that vision, everybody gets confused by what you are trying to do. Being innovative is about always looking at new ways of doing things and being clever about how you do it. Everyone is involved in that.'

He believes that a work culture that creates confidence is a necessary background for innovation. Staff need to be confident that their ideas will get a hearing and that they will not be unfairly blamed if a development does not work out as planned: 'Staff need to be given the confidence to be innovative. If people don't know what they are doing then you just get chaos and back-biting – and office politics are extremely destructive in a growing company. You also have to create an environment where bad news is as acceptable as good news. In every company there is bad news – it is how you deal with it that matters. You have to make people willing and able to come forward with bad news and willing to resolve it – not frightened.'

2   Making it happen

Having a terrific idea is only half the battle. An equally great challenge is to turn that inspiration into a reality – a saleable product.

- *Key people*. Research into Millennium Product companies suggests that having an ally on the board is crucial, as a director should have the clout to drive a project forward. It is worth, too, considering employing external consultants or advisers during the development process. These might include specialist designers, universities, manufacturing consultants and market research agencies. You might also benefit from informal links with customers or other business people.
- *Funding*. The right mix of funding is key if your innovation is to have a chance of making it to market (see funding section below). Smaller companies may have to rely on private funding, while established companies may have a research and development budget. Around a quarter of companies are unsuccessful in their attempts to raise funds, so it is important to concentrate on producing a solid business plan and taking time to impress possible backers.
- *Testing the market*. Most successful innovative companies conduct market research to find out whether there is a demand for the product. Research may be followed up by market testing with a prototype before going on to a full product launch. Market research and testing should help to improve your ideas and position them successfully.
- *Problems, problems*. The main problems experienced by innovative companies are technical difficulties and access to finance. On the technical side, problems can be overcome by intensive testing and experimentation, modifying the product, and making as much use as possible of any expert help available.

  In respect of financial hurdles, these can be overcome by targeting your efforts to raise funds in the most appropriate direction, and working hard on producing a convincing business plan.
- *Be flexible*. Recognise that you may have to change your existing ways of doing things in order to push your innovation forward. This might involve redeploying staff to provide the skills you need on the project. You might even set up a new

division to separate the product from your core business.

- *Be patient.* The average length of time from coming up with an idea to launching it on the market is two years. This may seem like a frustratingly long wait, but much of the time is likely to be spent fine-tuning the product and testing it. Exercising patience in order to get the product right is likely to pay off in the long run. Maintaining your belief in your innovation and not underestimating the time and costs involved are key to surmounting problems and pushing it through to launch.
- *Look through the customer's eyes.* Customers are unlikely to be impressed with technical innovation for its own sake – they want to see a benefit that is meaningful to them. An innovation is more likely to be commercially successful if it offers customers benefits such as greater convenience, uniqueness, lower cost or environmental friendliness.
- *Setting sales targets.* Your aim in business is not to be an inventor, it is to make a profit. So you need to assess the impact of your innovation on the bottom line. Set realistic targets for sales and monitor your actual performance against them. The research suggests that companies which have systems or procedures in place for generating ideas and innovation on a regular basis are more likely to exceed their own sales targets. Set up systems to gauge customer satisfaction to evaluate the success of your innovation and as a pointer to possible future refinements.

3   Protecting your ideas

Many entrepreneurs and inventors have come unstuck because someone has stolen their big idea. It makes sense to protect your inventions at an early stage, to make sure that someone else does not end up taking the credit – and all the earnings – from your brainwave.

The Patent Office helps small firms to protect their business ideas, inventions and logos by offering advice about patents, designs, trade marks and copyright, and provides a range of free literature. It is not just inventions that need to be protected – you may also want to protect designs, trade marks or copyrights. In simple terms, patents are concerned with the technical and functional aspects of products and processes, designs relate to the visual appearance of products, trade marks identify the products or services of particular traders and copyright covers certain types of original work such as novels or music.

- *Copyright*. This covers a range of areas including original literary works such as novels and song lyrics, as well as computer programs and some types of database. It also covers paintings and drawings, including technical drawings. It does not, however, protect ideas.

- *Design*. A registered design gives you the monopoly rights over the outward appearance of an article. It can last for a maximum of twenty-five years and a registered design can be bought, sold or licensed to another operator. In order to register a design it must be new and have 'significant eye appeal'.

- *Patent*. A patent gives inventors the right to stop anyone else from using their invention for a certain period. Normally, patents cover products that contain some technical innovation. The vast majority are not granted for wholly new inventions, but for gradual improvements in technology that already exists.

  The benefit of having a patent is that you win a window of time during which you can control the use of your invention free from interference from your rivals. This may allow you to make earnings to cover research and development costs. You must take great care not to disclose the invention whether verbally, in writing or any other way before you file a patent application because this could be counted as prior publication and might stymie your hopes of getting a patent. Only make disclosures under conditions of strict confidence.

  To be patentable your invention must fulfil a number of conditions including being new, and being capable of being used for some practical application, as opposed to purely aesthetic or intellectual uses.

A patent gives its owner the power to take legal action against others who attempt to muscle in on the invention. Bear in mind that your activities could possibly infringe someone else's patent, so it is worth checking before you embark on a new activity whether you would run into problems. It is vital to file a patent application early in your research as this gives you priority over rivals who may be watching what you are doing and seeking to overtake you.

- *Trade Marks.* A trade mark is a sign that denotes the goods and services of one trader as opposed to another, for example Marks & Spencer's famous 'St Michael' trade mark. It might include words, logos and shapes. Trade marks can be valuable marketing tools as they distinguish one company's wares from those of its competitors.

Case Study 2: ?What If! creating a culture of innovation

?What If! is a business dedicated to fostering innovation. Created in 1992 by Dave Allan, a former ski guide who then became a brand management executive at consumer giant Unilever, and Matt Kingdon, a former Unilever colleague.

?What If! is an innovation consultancy and training company. Having started out in a cramped office with two desks and a second-hand Apple Mac that neither of the founders knew how to switch on, the London-based firm now employs seventy people. It is jointly owned by four partners – Allan, Kingdon, Kristina Murrin, who previously worked at Procter & Gamble in the marketing department on brands such as Oil of Ulay, and Daz Rudkin, a third former Unilever staffer.

The idea behind ?What If! is to help other organisations to foster their creativity, through means such as 'ideas harvesting' and 'timelording', or releasing time for creative activity. Some of the questions ?What If! has tried to answer are: If fruit is so great, why don't people eat more? and, with fewer people getting married, how will the provision of financial services have to change?

Matt Kingdon believes that small firms can be more flexible and therefore find it easier to innovate than large ones. 'I just knew that a small business could out-innovate big ones and that was what I wanted to do,' he says. Daz Rudkin adds, '?What If! is more like a crusade to me than a company. We are here to change the way the world works by unleashing its creative potential.'

4   Financing your innovation

Innovation is often an integral part of growing your business. Getting an innovation off the ground may also mean that in the first few years you are spending far more on research and development than you are receiving in sales. So it is important to make sure you have the right financial backing to cover your investment in innovation.

Most innovations involve a mix of tangible assets, such as equipment and machinery, and intangible assets, such as a brand name. Investing in innovation means you will be spending money now in the hope of future returns. You are likely to be spending on a variety of things, such as design, staff training, market research and so on. You may find that potential backers such as banks are reluctant to give you money to finance an untried innovation, as it will be risky for them.

Business angels are one possible source of help and financial support, or you may be able to get involved in corporate venturing, where a larger company helps a smaller one to develop an innovation that would be mutually beneficial. As ever, the better quality the business plan and the more credible the management team, the greater the chance you have of winning over a backer. It is not enough to be a gifted scientist, designer or whatever to convince the financiers. They will also want to see evidence of skills and experience of marketing. In simple terms, it is no use coming up with a technically brilliant invention if no one will want to buy it. This is especially true for innovative products and services, since many innovations change the nature of the competition in existing markets, or have no established market to sell into. In addition, for many innovative firms the markets and competition will be international, so you may need to think globally from early on.

Backers will also want to see evidence that you will be able to sell your product. You should be able to demonstrate that you will be looking for customers and setting up distribution routes in readiness for your product hitting the market. Lenders or investors will be keen to see that the cash injection they provide will be well managed and are more likely to back you if you can show them that you have people in the business with sound management accounting skills. They will be pleased, too, to see strong project management and leadership. Someone needs to pull the project together and make sure things are happening at the right time. They also need to be able to motivate the team when times get tough, and to keep backers and others with an interest in the project informed on its progress. See Chapter 7, Finance for Growth, for more information on getting the right financial backing for your business.

Case Study 3: Innovation without tears

Everyone knows that people hate having injections. That simple insight, and the determination to produce an innovative, commercially viable product that could administer drugs without having to face the dreaded syringe, is behind PowderJect Pharmaceuticals.

Founded in 1993 by Dr Paul Drayson, a former robotics engineer, and Professor Brian Bellhouse, the inventor of the applicator, PowderJect, won the competitive advantage category in the 1999 Enterprise Awards, despite the fact that it had not yet made a profit. The PowerJect system works by driving powder painlessly through the skin at supersonic speed, using a device that uses a short-lived gas helium jet. Its applications could include local anaesthetics, fertility treatment and vaccines. Not only is delivery pain-free, it is also more efficient. In many cases smaller amounts of drugs can be used than competing techniques and in others the medical problem can be targeted more effectively. Drayson reckons that around 10% of marketed pharmaceuticals would be suitable for needle-free delivery, a huge potential market.

The stock market-quoted company, like many in the biotechnology sector, was set up in the expectation of several years of losses because of the costs of research. The key to PowderJect's success in the awards was that it spotted a gap for an innovation that would appeal to its direct customers, the drug companies, and the end user, the patients themselves, with a big potential market. It has also taken steps to protect its competitive advantage by making sure it has a strong patent position, protecting its technique until 2014.

Rob Budge, PR Manager, says, 'The combination of the talents of the two founders has been important in translating a technical innovation into a commercial product. Paul has a business background, while Brian is the scientist. The idea came out of Oxford University, but in terms of the vision of making it happen and making it a reality, that is where Paul Drayson comes in. The innovation is amazing – you are taking a tiny amount of powder that you are accelerating to the speed of Concorde, then bringing it to a halt in a split second. But the key is that the concept of a needle-free injection is not hard to understand, although the engineering is quite complex. It is something that people can relate to and there is a clear demand in terms of commercial potential. As a concept, people can buy into it.'

Joint ventures with the likes of Glaxo Wellcome and Serono, a Swiss company, are part of PowderJect's strategy to bring its innovations to market. Budge adds, 'We can use their development expertise with our technology. They understand the power of what we are doing here.'

At PowderJect, the emphasis is on constant innovation and the company has taken steps to protect its inventions through patents. Says Budge, 'Innovative culture is a process of evolution, it just keeps on moving. It is an exciting environment here. But it is important not to forget the practical side. We have strong patents, so our intellectual property position is very strong.'

5   To share or not to share?

One major dilemma for would-be inventors is whether to share ownership of their new idea with someone else. Often, their first reaction is to try to keep the innovation to themselves, out of fear that a financial backer will 'steal' the idea, or that they will lose out on potential profits. Unfortunately, few small businesses have the resources to develop and market an invention all on their own, so sooner or later you may have to reconcile yourself to the idea of sharing. If you want to receive backing from business angels, venture capitalists or other types of investor, you will be forced to accept a degree of shared ownership, as they will be unwilling to take on the risk of backing you unless they are getting a share of the returns. Another issue will be how much of your innovation you have to reveal to potential backers. If you tell them too much detail, you take the risk that they could simply run off with the idea themselves. Tell them too little and they may have insufficient information to convince them to invest.

You must be able to explain what your innovation is, and why and how it will sell. But you should not reveal technical details or trade secrets before a backer is fully on board.

6   Sources of help

There is no shortage of schemes on offer to help businesses, particularly those operating in the field of science and technology. The Department of Trade and Industry has a whole array of initiatives, ranging from grants to schemes facilitating partnerships between academics and industry.

Business Link and its equivalent offices outside England have innovation technology counsellors available to give you local advice and also to help you tap into European Research and Development initiatives. Local universities may run schemes making their expertise and research available on a paid-for basis to businesses in their area. There are a number of 'gateway' websites. The Department of Trade and Industry's Innovation Unit maintains the Innovate Now website to help business understand why innovation is important and how the best organisations manage it. The Design Council is also an extremely useful source of information on how successful companies innovate.

There are a number of specific initiatives to help firms exploit particular new technologies. For instance, in the field of bio-technology, there are initiatives such as Biowise and Manu-facturing for Biotechnology, and the Information Society Initiative can help with IT-related areas. The International Technology Service keeps companies aware of new technological developments and management best practice from across the world.

A host of other initiatives exist, aiming to bring together businesses and researchers from universities and other academic institutions, both in the UK and across Europe:

- *SMART.* This is an initiative under the Small Business Service that provides grants to help individuals, and small and medium-sized businesses to make better use of technology and to develop technologically innovative products and processes. The following help is available in England (Scotland runs its own SMART and SPUR schemes, and Wales and Northern Ireland also have their own initiatives).

  Technology Reviews: Grants of up to £2500 for individuals, and small and medium-sized firms (those with less than 250 employees) towards the costs of having an expert review how your activities shape up against current industry best practice.

  Technology Studies: Grants of up to £5000 for individuals, and small and medium-sized firms to help you identify the opportunities to use technological advances to create inno-vative new products and processes.

  Micro Projects: Grants of up to £10,000 to help individuals and micro-firms (those with less than ten employees) with the fund-ing to develop low-cost prototypes of their new products and processes, if these involve technical advances and/or novelty.

  Feasibility Studies: Grants of up to £45,000, awarded through competitions, for individuals and small firms (those with less than fifty employees) who want to carry out feasibility studies into their possible use of innovative technologies.

Development Projects: Grants of up to £150,000 awarded through competitions, for small and medium-sized firms undertaking development projects.

Exceptional Development Projects: A small number of exceptional high-cost development projects undertaken by small and medium firms may attract grants of up to £450,000.

You can get more information from your local Business Link or equivalent organisation. The Department of Trade and Industry supports a number of other schemes that may be useful, including Postgraduate Training Partnerships, which is aimed at increasing the number of high-quality postgraduates with skills, experience and training relevant to the needs of industry, and the Faraday Partnerships, where the aim is to establish a network of partnerships between academics and industry that will be recognised nationally as centres of expertise.

The TCS, formerly known as the Teaching Company Scheme, sends high-quality graduates to work for two years on projects in companies, with the aim of transferring knowledge and technology from the academic sector into industry. It is now managed by the Small Business Service.

A similar scheme known as CBP or College-Business Partnerships involves further education colleges in partnerships with small and medium-sized firms, and is also managed by the Small Business Service.

STEP, the Shell Technology Enterprise Programme, is a scheme giving undergraduates work experience at small- and medium- sized firms during the summer holiday. It is also managed by the Small Business Service.

7   Business incubators

Business incubation aims to help small businesses with high growth potential to achieve their aspirations. Incubators are normally hives of small work units for entrepreneurs provided by universities or larger companies. The idea is that high-tech firms have the use of subsidised work space in a supportive environment. They can also benefit from financial and management advice from an incubator director. Firms that go into incubation are normally at the seedcorn or very early stage. Many incubators provide a range of services such as accountancy and office management, and may also offer expertise from seasoned entrepreneurs on how to grow the business. Incubators are often plugged in to local networks for skills and finance such as business and knowledge, from, for instance, the local university.

The UK Business Incubation Centre, although not an incubator, can advise on business incubation matters. Its website also contains details of all the business incubators across the UK.

8   Tax incentives

The government announced proposals for a tax credit for research and development to help smaller companies in the 1999 Budget, and the credit has effect from 1 April 2000. Eligible companies can claim the tax credit as part of their tax return. Under the new rules, companies can claim tax relief of 150% of the qualifying expenditure. In other words, for every £100 of qualifying expenditure on R&D, the company will be able to claim relief of £150 against its taxable income. The enhanced tax credit will reduce the cost of spending on R&D by 30% for companies paying tax at the small-companies rate.

Companies that are not making any taxable profit can claim relief in the form of a cash payment, up to a maximum limit of the gross amount they have paid in PAYE and Class 1 National Insurance Contributions during the relevant period. To qualify, companies must have fewer than 250 employees, and have an annual turnover of no more than 40 million euros, about £25 million, and/or an annual balance sheet total not exceeding 27 million euros, about £17 million. In addition, the relief can only be claimed if the company spends £25,000 or more on R&D during the relevant accounting period. In the 2001 Budget, the government announced it is consulting on new tax incentives designed to encourage innovation in larger companies.

9
Export
Know-how

Britain has always been a nation of exporters and importers – indeed, the old Empire was founded on enterprise and commerce. In the twenty-first century, we are now told that we are living in a truly global economy, where the Internet and better transport and communications systems have diminished national barriers, cultural diversity and made distances easier to traverse.

Over the last fifty years, exporting – and importing – have grown in importance. In 1998, the Organisation for Economic Co-operation and Development noted that the volume of world merchandise trade is sixteen times greater than it was in 1950, compared with a six-fold increase in world production.

As might be expected, exports are of crucial importance to UK plc. They account for around a third of UK national income and around a third of jobs are reliant on exports. Britain's export trade is, unsurprisingly, dominated by big companies, with the likes of British Aerospace, BP and Shell UK in the top ten companies selling overseas. In addition, more than 100,000 small and medium-sized companies currently export, and there are many more which could grow, and increase their profits, by aiming at foreign markets.

Exporting is not easy and many small firms are daunted by the idea of entering foreign markets. Others dabble in exporting on an ad hoc basis, only selling abroad in response to unsolicited orders. But exporting offers significant advantages, including reducing the risks of a downturn in domestic markets, increasing profits and exposing your business to world-class competition. And the development of e-commerce is crucially important for growing firms looking to export. It can give the smallest business relatively low-cost access to even the most far-flung markets.

In this chapter we will look at how to set about exporting, how to develop an export strategy and how to make sure you get the practicalities right, such as delivery of goods and getting paid.

We will also look at the vexed question of the single European currency, which is vital to many exporters and, indeed, will have an impact on *all* UK firms. The European Union is the UK's biggest customer, accounting for almost 60% of our manufacturing sales and more than 40% of services. Many exporters support the introduction of a single currency on the basis that it will cut out exchange rate risks and reduce transaction costs. It is not the place of this book to take a political stance, but to try to supply an objective account of the implications for businesses.

A major theme in this chapter will also be to stress the relevance of the core messages that apply to domestic markets, such as concentrating on customer service, delivering added value and making sure that products match or surpass the best in the world. 'Made in Britain' is still a tag that carries a great deal of clout in other countries, representing values such as reliability, quality and value for money. The challenge for growing businesses is to capitalise on that in today's intensely competitive markets.[1]

1   Should your firm export?

Exporting can offer huge rewards, but innocents abroad are likely to come a cropper. It is important to be clear about whether now is the right time to begin exporting and to have a clear strategy. To succeed at exporting, there must be a genuine commitment throughout the whole company. Exporting should not be seen as a secondary activity to be undertaken only when the domestic market is in decline, but as a core activity, needing research, marketing, methods of delivery and payment, and staff training.

It is important when drawing up an export strategy to be clear about why you want to export. The reasons might include spreading the risks of limiting the business to the domestic market, as an economic downturn in the UK might not be happening overseas. Businesses may also wish to increase their sales by expanding overseas, or may believe that their goods can be sold more profitably abroad. The type of product or service provided by your business may be in particular demand overseas – for example, British professional services such as design, software and consultancy are well regarded in other countries.

Before embarking on an export programme, you need to conduct some pretty exhaustive market research. That may sound like a bore, but there are an enormous range of pitfalls, including linguistic and cultural differences, and potential political problems, not to mention the complicated business of actually selling goods, getting them to the customer, then getting paid.

Entrepreneurs need to consider the following questions:

- *Where should I export?* In other words, which markets are likely to offer the greatest profit, without taking on undue risks?
- *How will I promote my goods and services overseas?* Obviously, overseas customers must know about your products before they can buy them. You need to consider options such as trade fairs, a website aimed at overseas buyers and advertising abroad.
- *Do I need an agent abroad?* Many firms use an agent or distributor based in the overseas market. The relationship with the agent is, clearly, extremely important and it is vital to take on an agent or distributor whom you trust.
- *What are the practicalities I will face?* These will include methods of shipment and their cost, customs barriers, tax and VAT considerations, insurance cover for theft and accidental damage, and making sure that customers are creditworthy and you receive your money.
- *Will our products be saleable in their current form in overseas markets?* It may be that you need to make modifications to

your products or services in order to sell them abroad, because of cultural, linguistic or technological differences.

Pros and Cons of Exporting

It is worth thinking about the potential pros and cons of exporting. These include:

Pros

- Spreading your risks – sales overseas can counteract the effects of a downturn in the UK.
- If yours is a manufacturing business, exporting may enable you to expand production and thereby reduce your unit costs.
- You may be able to sell your products or services at higher prices in overseas markets, thus increasing your profit margin.
- Some products that have reached saturation point or are a declining market in the UK may still be saleable or a growth market abroad.
- Your business will be exposed to international standards and competition.

Cons

- Your business will be exposed to additional risks, such as currency movements and possible problems obtaining payment from customers.
- It can take a long time – and considerable expense – to establish a viable export business.
- Failure at exporting could jeopardise your entire business.
- Exporting can make big demands on the time of managers; for instance, travelling overseas to make personal contact with customers or agents.
- Overcoming logistical problems and cultural and linguistic barriers can be a real challenge for a growing firm.

2   Where to export

Choosing your export markets is a very important decision. Many firms find it easier to start off with countries close to home, such as the Republic of Ireland or the EU, or English-speaking markets such as the US, Canada and Australia. The European Union accounts for around 60% of our export trade. It has a number of advantages, including a lack of trade and customs barriers – theoretically, at least – easy travel and the fact that most countries enjoy a similar level of affluence to the UK. English-speaking countries have an obvious advantage in the form of a common language and a similar culture. Some of the countries in the old Commonwealth still retain links with the UK and British banks often have subsidiaries and agents there.

Developed markets such as the EU and the US all have the benefit of well-run banking, financial and legal systems, a relatively high level of political and economic stability and good domestic and international communications and transport. The downside is that they are highly developed and sophisticated markets, and can be hard to break into unless your products are high quality and correctly marketed.

Exporting to less developed markets, especially in the Third World and the former Eastern bloc, is a much more demanding enterprise. These markets are prone to political upheaval, corruption may be rife, and transport and communications could pose a serious stumbling block.

3   Researching overseas markets

Once you have decided which markets to target, it is worthwhile undertaking detailed research to give your export drive the best possible chance of success. There are plenty of sources of information, ranging from professional bodies such as the Institute of Export to commercial banks to government agencies like the Department of Trade and Industry. Local Business Links and

Chambers of Commerce should also be able to offer help and advice.

A good starting point is Trade Partners UK, a free government-backed self-service library for exporters. The British Chambers of Commerce also runs a very useful Export Zone on its website, signposting users to sources of detailed information and help. Contact details are provided in Appendix 2, Useful Contacts.

It makes sense to carry out some desk research first before embarking on a costly and time-consuming trip overseas to investigate a market. From desk research, you should be able to find out the following information:

- *General Market background.* Information on the country concerned, including any relevant demographic and climatic considerations, and a sense of the political situation.
- *Industry information.* You should be able to assess the size of the particular market you will be targeting, by obtaining industry statistics. Aim also to gain an insight into trends in the market for your products and services, and to find out how they are sold.
- *The competition.* Aim to glean data on the main competitors in your market in the country concerned, their market shares, products, prices and how they promote their wares.
- *Customers.* Information on potential customers including their financial profiles. If you are operating in the business to business market, this will include information on the companies you hope to target as customers, including key personnel.
- *Business environment.* Information on regulations, legislation and tariffs in the target country.

When carrying out desk research identify the key questions you need to answer and do not be sidetracked, keep a file of useful information and be wary of 'expert views' which are, in fact, driven by self-interest. The Internet is a great source of information but most sources can also be contacted by traditional means. Possible sources of information include:

- staff and managers in your own office;
- business contacts;
- market research reports by commercial organisations;
- the UK government, normally using your local Business Link as a first port of call;
- libraries, both local and specialist;
- Chambers of Commerce;
- trade associations in your industry;
- foreign embassies and consulates overseas and in the UK;
- company directories and databases, such as Hoover, or Dun & Bradstreet.

Case Study 1: Making hay in export markets

A growing firm responsible for tying up the bulk of Europe's hay bales scooped the top prize in the *Financial Mail* Enterprise Awards in 2000.

In just four years, UPU Industries of Dromore in Northern Ireland, under the vigorous leadership of founder Phillip Orr, carved itself a significant niche in the specialised and lucrative agricultural packaging market. It shows that even a small firm can become a world leader in its field by pursuing a well-planned and focused export strategy.

The success of UPU has come at personal cost to Orr. He spends months away from his family trudging across farmland persuading potential customers of the benefit of his plastic wrapping, which is specially designed to cope with individual climatic conditions. 'Last year I spent 500 hours on planes, but when we first started up it was longer,' he said. 'In 1996, when we began, I used to spend four to five months of the year abroad, but as we expand, I am hoping to take a back seat.' It is a measure of the success of the company that he is already thinking five years ahead, when he plans to bow out and concentrate on building a new business.

UPU, which also collected the export category award in 2000, was at that time selling 35% of its production overseas. It plans to dominate the French and German markets, and extend its influence in America. 'We expect to export about 40% this year,' said Orr. 'The strong pound has not helped, but our productivity is increasing all the time and our customers understand that we produce world-class goods on time, always.'

One secret of UPU's success is its commitment to training. Unusually for such a small company, it has a full-time trainer. As engineer Adrian Marks explained, 'Anyone can buy machinery, but it is skill that makes the difference.' The company was founded on the belief that the quality of imported twine and plastic bale wrappings was not good enough. Orr, whose father is company Chairman, said, 'We felt that we could do better. So I got together a business plan, went to the bank manager and asked him for £4.6 million. It was the best decision he ever made.'

Michael Lorimer, Head of Sales and Marketing at UPU, adds, 'We are concentrating on continued development in the US. When you are exporting you need to be aware that every market tells a different story as does every state in the United States. The one common denominator is that we spend time in the markets with the people that really matter, the local distributors. We put that effort in, because if you can identify the key routes to market you are well on the way. We place a very high emphasis on physically being there. There is no substitute, though it is a big investment in time and money, so it is important to plan to make sure you make best use of the time. Overseas trips should not be junkets.'

UPU exports to the US, Canada, Argentina, Australia, New Zealand, the Republic of Ireland, Germany, France and Scandinavia. Lorimer says, 'We do hedge and take steps to mitigate currency fluctuations, but in some markets we have just had to endure pain.'

Language has not been much of a barrier for UPU, which has several English-speaking distributors and uses business translation services for technical and marketing data: 'British firms are fortunate because English is one of the fastest-growing business languages. But you do need to take care, even in English-speaking markets. In the US the nomenclature is different and that can cause endless confusion. You have to use their language and think as they do.'

He adds, 'When we are selling overseas, we have to be aware of the reality that a company from Northern Ireland is not going to be high on anyone's agenda. There are always indigenous companies so we have to work very hard to convince them to do business with us. The Department of Trade and Industry and other government initiatives are very useful, as they can make it much more affordable to go overseas. The local embassy people can be tremendously helpful, too, and I would advise other businesses to make use of them. The other advice I would give is that you can never prepare enough on this side of the desk for an export trip. Your time there is so valuable.'

4   Selling overseas

You need to consider exactly how you plan to sell your products overseas. In most cases it makes sense to use a local representative who knows the market well, and can act as a valuable source of information and feedback.

Business Link can help you select an overseas representative. In order for the relationship to have the best chance of success, it must be founded on knowledge and trust. The representative should be briefed as fully as possible about your business, its products and services, and what your aims are.

Before taking on a representative, make sure you have carried out background checks on her or his financial and personal references, linguistic and technical skills, the premises, facilities and staff that are available, what other businesses she or he represents and registered details of the business. Make clear that both sides understand exactly what responsibilities the representative will assume. Draw up a document setting out both sides' rights and obligations, and have it checked by lawyers.

Firms may opt to appoint an agent or a distributor. A distributor buys goods from you and then sells them him- or herself. Distributors are often used by exporters of consumer goods. They are largely independent and will themselves set prices and terms for overseas customers, take on responsibility for the sale of goods to customers and the financial risk. The advantages of using a distributor is that you send your product to just one destination in a given market and you only take on one credit risk – that attached to the distributor – rather than that of many different customers. With an agent, you retain more control, with the UK exporter setting prices and terms for customers, and remaining responsible for any unsold goods. Within the European Union you normally have to pay compensation to an agent when the agency agreement is terminated.

It is always a good idea to visit overseas markets and major customers in person. Learning about a country second-hand is never a substitute for personal experience. Attending trade fairs is a good way of gaining exposure to markets overseas and of making useful contacts. It can also help you keep your profile with existing customers. Support for attending trade fairs may be available through the government. There are, however, a huge number of trade fairs across the world and it can be difficult to decide which are worth the expense and time of exhibiting. It may be worth attending an exhibition as a visitor before deciding to take part.

The British Chambers of Commerce also runs a series of events known as Partenariat, which put UK companies in touch with possible overseas partners.

5   Breaking down the language barrier

Differences in language and culture can be extremely important in making a success of an export drive. No one expects all entre-preneurs to become multilingual, but it is not an area that it is wise to ignore. To some degree this issue is lessening in importance in the European Union, where it is becoming accepted that English is the language of business.

There are also useful schemes to help exporters, such as the Languages for Export Advisory Scheme (LEXAS), run by the British Chambers of Commerce. LEXAS aims to make British companies more able to compete effectively overseas by helping them to avoid costly mistakes in culture and language, to tailor their products or services for overseas markets and to open up new foreign markets previously considered too difficult. It provides tailor-made recommendations to help companies improve their systems for dealing with foreign languages and practices, and a clear idea of what language training is appropriate; what is achievable and what it will cost. The service will also provide help in identifying appropriate external providers for translation, language training, cultural awareness and freelance language cover. Fees for eligible companies start at £50 plus VAT.

The British Chambers of Commerce also offers Chamber Translation Services, catering for business needs, covering languages from Arabic to Zulu.

6   Training staff

Exporting is not a job for the uninitiated and proper training of staff is essential. The Institute of Export offers short-course training programmes that can keep businesses informed of the constantly changing rules and regulations governing exporting. British Chambers of Commerce also offers short intensive courses under the National Export Sales Training programme.

7   Dealing with the practicalities

Actually getting your goods to an overseas market can seem like an extremely difficult task. However, following a few simple guidelines will make the process easier and help avoid the pitfalls.

- *Documentation.* The documentation required for exporting can be complicated and organisations such as the Institute of Export, Chambers of Commerce and Business Link can provide advice.
- *Incoterms 2000.* Incoterms are a set of guidelines drawn up by the International Chamber of Commerce for the inter-pretation of some commonly used terms in foreign trade. They divide the cost, risk and delivery between the buyer and the seller, and tell you who is responsible for the goods and

for insuring them, when the responsibility passes from buyer to seller, and who is responsible for costs incurred at any point in the transaction. Copies can be obtained from the Institute of Export and other bodies.

- *Taxes and tariffs.* Be aware of any customs tariffs and the situation regarding taxes such as VAT in countries to which you are exporting.
- *Insurance.* Goods in transit are at risk of being damaged, lost or stolen. Make sure they are properly insured. Be certain goods are properly packaged – incorrectly packaged goods can easily be damaged beyond repair, causing customers to be disaffected and loss of business to your company.
- *Use the experts.* Freight forwarders and international delivery companies can advise on documentation, insurance, packaging and similar matters.
- *Communication.* An international sale can involve discussions with lots of different people, creating plenty of scope for misunderstanding, so it is important to give instructions in writing.

The Simpler Trade Procedures Board provides useful information on export procedures.

8   Getting paid

With more people trading across borders, payments systems and cultures, payment for exports is becoming increasingly complicated. There can be even more risk of incurring bad debts with overseas customers than with those based in the UK, and research and checking at an early stage can help prevent problems later on.

It is worth gaining a general view on the risks attached to the country as a starting point. Check on the financial standing of individual customers and proceed cautiously in the granting of credit until you know the customer well. Exporters often insist on payment in advance for lower-value transactions where the customer is in a high-risk area or is not considered creditworthy.

The 'collect on delivery' method offers a degree of security if you have not yet established a relationship with the customer. You obtain payment by sending documents through your bank to the customer's bank. You retain control of documentation and in some cases goods, and your bank will help collecting the funds.

Letters of credit are written guarantees given by a bank to an exporter and offer a high degree of security for both buyer and seller. They are, however, complicated and it is wise to take advice from your bank, Business Link or other agency.

'Open account' involves giving the customer credit on agreed terms; for instance payment to be made thirty days from the date of the invoice. Only use this arrangement if you know the customer well.

Banks, Chambers of Commerce, Business Link and others can advise you on your options.

Case Study 2: Beating the currency blues

NDB Engineering, based in Wolverhampton in the West Midlands, is a young firm making machine components. It was founded in 1998 and began exporting in 2000, against the backdrop of a strong pound, which makes British goods more expensive abroad. At the time, there were also big problems in the West Midlands car industry. But NDB managed to buck the trend and reach the finals of the 2000 Enterprise Awards.

Managing Director David Tilley set up NDB with a £30,000 redundancy pay-off. Two years on it had fifteen staff aged from seventeen to fifty-eight – Tilley's own age – and was making a £30,000 profit on turnover of £800,000. Ageism, job demarcation and sexism are banned, and Tilley himself will go on the shop floor to operate one of NDB's state-of-the-art computer-controlled machines. As well as skills, applicants for jobs at NDB must have a sense of humour. 'We don't take on anyone who takes life too seriously,' says Tilley.

Nick Smith, Sales Director, says, 'We were able to begin exporting at a hard time because of our in-depth knowledge of the markets. We also have something special to offer because we make non-standard and bespoke products, so we are not just selling on price. People talk a lot about the barriers to exporting, but they are mainly psychological. You just need to build a relationship with customers.'

NDB sells employing fax, mail, telephone and e-mail, and has used the Department of Trade and Industry's Trade UK scheme. 'The thing to remember when you are exporting', says Smith, 'is that the world isn't actually that big.'

9 Currency risks and how to handle them

During the late Nineties and 2000, exporters were faced with difficulties because of the strength of sterling, which was making British goods more expensive abroad. In the seventeen months following the launch of the single currency in January 1999, Euroland currencies dropped 20% in value against the pound. The uncertainty caused by swings in the value of the pound is a very real challenge for all small and medium-sized exporters. But there are a number of actions which can help companies cope.

- *Become customer-focused.* The companies who have been hit hardest by the strength of the pound are those manufacturing commodity goods, which others in Europe – and elsewhere – can produce more cheaply. Instead, try to tailor products to the specific needs of customers. Offer excellent service and aftercare. Becoming an integral part of your customers' supply chains can help insulate you against foreign exchange movements. Remember, the strength of the Deutschmark for many years did nothing to dent overseas sales of BMW cars or other top-quality goods.
- *Prioritise value, not price.* If you can make customers perceive the quality in your products or services, they are less likely to dump you in favour of a cheaper supplier.

  If customers stubbornly insist on treating price as the most important criterion, look at setting psychological price points such as £1.99 or £9.99. Review your price lists in other currencies to establish whether such points exist and whether you can benefit from setting them.
- *Concentrate on becoming more efficient and competitive.* Look

at where you can make your processes more efficient and streamlined, and where technology can improve productivity. Lessons can be learned from looking at the way your competitors work, but also by finding out about companies in other industries. Study your inventory for products which sit in storage too long and price them to sell quicker. Establish whether you can make the strong pound work for you by sourcing raw materials or products you use in continental Europe.

- *Use technology to the full.* E-commerce makes it possible for businesses to cut layers of cost and streamline ordering, payment processing and data management. It also makes it possible to reach new customers in the UK and abroad more economically.
- *Reduce exchange rate risk.* Ask your bank about treasury products and services to reduce your exchange rate exposure. These include buying forward, so you set the price in advance, protecting yourself against the currency moving against you in the meantime.

10   What is the single currency?

Love the idea or loathe it, the single European currency is a reality that growing businesses cannot afford to ignore. The single currency, whose basic unit is the euro, is part of a wider process known as Economic and Monetary Union or EMU, which is designed to harmonise the economies of European nations. The euro, worth around 65p at the time of writing, is not the first attempt at a single currency: in medieval times, peppercorns were used as a unit of payment throughout much of Europe. But it is certainly one of the most ambitious – and the most contentious – attempts to unify money across a group of nations.

Supporters of the single currency say it will stimulate trade and economic growth, while opponents argue that it is forcing together disparate economies and will ultimately fall apart in chaos. Critics also fear that the UK will lose control over her economic and political destiny.

But behind the rhetoric, few are aware of the facts about the new currency and of the impact it may have on businesses – whether Britain joins or not. The government plans to hold a referendum on whether the UK should join the single currency after the next general election. If we do join, there will have to be an enormous public education exercise, similar to that undergone when decimal currency arrived. Around £20 billion of notes and coins will have to be replaced. There is also likely to be a transitional period where the euro and sterling are run in tandem. Cashpoints and tills will have to be converted, and goods and services repriced in euros. As with decimalisation, the public is likely to harbour suspicions that businesses are seizing the opportunity to raise prices surreptitiously.

While the UK debates the issue, however, the rest of Europe is already embracing the project. Eleven countries – Spain, Portugal, Italy, France, Finland, Ireland, the Netherlands, Germany, Luxembourg, Austria and Belgium – have signed up and Greece is also keen to join.

Euro notes and coins will not become the sole legal tender in 'Euroland' countries until 2002. But the new currency can already be used for transactions by cheque, credit card or electronic payment. Prices are often quoted in euros and the existing local currency. By 2002 the seventy or so different coins currently circulating in the European Union will be replaced by eight euro coins of different denominations. Each euro coin will have a map of Europe on one side and a national face on the other. The coins are to come in denominations of 1, 2, 5, 10, 20, and 50 cents, plus 1 and 2 euros. The notes will be E5, E10, E20, E50, E100, E200 and E500.

11   What will be the likely effects of the euro?

The full effects are likely to be complex and far-reaching, and way beyond the scope of this book. However, one effect is that many entrepreneurs – even some who do not export to the Continent – will have to deal with the euro whether the UK joins the single currency or not. This can be extremely daunting for owner-managers who have never before had to deal with foreign currencies, so all entrepreneurs should be aware of some basic points.

A fully developed Euroland – the nickname economists give to the single currency club – would be the world's largest trading bloc, with around 18.5% of global commerce. It will represent about one-fifth of world economic output, roughly the same proportion as the US. The fact that the UK is not joining in the first wave does not by any means mean that UK entrepreneurs are immune to the dramatic changes that will take place when the euro is introduced. More than half of UK exports go to Euroland countries and those firms will have to be equipped to deal with the euro.

Even those who do not export to Euroland may be required by larger multinational customers in the UK to invoice in euros – for example, German giant Siemens announced that from October 1999 it has asked all its suppliers to switch from invoicing in sterling to the euro. From 2002, exporters to Euroland will only need to deal with one foreign currency, instead of a dozen. Furthermore, if the UK joins, there will be no need to exchange currency and no currency risk when trading with the rest of Euroland.

Most experts believe that the single currency will lead to greater transparency of prices across Euroland, thereby increasing competition and driving prices down. In addition, economists believe that the single currency will usher in an era of lower interest rates. At the time of writing, the European Central Bank (ECB) base rate stood at 4.25%, compared with a UK base rate of 6%. If the UK joins, our interest rates will be set by the ECB instead of the Bank of England and will be the same as that of the rest of Euroland. Clearly, this will make it cheaper than at present for businesses to borrow money if these conditions prevail, but the true impact will also depend on the level of inflation.

If your business has income or assets in euros, it may make sense to borrow in euros rather than sterling – but be aware that so long as the UK remains outside the single currency bloc, any interest rate advantage can be more than wiped out by adverse currency movements. The expectation of lower rates is already having an effect in the UK, as long-term interest rates on the City money markets are heading downwards in anticipation of the single currency, among other factors.

12 What should businesses do?

Entrepreneurs should waste no time in addressing the implications of the single currency. Regardless of the political bickering, or business owners' personal convictions, British companies will effectively be 'in' the single currency from the beginning. Large European multinationals are already pricing and invoicing in euros and demanding that companies they deal with do the same. So what some people call the 'creeping' euro is having an effect as businesses further and further down the supply chain are having to adopt the euro. Even if your business has no contact with Europe, you may trade with businesses that do. No one, however domestically focused, can ignore the euro.

One example is tourism. Hotels and travel companies on the Continent are by now often quoting prices in euros and the local currency. This practice is likely to spread and UK operators may find customers demand that they follow this lead. Shops in tourist centres such as London, Edinburgh and York, for example, might begin quoting prices in euros and pounds to cater to continental purchasers. Steps to take now if your business will be affected include:

- *Opening a euro bank account*. All the major banks offer accounts denominated in euros – if you already operate Euroland foreign currency accounts then they may convert these for you automatically. A euro bank account is useful if you have income and outgoings in euros that can be set off against each other, as this reduces your exposure to foreign currency exchange risk.
- *Pricing in euros*. When pricing products in euros, bear in mind the perceptions of overseas buyers. It may not make sense

simply to translate sterling prices directly into euros – instead, be prepared to adjust for psychological price points, for example E9.99, or consider changing unit sizes to make prices more attractive.

- *Software systems.* Your systems will need an overhaul so that they can deal with the euro alongside sterling. Look to find a software supplier who can support your business as further developments occur; for instance, if the UK does decide to join. Don't forget to check out the impact of the euro symbol and the numerical euro amounts on your existing systems field sizes and keyboard.
- *Managing euro currency.* Ask your bank about Treasury products and services that can help you to reduce the exchange rate risk of dealing with the euro.

13   What if the UK joins?

If the UK does join the single currency, the implications for UK businesses will be dramatic.

- *Transition period.* There is likely to be a six-month transfer period, when businesses would have to run a dual pricing system, resulting in the need for multi-function cash tills. Slot machines would also have to be updated.
- *Training and staffing.* Staff would need to be trained in recognising and handling the new notes and coins, and in dealing with new accounting systems. In retail businesses, they should also be equipped to help confused customers.
- *Pricing.* The prices of goods and services would become more transparent across Europe. The euro, coupled with the Internet, which makes it easier to check on prices across several different countries, will equip buyers to make more informed purchasing decisions. This will increase competition and could put pressure on profit margins.
- *Reduced exchange rate risk.* On the plus side, businesses will no longer be exposed to currency risk when exporting to the rest of Euroland, and they will also save on Treasury and

exchange costs. Businesses that at the moment run several European currency accounts can pool the balances in one euro account, possibly earning more credit interest or reducing their overdraft interest.

- *Reduced administration costs.* Businesses that export to several Euroland countries may find scope to reduce accounting and admin costs if they only have to deal with one currency. This benefit will, of course, largely be present whether or not the UK joins.

14   Using the euro to gain competitive advantage

It is understandable that entrepreneurs find the arrival of the euro somewhat daunting. But supergrowth businesses prefer to see it as an opportunity to gain commercial edge over their rivals. These forward-looking businesses believe that they can gain advantages from price transparency and the possible elimination of exchange risks. To gain the competitive edge in the new single currency era, consider the following steps:

- *Review prices and products.* If you intend to export to Euroland, work out a pricing and quality strategy. Even though the currency will be the same in Euroland, remember that you still need to consider customer preference and behaviour in individual countries.

- *Building your brand.* Experts believe that the euro will lead to the increased movement of goods around Europe, coupled with transparency and convergence of prices. If this is the case, you will need to differentiate your product in order to make sales without eroding your profit margins. Concentrate on reinforcing your brand, and providing value and service to customers.

- *Reducing costs.* Talk to your bank about the opportunity of borrowing in euros. This should mean a lower interest rate than sterling borrowings – however, you will need a stream of income in euros sufficient to service the loan.

- *Spot the opportunities.* Are there any opportunities for your business to cash in on the introduction of the euro? Boom areas are likely to include accounting software, cash registers and so on. Opportunities will also exist in training, advertising, marketing and consultancy.

- *Alliances.* Commentators expect to see more cross-border mergers between large companies in Europe. Should you consider a partnership or joint venture with a company in another Euroland country?

- *Watching competitors.* It is more important than ever to keep a close eye on what competitors are doing. Ask yourself how they are handling the arrival of the single currency, and whether you should be doing the same.

- *Expand your markets.* If you do not already export, the single currency, coupled with the arrival of e-commerce, may present you with an opportunity. Evaluate whether you can begin selling your goods or services within the rest of Euroland. Bear in mind that within Euroland there will be little in the way of psychological barriers to a business selling to customers in another Euroland state, whereas the UK is still divided by a currency channel until or unless we join. Think about how to present your business, bearing that in mind.

- *Setting up shop abroad.* Ask yourself whether it would make sense to set up an operation overseas if, for example, you do a lot of business with a particular country. Bear in mind, obviously, that the currency may be easier, but there will still be formidable language and cultural barriers.

Notes

1   Figures from 'Exporting in the 21st Century' an Institute of Export discussion document published by the Institute of Export and DHL Worldwide Express, May 1999.

CHAPTER **10**

Risks and Rewards

Growth should be . . . like tending a bonsai tree: growing a
really strong, solid object very slowly.

Julian Richer, *Founder, Richer Sounds*

Many people see entrepreneurship as a very high-risk activity and
consider business people as a special breed who think nothing of
gambling millions on a commercial venture. Risk is an inevitable
part of business and, indeed, of life. No one can succeed at
anything, whether it is an examination, taking on a new job,
embarking on a marriage or running a business, without running
the risk of failure. Sometimes, in business as in life, entirely
unforeseen events will happen out of the blue and threaten your
security. But in many if not most cases, risks can be managed and
minimised by identifying, assessing and responding to them.

Successful growth entrepreneurs usually take a measured
approach to risk and do not embark on reckless courses of action.
They try to anticipate risks to the business in advance and to cover
themselves as much as possible against them. Managing risk
should be a dynamic process. As your business grows, your exposure to risk will change and, at times, increase. Risk occurs because
the world is constantly changing and we cannot always predict
events and outcomes. But for every risk there is an opportunity and
a potential reward. Taking a well-thought-out approach to risk

will boost your chances of harnessing the opportunities productively, and reaping the rewards for your business.

1   Managing growth risks

What is the biggest risk facing a growth business? The answer is probably complacency. It is human nature not to enquire too deeply into success – failure is normally what provokes a bout of soul-searching. If a business is performing well, it can be tempting simply to stick with a formula that works, and to become reluctant to try new things, ironically, often on the grounds that it would be 'too risky'.

But successful business growth in itself brings a host of new risks, including lack of inventiveness, loss of entrepreneurial spirit, a dearth of the right people to take the business to the next stage of growth, and losing touch with markets and customers. Often these risks do not become apparent all at once, but they creep up over time. If complacency is allowed to take root, a business can become the victim of its own success.

- *Complacency.* Businesses can fall prey to the trap of resting on their laurels and setting only soft and unchallenging objectives. The founders may be content with the way the business is performing and investors may be more than happy with their returns. The opportunity to relax a little may be more than welcome after the rigours of setting up the business, but complacency may lead to stagnation or even gradual decline. The business may well be under threat from competitors who are improving their products or services while you are standing still.
- *Lack of inventiveness.* 'If it ain't broke, why fix it?' The status quo may seem to be working, but are you investing enough in developments and ideas to drive the business forward in the future? Sticking to tried and tested methods may have become a habit, with little incentive for people to suggest changes or improvements. Will your business model still work in a year's time? What about five years?

- *Loss of entrepreneurial spirit.* As the business grows, you will have become more orientated towards planning and will have set up systems for the running of the company. This is an essential part of development, but care needs to be taken to prevent systems becoming inflexible or ossified. Is bureaucracy taking over from enterprise? Are people starting to say things like 'But we've always done it this way'? If so, you may be losing some of your entrepreneurial edge.

- *Lack of people for the next stage of business growth.* This is quite a common phenomenon, where the founder or founders are perfectly well equipped to run the business as it is, but lack the vision or the skills to take it up to the next stage. It can occur, for example, when a business makes the transition from a niche to the mass market, or when it changes from a private company to a stock market-listed one.

  Do you need to bring in new people to take the business into its next phase of development? Or should you consider selling and moving on to your next venture?

- *Losing touch with markets and customers.* A business which has been totally in tune with markets and customers can, over time, lose its seemingly magic touch. This can occur when a business fails to keep pace with economic, social or demographic trends, or by failing to keep abreast of new technology. One example would be the threat posed to conventional bookstores by the new Internet booksellers.

  To keep growing, and to guard against the business becoming a victim of its own success, those in charge must recognise the need for regular reviews and the importance of questioning assumptions. You cannot rely on the past, you must be ready to face the future.

Case Study 1: Marks & Spencer – how the mighty can fall

The recent woes of Marks & Spencer are an object lesson in how a business can become the victim of its own success.

M&S began life in 1894 as a humble Leeds market stall run by Russian refugee Michael Marks and cashier Tom Spencer. It grew to become the UK's favourite retailer, symbolising all that was best about British business, and virtually synonymous with middle-class taste in foods, clothes and furnishings. But after decade upon decade of growth, it all went horribly wrong.

In 1998 the company was forced to unveil a disastrous set of half-year results. Shortly after, a spectacular and embarrassingly public boardroom battle broke out over who would succeed long-term boss Sir Richard Greenbury as chief executive. Eventually, Peter Salsbury won out over rival Keith Oates, who departed with a large pay-off.

Customers, staff and the City were shocked at the troubles emerging at Britain's best-respected retailer. One commentator described the affair as being 'like discovering your efficient maiden aunt has been arrested on a drink-driving charge'.

What had gone wrong?

In large part the distinctive culture that had made M&S so successful had failed to move with the times. Sir Richard, a devoted M&S man with the business for forty-six years, was obsessive about making sure Marks & Spencer did things better than anyone else. But his powerful personality dominated the company to the extent that many critics thought harmful. It seemed as if M&S had failed to notice the retail revolution going on around it and was clinging to the belief that it could carry on doing things in the way it always had.

Yet in comparison with glossier high-street rivals, its stores looked drab and outmoded. Clothes were not well presented on rails and changing rooms were not welcoming. M&S was also out on its own in refusing to accept credit cards other than its own store card. Its designs were panned by fashion commentators and Marks had also seemingly failed to notice that its pricing was poorly pitched. Customers had shifted either to seeking high-ticket aspirational designer brands, or discounts. Offering neither, M&S was squeezed. Even its underwear, for so long a staple of the British public, was attacked by a female shareholder in her fifties at the 1999 annual general meeting for not being sexy enough.

New chief executive Peter Salsbury put all aspects of the

business under review. He is reforming the company's bureau-
cratic management structure, changing its buying system and
employing avant garde designers such as lingerie maker Agent
Provocateur to produce more exciting lines. Whether Marks &
Spencer can recover its place as the best retailer in Britain,
however, remains to be seen, and its complacency has cost it dear
both with customers and the City.

2   Recognising and responding to risks

Every business faces an array of risks, some of which pose a more
serious threat than others. These include:

> Market risk
> Operational risk
> Product risk
> Economic risk
> Currency risk
> Fraud risk
> Security risk

Some of the threats are external, while others come from within
your business itself. One can never eliminate risk. In many cases,
however, it can be dealt with by planning, insuring, setting up
recovery processes, or education and training.

The first stage is to identify as many as possible of the risks
your business faces. These may be within your business; for
example, your computer systems might fail, your products may be
overtaken by competitors, or key staff might defect to a competitor.

Your business is also likely to be vulnerable to risks from
outside, such as a change in the economy or the tax system,
political instability or unpredictable fashions.

The next step is to assess the possible impact of these risks. In
other words, how bad would it be for the business if the risk turned
into a reality? How likely is it that the worst will happen? When

considering how much a particular eventuality would cost the business, remember to include indirect costs such as loss of business following a fire, as well as the expense of repairing the damage done by the blaze. Here, the 'iceberg principle' often applies, in that most of the costs may not be immediately obvious. For instance, in the case of a product being contaminated, the main expense is unlikely to be the recall of the items, but in rebuilding your damaged reputation.

The third step is to respond to the risk. Consider what, if anything, you can do to mitigate the risk in question and what it will cost. Your response might be to avoid it altogether. For example, having assessed a new project such as branching out into a fresh line of business, embarking on a joint venture or buying another company, you might conclude that the risks are so great that you would be better off not to go ahead.

You may decide to accept and control the risk by taking preventative action and, if appropriate, by insuring and having a recovery plan in place.

Finally, you may decide to accept the risk but do nothing more, on the basis that the danger in question is unlikely to occur and the impact would not be too damaging.

The response should be proportionate: in other words if there is only a remote chance of a risk event happening, there is not much point in devoting huge amounts of time and energy to tackling it.

3   Risks within the business

There are a host of risks within the business, associated with your premises, your assets, your employees, your products and your finances. Make a list of those which might affect your business, using the examples below as a guide, then set out an action plan to eliminate or reduce them. Ask employees to give you feedback on any potential risks.

In some areas, there are legal requirements on you to manage risk. These include:

- *Fire regulations.* You must carry out a risk assessment of your premises and, in certain cases, have an inspection and certificate from a Fire Prevention Officer.
- *Employment.* The law insists that you follow set procedures when hiring, promoting or firing staff.
- *Health and safety.* You must carry out a risk assessment of your business and ensure the health and safety of employees and visitors.
- *Directors' responsibilities.* Directors of limited companies are under responsibilities set out in the Companies Act to protect the assets of the business.

In certain industries there may be other legal requirements to ensure you minimise risk; for instance, food safety or protection for investors set out in the Financial Services Act.

Other areas where your business is at risk include:

Your Premises

- *Fire and water damage.* Check all electrical items and wiring in accordance with Electricity at Work regulations.
Keep flammable and dangerous substances securely stored.

  Guard against arson by removing all waste – many fires break out because material is left lying around. Ensure you have adequate security.

  Bear in mind that 15% of fires are caused by smoking, according to the Fire Prevention Association. Make vulnerable areas 'No Smoking' zones and educate staff about smoking as a fire hazard.

  Install fire extinguishers, smoke alarms and sprinklers, and hold regular fire drills. Your local Fire Prevention Officer should be able to give you advice.

  Reduce the risk of water damage by regularly inspecting and repairing water pipes and tanks. Also check gutters, roofs and stopcocks regularly for leakage.
- *Burglary and vandalism.* Consider fitting a burglar alarm system. Only give out codes and keys to authorised and trusted people.

  Set up security procedures at reception. Make sure the

receptionist takes the name of all visitors and checks with the person they are visiting before allowing them to go beyond the front desk.

Encourage people to supply reception with a list of expected visitors in advance.

Make sure the premises are secure at the end of the working day.

Consider installing toughened glass or fitting bars to deter vandals from window smashing.

Ask your local Crime Prevention Officer for more advice.

Your Assets

- Equipment. Make sure equipment is well maintained and regularly serviced. Train employees to use the equipment properly.

  Back up computer data regularly and store back-ups off site.

  Consider installing a back-up system and an uninterruptible power supply so that data is not lost through power failure.

  Ban staff from installing their own software such as computer games until it has been checked or you may be vulnerable to viruses.

  Consider contingency plans in the case of systems breakdown.

- *Employees*. You must have Employer's Liability Insurance to cover you if you have to pay compensation for employees who are injured or suffer an illness as a result of working for you. Make sure you have set up effective health and safety procedures and be aware of risks such as Repetitive Strain Injury and even stress, where the courts have begun to make awards in favour of employees.

  Consider the risk of a key employee or employees leaving, falling ill or dying. Regular company medical checks and perhaps company medical insurance can reduce the risks of ill health. You should have succession plans in place for key roles, so that replacements are being groomed to take over from current occupants, reducing the risk of a crisis if they leave.

You can also take out 'key man insurance', covered below.

- *Theft and fraud.* Carry out checks on new employees by taking up references and checking that they have the qualifications they claim. Mark all equipment with the company name and keep a record of any items given to staff for use away from the office.

  Carry out internal audits to double-check invoices and expenses claims.

  Restrict access to confidential information to prevent employees selling it to competitors or using it for their own personal gain.

- *Vehicles.* Make sure all company vehicles are properly maintained and serviced.

- *Products.* Risks here could include being overtaken by competitors, products not meeting quality standards or, even worse, causing danger or damage to a third party, failures in delivery and service.

  Monitor your competition closely and consider whether your products are likely to be displaced through technological change.

  Set and maintain the highest quality standards, and consider introducing a quality assurance system. ISO 9000, the international quality system standard, is explained later in this chapter. Pay constant attention to meeting customer service standards.

  Consider your own supply chain management. If a supplier lets you down, that in turn can lead to your business failing a customer.

Your finances

Set up financial systems so you are alerted to potential cash flow or other problems. Bad or late debts are an enormous problem for many growing businesses, so reduce the risks by setting up credit checking procedures, and consider a factoring service or credit insurance. This topic was dealt with in greater detail in Chapter 6, Cash Management.

Be aware of the increasing danger of being sued by customers, suppliers or employees claiming unfair dismissal or discrimination. Contractual disputes are the main source of litigation, followed by employment disputes. Compile a written set of standard terms and conditions for everyday transactions. Obtain legal advice before drawing up major contracts.

Be aware of legislation and regulations affecting your business and make sure you comply.

Remember that product liability claims can be made against you if you supply faulty goods or a poor service.

You may also be sued if a member of the public is injured on your premises or by goods you have supplied.

Be aware of your responsibilities as a director under the Companies Act. There are a range of offences for which you can be held personally liable. You could also be sued for offences committed by another director.

4   Insuring against risks within the business

You must have employer's liability insurance to cover you against claims by employees for accidents or illnesses they suffer as a result of working for you. Cover must be for at least £5 million, but most policies cover £10 million.

You must also have at least third-party motor insurance for all company vehicles.

Certain professional bodies insist on you having professional indemnity insurance.

Other types of non-compulsory insurance you may consider include:

- *Buildings cover*. This protects you against a range of risks to the physical fabric of your premises, including fire and water damage. If you own the premises, they should be insured for the full rebuilding cost. If you rent or lease them, check what insurance the landlord has.

- *Theft policies*. These cover your stock and equipment against theft by an intruder who has made a forcible entry to or exit from the premises.
- *Staff honesty policies* protect against theft by your own employees.
- *All-risks policies* cover cash, cheques, stamps and so on.
- *Computer policies* protect you against the costs of breakdown and loss of data.
- *Credit insurance* covers you against losing money if creditors fail to pay debts because they have become insolvent.
- *Business interruption insurance* is designed to cover you against consequential losses following on from an initial loss; for instance, a flood.
- *Legal expenses insurance* covers legal costs if you take a case to court and can be valuable cover for growing firms if they need to sue or are being sued.
- *Public liability insurance* covers the business against claims for accidents to the public or damage to other people's property.
- *Product liability insurance* covers injury or damage caused by faulty goods.
- *Professional fees insurance* covers you against the cost of accountancy fees in case of a tax investigation, for example. These can run to several thousand pounds, even if you have done nothing wrong, and are not tax deductible.
- *Directors' liability insurance* covers you for liabilities caused by fellow directors. Can be worthwhile if you are a non-executive or non-active director.
- *Goods in transit insurance* covers goods which are lost or damaged while being transported by your own vehicle or a carrier.
- *Key man insurance* covers the cost of recruiting and retraining replacements for especially valuable employees.
- *Travel insurance* covers employees while abroad on company business. Note that personal travel policies often exclude business travellers.

Growing firms frequently take advice from a broker or company representative and then buy a package of policies tailored to their needs. Take care not to under-insure, and to take account of inflation. Be aware of any exclusion clauses.

5   Quality control

Setting up a quality assurance system can help reduce the risk of expensive mistakes. It can also improve procedures and attract new suppliers. Indeed, many large companies, especially European ones, insist that all suppliers have the international quality system assurance standard ISO 9000.

Implementing ISO 9000 while you are still small can avoid quality problems later on. Advantages include meeting customer demands and reassuring customers as to quality, and giving staff clear quality guidelines to meet. The standard aims to ensure that your system will maintain quality at a consistent level. It covers the full range of activities affecting the customer and will include measures to ensure that the system runs smoothly. You will be required to document your systems and to draw up a quality manual. To win certification, you will have to produce, implement and document your own quality system and it must be independently audited. There are a number of certification bodies but it is best to choose one that is approved by the United Kingdom Accreditation Service.

Your system cannot be audited before you have evidence that you are meeting the standard and most certification bodies will not carry out an audit before the system has been running for three months. The auditor will inform you of any problem areas and your company will be rechecked, normally twice a year.

You will probably need help and advice on designing and implementing a quality assurance system. The local Business Link or equivalent organisations may be able to offer advice and should be able to direct you to approved consultants. Business Link or its equivalent will also be able to advise you of any grants available towards the cost of ISO 9000. You will have to have trained internal auditors to monitor the system. The International Register of Certificated Auditors has details of training courses for internal auditors. The British Standards Institution has publications on ISO 9000 including guidance on the standards.

Case Study 2: Bread rising from the ashes

Breadmaker Hossain Rezaei has more experience than most of the risks that threaten a business. In his case a nightmare came true – but his business, Pride Valley Foods, a speciality flat bread manufacturer in Seaham, County Durham, managed to bounce back.

In December 1995, Iranian-born Rezaei had been running his business for five years, selling naan bread, pitta, chapattis and other ethnic breads. He had just opened two new state-of-the-art factories when the premises were burnt to the ground. To his horror, the insurers refused to pay up on his claim, saying it was invalid. Far from being defeated, Rezaei reorganised and swiftly went back into business using borrowed premises. By April the following year, with help from his bank, he had a new factory up and running.

At the time Rezaei had not had a holiday for three and a half years and was starting again £4 million in the red. To make his life even more difficult, supermarkets began using bread as a weapon in their price wars. Rezaei analysed the issue and then decided to maintain his products' premium pricing at a time when competitors were discounting and suffering huge losses. He realised that despite the price wars, supermarkets still wanted to make profits from bread, so they needed products like his that they could sell for a higher gross profit. Customers were prepared to pay extra for his breads, as they are high quality and fill a specialist niche.

Rezaei's persistence, resilience and measured response to competitive risk has paid off. Pride Valley now controls half of the speciality flat bread market in Britain and in 2000 made profits of around £1 million.

6   Risks outside your business

Growing businesses are exposed to risks from outside the company as well as from within. External risks are usually harder to deal with than internal ones, because you do not normally have much, if any, control over them. However, considering the possible risks from outside can help you to prepare responses.

- *Political risk*. Your business may be affected if, for example, there is a change of government here in the UK. A new government may alter the tax system in ways which have an impact on the business or on your personal affairs as an entrepreneur. Governments of different political persuasions could, moreover, pass legislation in other areas that are likely to affect businesses; for example, labour market law. UK businesses can also be affected by directives from the European Union that are adopted by the UK government.

  There is often little a business can do to prevent governments bringing in changes they consider to be damaging, other than to add their voice to campaigns run by business lobby groups such as the Federation of Small Businesses, the Confederation of British Industry or the Forum of Private Business. It is worth, however, keeping up with proposed changes to the law and the tax system, and taking professional advice to see if any adverse effects can be minimised. For example, the impact of certain tax measures can be reduced by planning, with advice from a professional accountant. Businesses should also make sure they comply with changes in the law, or run the risk of incurring fines and other penalties.

  Companies doing business overseas are, of course, also exposed to political risks in other countries. These are worth taking very seriously, as they can have a devastating effect on a business. For instance, many UK companies doing business with Russia pulled out in 1998 when that country fell into a state of political and economic turbulence.

  Before exporting to a country, make sure you are fully acquainted with the political situation there and any likely dangers.

- *Economic risk.* Businesses are obviously affected by the state of the economy as a whole. For instance, in the mid to late 1990s UK exporters suffered because the pound was very strong against European currencies, making British goods expensive for continental purchasers. Many economic factors can have a major impact, good or bad, on your business, including exchange rates, interest rates, inflation, deflation and employment levels.

   It is extremely difficult to forecast economic trends and different economists in any case reach completely opposite conclusions from the same data. However, there is an increasing amount of research available, often readily accessible in newspaper articles. Independent surveys of growing businesses, in particular, can give you a reasonable indication of how optimistic or pessimistic your peers are about the economic climate.

   New business formation tends to rise during periods of economic boom, as banks become more willing to lend, asset prices are usually rising and confidence is high. But in a downturn interest rates may rise, banks may review or recall their loans, the value of assets may fall and hard-up customers will stay away, creating a cycle of gloom.

   Entrepreneurs who start up during a boom period need to ask themselves whether their business proposition can survive in a less rosy economic climate. We will deal with managing through difficult economic conditions in the next chapter, but at this stage two simple points are worth remembering.

   First, good businesses can survive adverse economic conditions and even come out stronger at the other end.

   Second, downturns in the economy tend to expose weaker businesses that might have been coasting along thanks to the general economic prosperity.

- *Social and demographic trends.* Societies change in their views, their ideas of fashion, and the goods and services they want to buy. Of course, each individual has somewhat different opinions, needs and purchasing habits. However, major demographic trends can have a major impact on businesses. For example, the ageing population, the tendency for older people to stay in better health for longer and the relative prosperity of many over sixty-fives means that there is a whole market for purchases such as holidays and cars that scarcely existed thirty years ago. Similarly, the 1960s baby boom generation is now producing its own offspring, with a major effect on the items they buy – prams rather than Prada handbags.

Not taking account of social and demographic trends leaves a business at risk of losing touch with the market, serving a dwindling number of customers. Businesses also need to take note of shifts in what is considered socially or politically 'correct', or risk damage to their reputation and perhaps even a customer boycott.

- *External disasters*. The outbreaks of foot and mouth disease in 2001 was a disaster not only for many farmers but also for large tracts of the tourist industry. Try to build a protective cushion of cash and make sure you are aware of any compensaition arrangements.

Case Study 3: Bank of Scotland

Failing to take account of prevailing social views can be extremely damaging to a business. A case in point is the story of the Bank of Scotland's collapsed deal with US televangelist Pat Robertson in 1999.

The Bank wanted to do a deal with Robertson that on paper sounded wonderful. It would have given them access to 55 million customers across the US, through Robertson's Christian Broadcasting Network, to whom the Bank intended to sell telephone banking services. Unfortunately, the Bank did not anticipate how unacceptable its customers would find Robertson's controversial views, including the observation that feminism leads to 'child-killing, witchcraft and lesbianism'.

The Bank initially stuck by the deal in the face of threats by customers to move their accounts in protest. The Bank itself confirmed it had lost at least 500 accounts over the issue. The final straw came when Robertson described Scotland on his television channel as a 'dark land' because of its acceptance of gay people.

The mistake the Bank made was not realising quite how far Robertson's fundamentalist views were out of line with mainstream opinion in this country. In a climate where social views towards homosexuality have become much more liberal, many people found Robertson's remarks about gays deeply offensive. Similarly, his comments about Scotland upset many of the Bank's core customer base north of the border. The Bank finally broke the deal, at a cost thought to run to at least £2 million in compensation to Robertson and was forced to apologise to shareholders for its error of judgement.

7   Personal attitudes to risk

Entrepreneurs' personal attitudes towards the level of risk they are prepared to take are likely to vary as they go through life. Young entrepreneurs are often prepared to take on more risk than older, more established ones, and indeed will probably have to in order to kick-start the business. A single man in his early thirties, for instance, is probably more likely to be prepared to take risks than a family man in his late forties, because the former has less to lose and no one else depending on him.

People often become more risk averse as they get wealthier and want to protect their gains. The approach of retirement also normally leads to a downscaling in the risks individuals feel they can live with. On the other hand, some older people become more relaxed about risk because they no longer have children at home to support or a mortgage and are prepared to 'punt' a proportion, say 10%, of their wealth on a business venture.

It is important to think about your own attitude to risk and how it might change in future. Discuss this with your family, spouse or partner if relevant – their views are also important and conflicts could arise if differences with your own views remain unresolved. From an individual financial risk viewpoint, it makes sense not to tie up all your assets in the business long-term.

To take one common example, business owners often neglect to save for a pension for themselves, relying instead on the sale of the business to provide them with an income on retirement. But taking out a separate pension plan means that your security in old age is not solely dependent on the fortunes of your business and that it will not be destroyed if the business goes wrong as you near retirement.

11

Avoiding the Pitfalls

There is much to be said for failure. It is more interesting than success.

Sir Max Beerbohm

Experience is the name everyone gives to their mistakes.

Oscar Wilde

At some point every entrepreneur has to think about the un-mentionable 'F' word – failure. For many, unfortunately, it is a reality. The mortality rate for new businesses is frighteningly high. Statistics from Barclays Bank[1] show that in the period from 1988 to 1999, almost one in ten businesses ceased trading within six months after being set up. Fewer than 30% of firms survive for longer than five years and fewer than 15% ever celebrate a tenth birthday.

When an entrepreneur is pushing for growth, the last thing he or she wants to think about is failure. But knowing how and why firms typically fail, and knowing how to handle difficult business conditions, can help you avoid the same fate.

Failure, of course, is a natural part of business life. Some experts attribute the vibrant US enterprise economy to the relative lack of stigma that country attaches to business failure and to its forgiving insolvency regime, which allows entrepreneurs who failed honestly to have another go.

The Department of Trade and Industry is currently looking at ways of making it easier in this country for entrepreneurs who have gone under to try again.

In this chapter we will look at the most common reasons for business failure and how to trade through difficult conditions. We will also examine how to avoid being dragged down by other people's failures and, if you do hit the rocks, how your business might be rescued.

1   Why do businesses fail?

People tend to associate insolvencies with either a recession or fraud. In fact, business failures are always present, even when the economy is booming. In 1998, for example, a relatively good year for the UK economy, 13,203 companies went into insolvency, according to the Society of Insolvency Practitioners.[2] These figures are, of course, the tip of the iceberg as many more companies are rescued or remain hovering on the brink.

Insolvency figures usually increase in times of economic growth, as a rise in company start-ups normally leads to a hike in failures a few months down the line. Fraud is a significant factor – it is cited as the main reason for failure in 3% of cases but it is a contributory factor in a total of 14% of insolvencies.

But the main reasons for business failure are neither the economy nor fraud. They are poor management, financial constraints and loss of market, which between them are cited as a primary cause in around three-quarters of all insolvencies.[3]

One might argue that poor management, which is a prime cause in 26% of cases, is the worst of these as few factors ought to be beyond the control of those running the company. Usually, disaster does not strike as a lightning blow. Businesses frequently collapse because problems, such as failing to keep in step with a changing marketplace, have been allowed to build up over a number of years. Although people often blame the economy when businesses go under, the truth is usually that an economic downturn exposes, rather than causes, failures.

2   Poor management

No one believes they are a poor manager any more than they would admit to being a bad driver. But the most damaging form poor management takes is self-delusion – over the value of assets, the likely volume of sales, your ability to pay back debts – and the idea that you are always right. It is worth taking an honest look at your behaviour – or asking a trusted confidant to do it for you. A couple of the points probably apply to practically all companies. No business, or manager is ever ideal. But if you are answering 'yes' to several of the questions below, there could be trouble ahead.

- Are you unable to make tough decisions, instead letting problems drift?
- Does the management team lack direction?
- Are there serious disagreements or lack of clarity over strategy?
- Have the management failed to analyse how your market is developing?
- Are there serious problems in the relationship between you and other key people in the business, such as co-founders, co-owners, a major shareholder, finance director, bank manager? Is there a possibility the relationship could break down?
- Are you suffering personal problems that are affecting your ability to run the business?
- Is there in-fighting over who will take over the business when you step down?
- Are you over-reliant on a few products or customers? A few suppliers? Key personnel, such as your marketing director?
- In your heart of hearts, do you feel you have been over-optimistic in your budgets and cash-flow forecasts? Has your lender voiced concerns about this?
- Again, in your heart of hearts, have you been imprudent in your accounting, hiding problems such as obsolete stock?
- Are you losing sleep over the level of borrowing you have taken on?

3   Financial constraints

Financial constraints are the main cause in 26% of insolvencies. Here, it is useful to draw a distinction between liquidity and solvency. Solvency is the ability to clear all debts, whether from profits if the business is a going concern, or from assets if it is being wound down. Liquidity is the ability to pay debts as they fall due. The latter is essentially a dynamic cash-flow concept. Looking at short-term assets and liabilities might not be the best guide as to whether you have liquidity. You might have lots of debtors and stock, but can they be converted into cash quickly enough to pay creditors?

The main problems include:

- lack of long-term finance;
- failure to manage working capital;
- assets out of balance with short-term liabilities;
- poor management of the exchange rate.

The business may also run into problems because of poor accounting and financial controls, such as:

- failure to cost supplies properly;
- under-pricing products;
- overheads are too high;
- poor stock management;
- failing to produce management information and accounts on time, causing a delay in becoming aware of potential problems;
- poor credit control. This has been dealt with in more detail in Chapter 6, Cash Management.

Around 14% of business failures are mainly brought about by bad debts and a further 4% are caused by the knock-on effect of another insolvency, usually that of a major customer. Good credit control, screening new customers, monitoring credit limits and chasing debts is vital.

4 Loss of market

Loss of market is given as the main cause of insolvency in 23% of cases. It can be brought on by:

- lack of demand for the product;
- being overtaken by new competitors;
- problems with location; for instance, a high-street shop running into trouble after the opening of an out-of-town retail park;
- being unable to comply with regulatory changes, such as new hygiene rules in the catering or food-selling industry;
- poor marketing, leading to overspend and low returns;
- failure to watch and understand competitors;
- poor product quality, prompting customers to defect;
- lack of technical knowledge and ability leading to obsolete or out-of-date products;
- poor fulfilment and aftercare leading to loss of customers as a result of late deliveries, poor complaints handling and so on.

Case Study 1: C&A

Loss of market as customer demands change is a particularly hot issue in the fast-moving world of fashion retailing. In June 2000, famous name C&A, a fixture on the high street since 1922, announced that it was closing down its 109 UK stores, following losses of £250 million last year in Britain and Ireland, to concentrate its activities on the Continent. The company, which in the Sixties was successful at supplying high fashion at a low cost, was forced into the move by the disappearance of its market, due to a combination of changing shopping habits, rising property costs and new competition. In the Nineties shoppers' tastes changed so that people prefer designer labels. At the same time C&A faced competition from discount chains and from new entrants such as New Look, Matalan and Zara. Property costs also played a part with huge high-street premises becoming increasingly unfashionable and expensive. Many shops moved out of town to retail parks, or alternatively switched to small, boutique-style outlets, such as Kookai or Morgan. In addition, trendy shoppers in London and other large cities are shunning high-street chains in favour of independent boutiques in areas such as Notting Hill.

C&A failed to follow other retailers in similar straits such as Marks & Spencer and Debenhams, both of which launched their own designer ranges. It failed also to rejuvenate its dowdy image or store displays and tried fruitlessly to lure young trendy customers when its remaining loyal following consisted mainly of middle-aged women of a certain size.

5   What happens when businesses fail?

It depends on the nature and degree of the business's problems – but only in the worst cases are the liquidators called in and the company terminated completely. In many instances the owners understand that it is on a downward slope and therefore decide to sell off all or part of its operations. This route may be appropriate if the current owners realise that the business still has the scope to be successful, but that it needs a new proprietor to provide additional capital, say, or management skills. Alternatively, they may decide to wind down the business in an orderly fashion, selling off assets to pay off creditors.

Although either of these options is less traumatic than having the receivers called in, it can still be heartbreaking for owner-managers. It may be particularly difficult in family businesses where owners could feel they have let down older family members, or perhaps deprived their children of their 'inheritance'. They may also feel guilty about job losses for loyal staff members.

In other cases the company may be in such a bad way that it needs to be 'rescued'. After rescue, it may continue to be run by existing management, or be sold off to others. Rescues may be carried out either informally, or through formal insolvency procedures such as a Company Voluntary Arrangement. There are a variety of formal insolvency procedures which are explained later in this chapter.

A Quick Survival Course

Crises can – and will – hit any company. The survivors tend to be those which are well prepared and robust, and therefore in good shape to fight back against the blows.

Many if not most insolvencies can be prevented by early action, but in a lot of cases managers do not have the information they need to recognise a looming disaster, or choose to ignore the danger signals.

The three golden rules for survival

1   Act early. Take action promptly whenever you think there may be a problem. Don't wait until it has actually hit you, by which time it may be too late.
2   Recognise your business's weaknesses honestly and try to overcome them.
3   Keep an eye on the economy and the business environment for developments that might affect your company.

To maximise your chances of survival, follow the tips below to make sure you have early warning systems in place.

- Make sure you have an up-to-date business plan and that you regularly measure progress against it. Meet with co-directors regularly to review performance and to highlight any problems. If you are a sole entrepreneur, set aside time to get to grips with the financial position.
- Don't assume that just because sales are rising, your business is doing fine. Keep a grip on costs and overheads as well.
- Monitor debtors and creditors carefully. Prepare lists to identify any debtors that are behind with their payments and of any creditors that you have not yet paid.
- Prepare regular management accounts and cash-flow forecasts at least monthly. These should help with the early identification of any problems.

Alarm Bells

There are a number of common warning signals that can indicate a company is on the slippery slope. If any apply to your company, it is time to take action.

- Is your bank balance going steadily downwards?
- Have you gone beyond your overdraft?
- Are you receiving writs and final demands?
- Are you having to increase your borrowings just to keep the business running?
- Are you unsure how much you owe and how much others owe you?
- Are you failing to pay the Inland Revenue or the VAT-man on time?
- Are you failing to collect debts efficiently?
- Are your key customers failing to pay, or asking for extended credit?
- Are sales static or falling, with stock levels rising?
- Are you having to absorb ever higher costs that cannot be passed on in higher prices?

6   Managing through difficult times

Whenever the economy takes a downturn, businesses begin to go under, many of them loudly blaming 'the recession', 'the pound', 'interest rates' or whatever for their plight.

Obviously, when the economy is going through a tough time, life becomes harder for individual businesses. But any entrepreneur serious about building a business is likely to face a downturn sooner or later, and must learn how to live through it.

In fact, few businesses are killed off purely by a recession. Those that fail to survive are usually harbouring serious weaknesses that have been exposed by difficult economic circumstances. Recessions represent opportunities for those who do survive – opportunities to take business from weaker competitors and to buy assets at cheaper prices, to name just two.

To survive difficult economic circumstances, you need to take a hard look at the business, preferably before the crisis hits. Review each part critically and take steps to make it leaner and fitter, to boost competitive advantage and withstand financial problems.

- *Keep up to date.* Make sure you have timely management information. Comparing actual performance with forecasts should alert you to trends and any action that needs to be taken. Look out for danger signs such as obsolete stock or deteriorating profit margins.

  Again, do not be shy of consulting an experienced bank manager or accountant. They will have seen many businesses suffer problems and should be able to save you a lot of time and trouble by passing on the benefit of their experience.

  Benchmarking yourself against competitors can show up where you are going wrong – a large amount of comparative information and benchmarking is done by the Department of Trade and Industry and can be accessed through your local Business Link or equivalent.

- *Be honest with your bank.* It is tempting, when difficulties hit, to retreat into silence, in the hope that things will get better. A far more sensible strategy, however, is to keep talking to your bank manager. Contrary to popular myth, bankers are not desperate to pull the plug at the first opportunity – it is not in their interest to accumulate bad debts from a welter of failed firms. But bank managers deeply dislike having bad news come as a shock. If you give the bank early warning of any problems, it may be able to help you avert or mitigate them. In particular, make sure you warn the bank if you know you are about to breach overdraft limits or covenants.

  Do not be shy of taking advice from other sources, such as your accountant or Business Link adviser.

- *Concentrate on cash.* When trouble hits, cash is paramount. Many inherently profitable businesses go under because their cash dries up – conversely, if a business is unprofitable, but has cash in the bank, it can buy time to restructure, or to provide investors with an exit route. Reduce cash requirements to a minimum, convert all non-performing assets into cash and direct management attention towards making sure as much cash is kept within the business as possible.

Draw up short-term cash forecasts examining the requirements to run the business on a day-to-day basis, so that you can identify any danger of breaching bank facilities.

Draw up longer-term forecasts also, so that you can spot potential problems further ahead. Remember that the more time you give yourself to negotiate with your bank, the more favourably they are likely to deal with you.

- *Be efficient over collecting debts.* Pursue debts on a daily basis if necessary. In a difficult economy other firms will also be facing a crunch and are likely to try to boost their own cash flow by delaying debts.

  Make sure you chase debts hard to avoid being brought down by a tardy or non-paying customer. Remember that if cash is tight, the customer is likely to pay the creditor who causes him or her the most hassle.

  Get invoices out on time and try to negotiate electronic payment to be sure of being paid on the due date, and consider using a factoring service.

- *Prioritise profit.* It may sound obvious, but it is only worthwhile making sales if they are profitable. When the economy hits trouble, customers often attempt to squeeze suppliers and firms are tempted to comply with their demands for the sake of keeping a customer and doing business in future. Be aware, however, that this is likely to increase the financial strain on the business.

  Concentrate on the areas of your business that are the most profitable. Make sure customers are aware of the non-price advantages of your product – for example, the export businesses that coped best with the high value of sterling during the late 1990s were those that did not sell on price alone, but had other product qualities to attract and keep buyers.

  Keep a close eye on your competitors and be constantly aware of the prices they are charging.

- *Maximise marketing.* Examine your marketing strategy carefully and concentrate on areas that are likely to produce the quickest return. Do not be tempted to axe marketing expenditure altogether in an attempt to save cash, but take care to target it effectively.

  Talk to customers to find out if they need improvements to your products or services. Remember that if you are not serving them well, you are particularly vulnerable to losing them during a downturn.

  Consider talking to ex-customers to find out why they left.

  Try to spread out your customer base so that you are not over-dependent on one or two customers who could themselves go under or could exert unfair pressure over you.

- *Dealing with suppliers.* Review your suppliers to check whether you could make savings by switching your business elsewhere. Do not become over-reliant on one supplier. Always have two or three sources for vital materials. Negotiate hard with suppliers – ask for discounts for early settlement of bills, if appropriate, or for extended credit periods if that would help.

  Question any price increases a supplier tries to impose upon you.

  Consider forming an association with other businesses to drive down the costs of supplies and make full use of buying over the Internet to keep costs down.

  Remember, however, that a good partnership with suppliers can ensure that you get the best service and goods tailored to your needs. Do not lightly sacrifice such a relationship.

- *Managing stock.* The number one rule is: don't be a hoarder. Holding on to obsolete stock is a drain on the business, so review all old stock and sell off as much as you can.

  Use 'just-in-time' techniques to reduce the period that materials are held before being sent to a customer to free up working capital. If necessary, take advice from a consultant in order to reduce to a minimum the time you have stock hanging around idly.

- *Cut overheads.* It is important not to be spending money unnecessarily, so cast an eagle eye over all outgoings. Examine your ordering procedures for goods such as stationery – you may be able to improve cash flow by ordering smaller amounts more frequently.

  Examine any research and development programmes to distinguish essential from inessential work. Thoroughly check any proposed major expenditure; for example, on repairs or replacing fixed assets, to see if it can be postponed.

  Look at utility and telephone bills, and consider switching to a cheaper supplier, and examine patterns of usage to see if you could cut bills by making use of cheap-rate tariffs and the like. Specialist consultants can advise in this area. If fixed costs can be turned into variable costs you have more flexibility when income goes down.

  Check staff and management expenses, and make sure you are only paying for essential work-related outgoings.

- *Handling creditors.* It may be tempting to delay paying your creditors, but if you can afford to pay on time, do so. That way, you will retain their goodwill. If you do run into payment problems, talk to creditors and keep them up to date. If you are midway through purchasing a fixed asset from a leasing company or the like, talk to them and see whether you can arrange a payment holiday until the business is in better shape.

- *Share the burden with staff.* Dealing with staff is one of the most difficult and sometimes heartbreaking aspects when a business hits problems. Entrepreneurs often feel deeply guilty and responsible towards employees and find it extremely hard. However, it is important to deal fairly and honestly with your staff as you will need their support. Do not try to hide problems from them, especially if tough decisions, such as freezing pay or shedding staff are involved.

  Try to cut out unnecessary overtime and perks, and

review production to see if you can reduce costs and cut out inefficiencies.

Put a freeze on wage increases and do not hire new staff unless absolutely necessary.

Review staffing, to see whether there are any employees whose contribution does not justify their continued employment, but assess redundancy costs and how these will be met. If you do have to embark on a redundancy programme, do it thoroughly and all at once. A bit-by-bit programme is likely to prove highly damaging to morale.

Equally, give some thought to how you will try to retain key staff. Simply talking to them honestly can work better than you might imagine, but you may also consider incentives directly linked to improvements in performance.

7   Others in trouble

Others who run into difficulty can cause you problems too. Many businesses are thrown seriously off course, or even go under, if a customer goes bust or fails to pay her or his bills on time. Equally, a supplier who goes under might leave you without crucial supplies or services.

Warning signs that a customer may be in danger include taking longer to pay bills, or not paying at all, paying by post-dated cheques and using disputes as a delaying tactic. Try to achieve open and honest communication channels with customers and suppliers. Set up clear credit control procedures to identify customers in difficulty and only deviate from these after careful consideration. Check customers' credit references before taking them on and review credit limits regularly.

Consider including retention of title clauses in your terms of trading so that you can repossess goods if you are not paid.

Also consider taking out credit insurance or using a factoring service.

Even after taking these steps, you may still be faced with a customer in difficulty. In this case you need to make a rational and considered decision on how supportive you are prepared to be. Remember that keeping a company going can produce a better return to creditors than pushing it under. Factors to take into account include whether the customer has been honest and trustworthy with you, whether the problems are short- or long-term, whether you actually need to keep the business and how critical your support is.

It is sensible to seek professional advice about your rights and the best course of action. Take steps to inform yourself as fully as possible about the situation, for instance, by attending creditors' meetings.

8   Intensive care

If, in spite of your efforts, the business continues running into crisis, it may still be capable of being rescued. Contrary to popular myth, banks and other lenders do not want to force businesses under – it is not in their interests to do so, because they have far more chance of recouping their loans from a firm that is a going concern than from one that is insolvent. UK law always puts the interests of creditors first, so a rescue can only be achieved if they believe they will get a higher return through the company being saved than by putting it into insolvency.

After the experience of the early Nineties recession, when thousands of businesses went under and the banks ran up huge losses, the Big Four have set up 'intensive care units' to nurture businesses back to health. The banks say they will support realistic rescue plans, so long as the firm communicates with them honestly and keeps its commitments. The British Bankers' Association has produced a Statement of Principles 'Banks and Businesses: Working Together', which sets out banks' policies concerning firms in crisis.[4] According to figures from the Society of Practitioners of Insolvency, more than half of firms that enter bank intensive care procedures go on to recover.

Most bank-led rescues begin with the appointment of an investigating accountant, who will compile a report on the state of the business's affairs for the bank. The investigating accountant is often understandably viewed by business owners as a 'Grim Reaper' figure – but this is frequently unjustified. His or her report will examine the firm's current position, a summary of its future prospects and recommendations for how it should move forward. It is often the starting point for a firm's journey back to health and it is in directors' interests to co-operate, not to obstruct the accountant. The reports are confidential and provide an independent view of the company – as such, they are valuable documents both to the company and its lenders.

Since it is your business which pays for the report – even if it has been commissioned by a bank or a trade creditor – it makes sense to derive as much benefit from it as you can. It may make recommendations including cutting costs, strengthening management, raising additional capital and so on. Only in one out of five cases, according to the Society of Practitioners of Insolvency, does a report recommend bringing in the receivers.

9   Your personal responsibilities

As the owner of a business in crisis, you have a whole raft of legal and moral responsibilities. It is not necessarily easy to face up to these – but it will undoubtedly be worse if you take an ostrich attitude.

When a business runs into trouble, it puts tremendous strain on the entrepreneur, who may begin working longer and longer hours in an attempt to ward off disaster. Family life frequently becomes strained. Partners and children may themselves feel anxious and stressed at their inability to help, or worried about the financial impact on them if, for instance, the family home is at risk. Staff and fellow directors may be recriminatory and hostile, and relations with the bank are frequently difficult, to say the least.

Some entrepreneurial personality types, who thrive on optimism and self-belief, are not best equipped to deal with these issues. Others simply feel that they have invested so much, personally and financially, that they absolutely cannot countenance the reality around them. But honesty, with yourself and others, is the only approach likely to result in a successful survival strategy, as things cannot start to be put right until the problems are acknowledged.

You may be surprised at how positively others respond to an honest admission of the situation on your part, and at their willingness to help. Remember that in the majority of cases where banks or other creditors trigger an insolvency it is only when they have totally lost confidence in the company. Normally this happens because the entrepreneur or directors have refused to admit to problems and made unrealistic commitments, which they have then failed to meet. However persecuted and lonely you feel, it is worth remembering that everyone has a stake in recovery – your family, your staff and your lenders will all be better off if the business revives than if it fails. No one wants to bring you down.

In addition, it is worth being aware of your legal responsibilities. Directors of limited companies are held personally responsible for debts of a company if it continues to trade after there is no reasonable prospect of it avoiding insolvency. You may also be personally liable for debts if you have given personal guarantees against bank borrowings, property leases or HP agreements. If your company is insolvent, you might be liable for any cheques issued if it is clear they will bounce, running up credit when there is little chance of it being paid, taking deposits from customers for goods and services they will never receive, and selling goods off at less than their market value to raise cash.

Directors who fail to live up to these responsibilities face disqualification – sometimes for up to fifteen years and, in extreme cases, a prison sentence. In most cases unthinking or incompetent directors will not be banned but it is worth taking professional advice on your position as soon as you see warning signs. This is not just to avoid possible legal penalties, but also to give yourself the very best possible chance of avoiding seeing the years of hard work and money invested in your business disappear.

> ## The Personal Consequences of Business Failure
> Too many businesses fail because the owner refuses to believe it can happen. But the personal consequences can be very damaging. They include any, or even all, of the following:
> - personal bankruptcy;
> - losing your home to pay the firm's debts;
> - inaction or misbehaviour on your part leading to fines, disqualification as a director or even prison;
> - breakdown of marriage or other close relationships as loved ones are unable to cope.

10   The four most dangerous words in the English language . . .

A wise economist once told me that the four most dangerous words he ever hears are: 'This time it's different.' Usually, they are being used to justify the suspension of common sense and the normal rules of gravity about a business or economic trend.

The frenzy over dot.com businesses in late 1999 and early 2000 in the UK is a case in point. Many of these companies were set up by young entrepreneurs, with the backing of venture capitalists and wealthy individuals who seemed to have thrown their critical faculties out of the window. The investors' thinking was that the Internet is transforming business beyond recognition and that vast fortunes would be made from those companies that succeeded in cashing in. They were not unduly concerned if most dot.coms they backed went under, as the few success stories, they believed, would more than compensate. Some of the dot.com entrepreneurs, in turn, behaved as if the usual rules of business did not apply to them. They prioritised marketing, groovy websites and trendy staff at the expense of such mundane matters as making sales, or even a profit.

This kind of frenzy seems to sweep the business world at regular intervals. In the early Nineties, biotechnology companies were the height of fashion and, in the Eighties, advertising agencies filled the role. The outcome is always the same – a few well-run companies do make the grade, most simply vanish.

The moral for entrepreneurs is simple: just because it is a dot.com company does not mean that any of the other rules of business change.

Case Study 2: Boo.com

The collapse of Internet sportswear retailer Boo.com in May 2000 was interpreted by many as a grim warning of the fate ahead of many other ill-managed e-commerce companies – and as a classic example of how not to run a successful business of any type.

Boo's founders Kasja Leander and Ernst Malmsten, both aged twenty-nine at the time of the collapse, were young, attractive, plausible – and inexperienced. The pair already had one failed venture, a publishing house in their native Sweden, behind them. In spite of their lack of track record, the pair won backing from high-profile investors including Italy's Benetton family and Bernard Arnault, chairman of luxury goods retailer Louis Vuitton. The firm generated acres of free publicity from commentators seduced by the idea that dot.coms were transforming the normal rules of commerce.

But the company appeared to believe in its own hype and did not take any account of good business principles. Instead, it indulged in a policy of 'spend, spend, spend'. Persuaded that the dot.com boom had created a shortage of good staff, Boo.com pampered employees with first-class air travel, champagne receptions and plush offices in central London. In addition, the company spent around 75% of turnover on marketing, which experts say was far too high. The company's website was state of the art – so much so that many home computers were not capable of accessing it.

Boo's problems began to emerge in January 2000 when it started to slash some prices and cut around a hundred staff. Five months later it had earned the dubious distinction of becoming the first dot.com liquidation, owing creditors around £110 million and leaving more than 300 staff without a job.

11   What is insolvency?

Insolvency is the state a company finds itself in when it cannot pay its debts as they fall due, or its assets are worth less than its liabilities. It is perfectly possible for a company to be on track to making a profit but to be made insolvent because it cannot pay a large tax demand or trade creditor. When determining whether a company is technically insolvent, it is not just current borrowings that must be taken into account, but also liabilities that normally only bite if you go under, such as redundancy payments.

12   Insolvency procedures

There are a number of formal insolvency procedures in the UK: Company Voluntary Arrangement; Administration; Administrative Receivership; Receivership (Scotland); Creditors Voluntary Liquidation and Compulsory Liquidation. The first four may be used to effect a rescue, by maintaining the business as a going concern. The outcome may be either a sale of the business as a going concern, in which case it will attract a higher price than its break-up value, or the rehabilitation of the company, so that it can return to the care of its existing management.

Rescue, however, is not always possible. Some businesses cannot be sold or rehabilitated, perhaps because, as in the case of advertising agencies, for instance, their main assets are people and everyone has left. A company may also be incapable of surviving under current conditions. In this case it is likely to be placed in liquidation and its assets sold off, with the proceeds distributed to creditors.

Normally, liquidation is terminal for a company.

- *Company Voluntary Arrangement.* CVAs are intended primarily as a rescue vehicle. Proposals for a CVA can be made by the directors of a company, its administrator or its liquidator. In a CVA, plans are drawn up so that a company can order its affairs by, for example, delaying or restructuring its debts, or disposing of assets in an orderly manner.

  The proposals will be presented to creditors at a meeting and 75% of the creditors by value must vote in favour for the arrangement to be binding. The arrangement is supervised by an insolvency practitioner. If it is successfully completed, the directors will remain in charge and will be able to take the business forward in whichever way they choose, or sell it to new management.

- *Administration.* Administration orders are orders of the court and are meant to be a constructive way of attempting to save a business. Usually, a company that is insolvent, or believes it is about to be, will seek an order to keep creditors at bay.

  Under administration, the day-to-day running of the company is placed under the control of an administrator, who is an officer of the court. He or she has a great deal of power and can, for instance, hire and fire staff or enter into contracts on the company's behalf. The company is protected from creditors who cannot disturb the business or recover any assets without the court's permission.

  The idea is to keep the business running while a plan is put in place either to rescue it, or to realise the maximum from a sale of its assets. The administrator may put forward other options such as a CVA.

  Although administration has achieved some successes, it is only suitable for larger companies because of the expenses involved.

- *Administrative Receivership.* Administrative receivership, usually just known as receivership, is normally initiated by a bank or consortium of banks which have a floating charge over a large proportion of a company's assets.

  The receiver has similar powers to the administrator. He or she will continue to trade the business and attempt to sell it as a going concern. In many cases the result is a management buyout, with the business being sold to its managers. Around half of all receiverships end in the rescue of all or part of the business.

- *Receivership (Scotland).* The procedure in Scotland is somewhat different but the Scottish receiver has similar powers and aims to the receiver in England and Wales.

- *Creditors Voluntary Liquidation.* A creditors voluntary liquidation is the most common way for directors and shareholders to deal voluntarily with insolvency.

  It is in the interests of directors to take action early on to minimise the risk of being held personally liable for wrongful trading. Under a CVL, the liquidator is appointed by shareholders but is subject to the approval of creditors. He or she is required to report to the Department of Trade and Industry on the conduct of the directors, but their behaviour is not brought under the beady eye of the Official Receiver.

  A different procedure, known as a Members Voluntary Liquidation, may take place if the company is solvent – if its assets are enough to settle its liabilities, plus interest, within a year. This might happen if the owners wish to realise their assets and retire, or if a group of companies want to close down a defunct subsidiary. In this case a liquidator is appointed by shareholders to wind up the business.

- *Compulsory Liquidation.* Compulsory liquidations are ordered by the court normally following a petition from a creditor, shareholder, or the company itself, usually because the company is insolvent. A petition may also be brought by the President of the Board of Trade on the grounds of the public interest. The Official Receiver, who is a member of the Department of Trade Insolvency Service, is brought in as liquidator and will investigate the company's affairs and report to creditors. He or she is also responsible for investigating the conduct of directors.

Notes

1 Barclays Bank Group Economics Department 'The Lifespan of the UK Business Stock', July 1999.
2 Society of Insolvency Practitioners Survey of Company Insolvency in the United Kingdom.
3 Ibid.
4 Copies available free from the British Bankers' Association on 020 7216 8820.

APPENDIX 1

Moving On

Many entrepreneurs may not be able to imagine life outside their business. But believe it or not, it does exist – and at some stage most will want to return to it. Planning your move on, whether it is to retirement or to other interests, is important, as it will enable you to maximise the financial and personal benefits you take with you, and possibly to minimise your tax bills. Moving on can be an emotional process, as entrepreneurs have invested a lot of time and work as well as money in their businesses.

There are several exit routes that an entrepreneur can take, including selling the business or passing it on to a family member or another 'heir'. Some prefer not to think about what will happen when they leave the company or scale down their involvement, and one of the most neglected areas in all too many businesses is planning for succession. That is understandable, as we all like to believe we are irreplaceable. The problem is that if you fail to plan for who will succeed you – particularly in a family firm – you can cause tension and rows that sour the atmosphere while you are still there and chaos after you leave.

In this appendix we look at how to groom your business for sale, and Helen Riley, Tax Partner at accountant RSM Robson Rhodes, gives her advice on how to manage the succession issue.

1   Selling out

Most people set up their own business because they hope to realise their dreams – whether of becoming a billionaire or retiring to the Bahamas at forty. But few give a great deal of thought to the practicalities of making a graceful and profitable exit from the business they have built.

Once you have set up a thriving business there may be a number of personal reasons why you need to make an exit from it, including retirement, setting up a fresh venture, releasing capital for yourself or realising a return for your backers.

There may also be commercial reasons pointing to your exit as the most sensible step. For instance, you may recognise that in order to grow further, the business needs a different structure and management from the one you can provide. The government is also trying to encourage serial entrepreneurship, where people start up one business, exit from it after they have grown it to a certain point and then begin again with another new company.

Entrepreneurs can choose from a number of potential exit routes, including floating on the stock market, passing the business on to the younger generation and management or employee buyouts. But the most common exit route, and the one we deal with here, is to sell up.

Selling your business is one of the most important deals you will ever do in your life, so it makes sense not to stint on time, effort and money in order to get it right. Experts recommend beginning preparations as much as three years before the intended sale. Once you have identified a buyer, it is likely to take between four to six months to complete the deal. Like selling a house, it can also be an emotional and frequently very stressful affair. Owners have made an enormous emotional investment in their firm and frequently find it hard to let go. They may find they take it very personally if a potential buyer pulls out or attempts to beat down the price. They often also have concerns about employees, many of whom may have been colleagues for years.

All of this means that you need to plan the sale as rationally as possible. The following pointers should help you to get the best deal – and keep you sane.

- *Wise counsel.* Good advice is absolutely key. Having the right advisers can make the difference between a smooth sale at a price you like, and a nightmare of wrangling and stress or, worse, the business remaining unsold. If you have non-executive directors, make full use of their expertise.

  It is best to engage advisers at an early stage of the process. As sales can be quite protracted and stressful, it is important that advisers are not only well-qualified and experienced, but that you trust and like them. Depending on the size and complexity of the transaction it may be appropriate to seek advice from an accountant, solicitor, or a corporate finance expert. Pay fees on a success basis to give them an incentive to get you a good deal.

- *Good timing.* The first point to bear in mind is timing. You may not be fully in control of the timing of your exit, for instance, if a sale is forced on you by ill health. But ideally, try to sell when your business is growing. It also helps if your market as a whole is heading upwards. If not, it may make sense to delay in the hope of an upturn.

- *Be well groomed.* Grooming is also important. Time and effort spent putting the business in the best possible shape for a sale is likely to pay dividends.

  In the run-up to a sale, concentrate on maximising profits by controlling overheads and making sure you are extracting maximum value from your assets. Concentrate on profitability, not trappings and status, by stripping out any assets that do not produce profit, such as directors' cars, as this can affect the valuation of your business. You should have time to enjoy your lifestyle after the sale.

- *Take a memo.* You and your advisers will need to prepare a full memorandum of sale, a document enabling potential buyers to make an assessment of your business.

  It should include the history and ownership of the company, the nature of its business, the reasons for sale, details of suppliers, customers and competitors, the management, information on plant, IT systems and so on, and financial information. Identify any 'hidden' assets such as intellectual property, but also any problem areas such as litigation.

- *Seek a prime buyer.* Try to identify a prime buyer – one who would benefit strategically from buying your business and therefore will be prepared to pay a good price, perhaps even above the market value.

  You might be able to find potential prime purchasers through existing contacts with suppliers, competitors and customers, through using business directories, through an advertisement or through your adviser. Having obtained a long list of possible buyers, narrow it down to those who can afford to buy and would achieve either cost savings, access to new markets, or other strategic benefits from the purchase.

- *Sensitive secrets.* Your advisers can make contact with potential buyers on a confidential basis. They should put in place a confidentiality agreement before releasing the memorandum of sale to prevent the misuse of information you give.

  The memorandum of sale should also avoid giving out sensitive information that may fall into the wrong hands of competitors.

- *What's it worth?* Valuations are subjective and there is no simple answer to the question: 'How much is my business worth?' However, your advisers should assess the market value of the company before embarking on the sale. The most common method of valuing profitable private companies is to apply a multiple to the firm's estimated future earnings. A range of values from a conservative price to a bullish valuation will be calculated.

  Obviously, negotiation by your advisers is vital in getting the best price and this process can take six months or more. During negotiations, concentrate on big issues and avoid the temptation to fixate on smaller items that may seem important to you but are not really germane to the deal.

Have a clear idea of your bottom price – that below which the business will not be sold.

- *How will you be paid?* It is worth thinking about how and when the buyer will pay you. Most sellers clearly would prefer to receive the total proceeds in cash, but you may find it makes sense to defer part of the payment or accept shares rather than cash. Leading corporate financiers recommend that you only take up to a third of the payment in the form of deferred consideration or shares. If you do agree to defer part of the payment, make sure your adviser carries out stringent checks to protect against the risk of the purchaser defaulting.

  Similarly, if the buyer offers you shares in her or his company, satisfy yourself that they will prove a good investment.

- *The taxman cometh.* Chancellor Gordon Brown has taken steps to reduce the capital gains tax burden for entrepreneurs, but the demands of the Inland Revenue are still a major consideration for many sellers. Tax planning considerations can affect the timing and the structure of the deal, so get good advice early.

- *What next?* The purchaser may want you to stay on after the sale to smooth the transition. Staying on for up to a year is not unusual.

It is worth looking further ahead at what you will do with your life once you finally leave. Entrepreneurs used to throwing their whole lives into the business are often left at a loss once they have sold and depression is a common consequence. Start laying plans for your new life. If you are not starting a new venture, make sure you take good personal financial advice on investing the proceeds.

2   Managing succession

Most companies are managed on the assumption that they will exist for ever. All too often they have no formal succession planning policy in place to effect the transfer of ownership. Hand on heart, have you identified successors for your key senior managers? The majority of businesses will be familiar with the various maxims advising you not to become reliant on a few key stars. Nevertheless, it is not unusual for succession planning to be relegated to something the human resources department has responsibility for. Alternatively it can become a victim of political concerns. Whoever is the champion of a company's succession planning policy needs to have sufficient clout to ensure the longevity of the policy and to have the company's and its stakeholders' best interests at heart. The board should drive and own the policy but it does require input both from human resources and finance teams or the company's advisers in these areas.

Recruiting senior people is expensive and can easily cost in the region of £20,000 per position. However, against this cost you need to weigh up the long-term investment required to 'grow your own' future top management. Clearly, a balance is required. Increasingly, retaining key staff is a major issue for companies in all fields. Those not offering stock options are at a disadvantage when trying to attract the very best people, some of whom will be benefiting from the sophisticated packages offered by big blue-chips.

Recent changes to Capital Gains Tax Taper Relief (see below) will have important implications for the commitment of share-holding directors and employees.

Our top tips for putting you on the right road focus on four key areas: management structure, the importance of assessment, preparation and anticipation, and financial planning.

- *Management structure.* As far as possible the structure of the company should be such that you avoid having roles which can only be filled by one person. Companies heavily dependent on personalities can be more vulnerable in this respect. Some companies – particularly those of a certain size – try to expose their best managers to all facets of the company in an attempt to create a well-rounded pool of talent.

- *Importance of assessment.* While forward planning – along the lines of imagining what your company may be like in the future – is intuitively a sensible basis to start, it is increasingly difficult in today's dynamic business environment to anticipate the future beyond a few 'what ifs'.

    Be realistic. Having a cadre of people who have the fundamental skills of senior managers and who can really operate in your culture should mean that your company is in safe hands – at least in the short term. Sensible assessment of the potential of tomorrow's high flyers is expensive but helps senior management to navigate political barriers which can make it difficult to put the 'right' person in the right job. This helps bring a longevity and continuity to the policy.

- *Preparation and anticipation.* For the really top positions prepare in advance. Human resources experts estimate it can take up to eighteen months to 'groom' someone for a job and another eighteen months for them to become fully effective. Listed companies know to their cost the impact a 'shock' departure can have on share price, particularly if that person was one of the founders of the business. Companies who fail to fill a vacuum at the top for any length of time can become a target for predators. Appoint an appropriate team of professional advisers to help project-manage the succession or exit. Appoint a committee of the board who should work with the appointed professional advisers.

- *Financial planning.* The succession policy must be reviewed regularly in light of changes to legislation. There are two particular areas of tax to think about in relation to succession planning: inheritance tax and capital gains tax (CGT).

    Currently the situation with respect to CGT is interesting, given the government's objective of increasing the liquidity of shares. Changes to Business Asset Taper Relief introduced in last year's Finance Act may mean that companies experience an increase in executive departures.

    A reduction in the Business Asset Taper period might encourage executives to sell their shares after four rather than ten years as they will qualify for a reduced rate of CGT at an earlier date.

Prepare the business for change by concentrating on wealth creation and not lifestyle – whether it is 'grooming' the company for a sale or making it ready for outside investors.

Helen Riley
Tax Partner
RSM Robson Rhodes

APPENDIX 2

Useful Contacts

Government-backed services
The Small Business Service, the new government-backed support
agency for growing firms supplies advice on its website at
www.businessadvice.online.org or contact via Business Link.
In England, advice on general business matters can be obtained
from your local Business Link. Website: **www.businesslink.co.uk**
Tel: **0845 7567765**.
For most areas of Scotland, business advice is provided by the
network of Scottish Business Shops. Website:
www.sbgateway.com
For Wales, Business Connect provides advice services. Website:
www.businessconnect.org.uk Tel: **0845 7969798**.
In Northern Ireland, an information service is provided by the
Local Economic Development Unit (LEDU) for firms that employ
up to fifty employees and by the Industrial Development Board
(IDB) for firms with more than fifty employees. LEDU website:
www.ledu-ni.gov.uk Tel: **0 28 90 491 031**. IDB website:
www.idbni.co.uk Tel: **01232 233233**.

Useful websites
www.barclaysb2b.com Barclays Bank's on-line business advice
with accountancy and e-procurement services.
www.bizwise.co.uk Bizwise is an Internet portal for small- and

medium-sized businesses, and is a very useful source of advice on a variety of topics.

www.btclickforbusiness.com British Telecom's portal for small business subscribers – requires registration and monthly subscription.

www.clearlybusiness.com An alliance between Freeserve and Barclays Bank with advice on enterprise, business planning and managing staff.

www.dti.gov.uk Department of Trade and Industry site with useful round-up of government policies to small firms and links to other sites.

www.enterprisezone.org.uk The Enterprise Zone was launched by the DTI and Business Link. Has a useful small business directory.

www.isi.gov.uk Information Society Initiative site. Useful gateway for those interested in electronic trading and Internet security.

www.marketinguk.co.uk Site allowing you to check how your marketing shapes up.

www.sage.com Established software company now provides many successful programmes as Internet modules.

www.smallbusinessadvice.org.uk National Federation of Enterprise Agencies and NatWest bank offer this site, with a facility to e-mail questions to a local enterprise agency adviser.

www.success4business.co.uk Lloyds TSB's small business portal and website production service. Lots of useful help and advice.

Professional organisations, trade associations and business lobby groups

British Chambers of Commerce website: **www.britishchambers.org.uk** Tel: 020 7565 2000.

Confederation of British Industry website: **www.cbi.org.uk** Tel: 020 7379 7400.

The Forum of Private Business is a representative group that regularly surveys members and represents their views to government. It also provides self-help services. Website: **www.fpb.co.uk** Tel: **01565 634467**.

Federation of Small Businesses is a small-business representative group with a local, regional and national committee structure lobbying on behalf of small firms and providing services. Website: **www.fsb.org.uk** Tel: **020 7592 8100**.

Institute of Directors website: **www.iod.co.uk** Tel: **020 7839 1233**.

People

The Chartered Institute of Personnel and Development website: **www.cipd.co.uk** Tel: **020 8971 9000**.

The Employee Share Ownership Centre is a first port of call for companies wanting to set up employee share ownership plans. Contact Fred Hackworth, ESOC Director, 2 Ridgmount Street, London WC1E 7AA. Tel: **0207 436 9936** or e-mail: **fhackworth@mhcc.co.uk**

Investors In People website: **www.iipuk.co.uk** Tel: **020 7467 1900**.

E-commerce

The Business Bureau (UK) provides information for growing firms on its website at **www.businessbureau-uk.co.uk**

Business Researchers' Interests is another useful information site at **www.brint.com/interest**

Inkspot at **www.inkspot.com** is a community site for writers, which may be useful to those attempting to write their own content for their websites.

Internet Fraud Watch at **www.fraud.org** is a North American site but gives useful information that is relevant to the UK.

Netlink at **www.netlink.co.uk** claims to be Europe's biggest business-only web space provider.

Net Profit, an electronic publisher, is an excellent source of sensible, clearly written advice on the Internet for growing firms. Its book, *The Electronic Business Manual: How to Make the*

Internet work for your Business, is an invaluable source of advice for first-timers. It also offers a monthly newsletter, a research database, specialist reports and tailored research. Website: **www.netprofit.co.uk** Tel: **020 7403 1140.**

Net Savvy at **www.netsavvy.co.uk** is an excellent e-commerce site.

First Tuesday at **www.firsttuesday.co.uk** is a meeting group for venture capitalists interested in investing in e-commerce companies and entrepreneurs setting up such businesses.

Thisismoney.co.uk, the financial website of the *Mail on Sunday*, the *Daily Mail* and the *Evening Standard*, offers articles, useful information and links to helpful websites for small businesses.

Marketing

Advertising Association website: **www.adassoc.co.uk** Tel: **020 7828 2771.**

Advertising Standards Authority website: **www.asa.org.uk** Tel: **020 7580 5555.**

Chartered Institute of Marketing website: **www.cim.co.uk** Tel: **01628 427500.**

The Direct Mail Information Service (for industry statistics, research and general information) website: **www.dmis.co.uk** Tel: **020 7494 0483.**

Direct Marketing Association website: **www.dma.org.uk** Tel: **020 7321 2525.**

Institute of Public Relations website: **www.ipr.org.uk** Tel: **020 7253 5151.**

Market Research Society website: **www.marketresearch.org.uk** Tel: **020 7490 4911.**

Royal Mail Sales Centre website: **www.royalmail.com** Tel: **0845 7950 950.**

Cash management

The Better Payment Practice Group offers material on credit management at tel: **0870 150 2500.** It also has a website with useful information at: **www.payontime.co.uk**

The British Insurance and Investment Brokers' Association will help you find an insurance broker who can deal with your credit insurance needs at website **www.biiba.org.uk**
Tel: **020 7623 9043**.
Dun & Bradstreet website: **www.dunandbrad.co.uk**
Tel: **01494 422000**.
Export Credits Guarantee Department website: **www.ecg.gov.uk**
Tel: **020 7512 7000**.
Experian website: **www.experian.co.uk** Tel: **0115 941 0888**.
Factors and Discounters Association Ltd website:
www.factors.org.uk Tel: **020 8332 9955**.
Her Majesty's Customs and Excise website: **www.hmce.gov.uk**
Tel: **020 7620 1313**.
Inland Revenue website: **www.inlandrevenue.gov.uk**
Tel: **020 7438 6420** or call your local tax office.
Institute of Chartered Accountants in England and Wales website: **www.icaew.co.uk** Tel: **020 7920 8100**.
Institute of Chartered Accountants in Ireland website:
www.icai.ie Tel: **003531 668 0400**.
Institute of Chartered Accountants in Scotland website:
www.icas.org.uk Tel: **0131 225 5673**.
To check whether companies or individuals have a County Court judgement against them, write or visit: Registry Trust Ltd, 173–5 Cleveland Street, London W1P 5PE, tel: **020 7380 0133**.
To check that a debt collector is licensed by the Office of Fair Trading, tel: **020 7211 8608**.

Finance
Small Firms Loan Guarantee Section, tel: **0114 259 7308/9**.
The Prince's Trust website: **www.princes-trust.org.uk**
Tel: **020 7543 1234**.
Shell LiveWIRE website: **www.shell-livewire.org**
Tel: **01352 710199**.
BCE Business Funding Ltd, tel: **01623 421200**.
British Steel (Industry), tel: **0114 273 1612**.
First Tuesday website: **www.firsttuesday.co.uk**

For an information pack about how to find (or become) a business angel contact National Business Angels Network, tel: **020 7329 4141**, or go to website: **www.bestmatch.co.uk**
The British Venture Capital Association website: **www.bvca.co.uk** Tel: **020 7240 3846**.
RSM Robson Rhodes is a UK partnership of chartered accountants and management consultants. The firm is the UK member of RSM International, the world's eighth-largest international organisation of accountants and business advisers, and it provides a full range of advisory services to help businesses and individuals maximise their potential and profitability. Contact: Charli White, RSM Robson Rhodes, 186 City Road, London EC1V 2NU, tel. **020 7251 1644**.

Innovation
DTI Innovation Unit website: **www.innovation.gov.uk**
Information Society Initiative website: **www.isi.gov.uk**
The Patent Office website: **www.patent.gov.uk**
Tel: **01633 814000**.
The Design Council website: **www.design-council.org.uk**
Tel: **020 7420 5200**.
UK Business Incubation Centre website: **www.ukbi.co.uk**
Tel: **0121 250 3538**.

Exporting
British Chambers of Commerce website at **www.britishchambers.org.uk** has an Export Zone section run with express delivery service UPS, which is a useful source of information.
Institute of Export website: **www.export.org.uk**
Tel: **020 7247 9812**.
The Institute of Export and international delivery company DHL runs an information helpline for exporters. Tel: **020 7377 8442**.
Export Credits Guarantee Department website: **www.ecg.gov.uk**
Tel: **020 7512 7000**.

Trade Partners UK is a free government-backed self-service
library for exporters with a website at **www.tradepartners.gov.uk**
Tel: **020 7215 5444/5**.

INDEX

barriers to, 57–58
business theatre groups, 58
case study, teamwork at
    Paper White, 52–53
confrontation, dealing with,
    57–58
ethos, 55
goals, 55
innovation and, 192
meetings, 56–57
team building, 53–55
team spirit, 51–53
tips for top teams, 55
television advertising, 123–124
teleworking, 75–77
Tesco, 174
theft, 236
thisismoney.co.uk, 278
Thompson, Yvonne (ASAP
    Communications),
    127–128
Thomson's Directory, 125
Tilley, David (NDB
    Engineering), 219
tips for
    attracting backers, 186–188
    choosing effective
        accountants, 179–181
    getting newspaper coverage,
        130–131
    getting the best from banks,
        148–149
    marketing, 112
    survival, 252
    teamwork, 55
TNT, 104

tracking progress, 119
trade marks, 199
Trade Partners UK, 126, 162,
    212, 281
trade references, 152–153
Training and Enterprise Agency
    (Northern Ireland), 64
Training and Enterprise
    Councils, 63, 64
training for exporting, 217
training for staff, 63
training for the euro, 225
Translation Services (British
    Chambers of Commerce),
    217

U
unfair discrimination, 59
Unilever, 199
United Biscuits, 175
unsolicited media contact, 131
UPS, 104
UPU Industries, 213–215
URL (uniform resource locator),
    108

V
valuation, selling your business,
    270–271
vandalism, 234–235
VAT, 165–166, 253
venture capital, 182–184
Venture Capital Association,
    British, 177, 183, 280
Venture Capital Report, 177
Virgin Group, 7, 13–14, 36, 120

virtuality, 88, 108
viruses, 108
vision, 5, 55
Vyakarnam, Professor
     Shailendra, 83

W
Waitrose, 174
Wall Street Journal, 109
WAP (wireless application
     protocol), 108
Waterstone, Tim, 1, 3
wealth, desire for, 11–12
web address, 106
website effectiveness, 97–99
website planning, 95–96
Welsh Development Agency,
     133, 170
WFTC (working families tax
     credit), 83
What If?, 199–200
Wilde, Oscar, 246

winning in the marketplace, 192
working capital, 140–141
working hours, flexibility in,
     73–75
working time, directive on, 82
world wide web, 86–87, 108
Worldpay, 102
Wrightson, Martin (BLP Print
     Solutions), 37

X
Xyratex, 112

Y
Yahoo!, 98
Yellow Pages, 125
Young, David, 100

Z
Zara, 250
zero hours contracts, 74–75
Zoom the Loom, 149–150